ABOUT THIS PUBLICATION

FOR SERVICE ASSISTANCE

Customer Service
1.704.898.0770

North Carolina General Statues is published by The Muliti-Media Group of Greater Charlotte in Charlotte, North Carolina. Copyright 2015 by the Multi-Media Group of Greater Charlotte. This book or parts thereof may not be reproduced in any form, stored in a retrieval system, or transmitted in any form by any means—electronic, mechanical, photocopy, recording or otherwise—without prior written permission of the publisher, except as provided by United States of America copyright law.

The records required by U.S. Code 2257(a) through (c) and the pertinent regulations 28 C.F.R. Cli. 1, Part 75 with respect to this publication and all materials associated with such records are maintained by The Multi-Media Group of Greater Charlotte, Publisher and available for review by Attorney General.

www.visionbooks.org

Copyright © 2015 by MMGGC
All rights reserved!

TID: 5064396
ISBN (10) digit: 1502934019
ISBN (13) digit: 978-1502934017

123-4-56789-01239-Paperback
123-4-56789-01239-Hardback

First Edition

090520140547

Printed in the United States of America

2

2015 EDITION

North Carolina Criminal Law And Procedure-Pamphlet # 56

Printed In conjunction with the Administration of the Courts

North Carolina Criminal Law and Procedure
Pamphlet Reference Guide

Chapters	Pamphlet
Chapter 1 Civil Procedure	1
Chapter 1 Civil Procedure (Continue)	2
Chapter 1A Rules of Civil Procedure	2
Chapter 1B Contribution.	2
Chapter 1C Enforcement of Judgments.	2
Chapter 1D Punitive Damages.	2
Chapter 1E Eastern Band of Cherokee Indians.	2
Chapter 1F North Carolina Uniform Interstate Depositions and Discovery Act.	2
Chapter 2 - Clerk of Superior Court [Repealed and Transferred.]	3
Chapter 3 - Commissioners of Affidavits and Deeds [Repealed.]	3
Chapter 4 - Common Law	3
Chapter 5 - Contempt [Repealed.]	3
Chapter 5A - Contempt	3
Chapter 6 - Liability for Court Costs	3
Chapter 7 - Courts [Repealed and Transferred.]	3
Chapter 7A – Judicial Department	3
Chapter 7A – Continuation (Judicial Department)	4
Chapter 7A – Continuation (Judicial Department)	5
Chapter 7B - Juvenile Code	5
Chapter 8 - Evidence	6
Chapter 8A - Interpreters for Deaf Persons [Recodified.]	6
Chapter 8B - Interpreters for Deaf Persons	6
Chapter 8C - Evidence Code	6
Chapter 9 - Jurors	6
Chapter 10 - Notaries [Repealed.]	6
Chapter 10A - Notaries [Recodified.]	6
Chapter 10B - Notaries	6
Chapter 11 - Oaths	6
Chapter 12 - Statutory Construction	6
Chapter 13 - Citizenship Restored	6
Chapter 14 - Criminal Law	7
Chapter 14 –Criminal Law (Continuation)	8
Chapter 15 - Criminal Procedure	9
Chapter 15A - Criminal Procedure Act (Continuation)	10
Chapter 15A - Criminal Procedure Act (Continuation)	11
Chapter 15B - Victims Compensation	11
Chapter 15C - Address Confidentiality Program	11
Chapter 16 - Gaming Contracts and Futures	11
Chapter 17 - Habeas Corpus	11

Chapter 17A - Law-Enforcement Officers [Recodified.]	11
Chapter 17B - North Carolina Criminal Justice Education and Training System [Recodified.] Chapter 17C - North Carolina Criminal Justice Education and Training Standards Commission	11
Chapter 17D - North Carolina Justice Academy	11
Chapter 17E - North Carolina Sheriffs' Education and Training Standards Commission	11
Chapter 18 - Regulation of Intoxicating Liquors [Repealed.]	12
Chapter 18A - Regulation of Intoxicating Liquors [Repealed.]	12
Chapter 18B - Regulation of Alcoholic Beverages	12
Chapter 18C - North Carolina State Lottery	12
Chapter 19 - Offenses against Public Morals	12
Chapter 19A - Protection of Animals	12
Chapter 20 - Motor Vehicles	13
Chapter 20 - Motor Vehicles (Continuation)	14
Chapter 20 - Motor Vehicles (Continuation)	15
Chapter 20 - Motor Vehicles (Continuation)	16
Chapter 21 - Bills of Lading	17
Chapter 22 - Contracts Requiring Writing	17
Chapter 22A - Signatures	17
Chapter 22B - Contracts Against Public Policy	17
Chapter 22C - Payments to Subcontractors	17
Chapter 23 - Debtor and Creditor	17
Chapter 24 – Interest	17
Chapter 25 – Uniform Commercial Code	18
Chapter 25 – Uniform Commercial Code (Continuation)	19
Chapter 25A – Retail Installment Sales Act	20
Chapter 25B - Credit	20
Chapter 25C - Sales of Artwork	20
Chapter 26 - Suretyship	20
Chapter 27 - Warehouse Receipts [Repealed.]	20
Chapter 28 - Administration [Repealed.]	20
Chapter 28A - Administration of Decedents' Estates	20
Chapter 28B - Estates of Absentees in Military Service	20
Chapter 28C - Estates of Missing Persons	20
Chapter 29 - Intestate Succession	21
Chapter 30 - Surviving Spouses	21
Chapter 31 - Wills	21
Chapter 31A - Acts Barring Property Rights	21
Chapter 31B - Renunciation of Property and Renunciation of Fiduciary Powers Act	21
Chapter 31C - Uniform Disposition of Community Property Rights at Death Act	21
Chapter 32 - Fiduciaries	21
Chapter 32A - Powers of Attorney	21
Chapter 33 - Guardian and Ward [Repealed and Recodified.]	21

Chapter 33A - North Carolina Uniform Transfers to Minors Act	21
Chapter 33B - North Carolina Uniform Custodial Trust Act	21
Chapter 34 - Veterans' Guardianship Act	22
Chapter 35 - Sterilization Procedures	22
Chapter 35A - Incompetency and Guardianship	22
Chapter 36 - Trusts and Trustees [Repealed.]	22
Chapter 36A - Trusts and Trustees	22
Chapter 36B - Uniform Management of Institutional Funds Act [Repealed.]	22
Chapter 36C - North Carolina Uniform Trust Code	22
Chapter 36D - North Carolina Community Third Party Trusts, Pooled Trusts	23
Chapter 36E - Uniform Prudent Management of Institutional Funds Act	23
Chapter 37 - Allocation of Principal and Income [Repealed.]	23
Chapter 37A - Uniform Principal and Income Act	23
Chapter 38 - Boundaries	23
Chapter 38A - Landowner Liability	23
Chapter 39 - Conveyances	23
Chapter 39A - Transfer Fee Covenants Prohibited	23
Chapter 40 - Eminent Domain [Repealed.]	23
Chapter 40A - Eminent Domain	23
Chapter 41 - Estates	23
Chapter 41A - State Fair Housing Act	23
Chapter 42 - Landlord and Tenant	23
Chapter 42A - Vacation Rental Act	23
Chapter 43 - Land Registration	23
Chapter 44 - Liens	24
Chapter 44A - Statutory Liens and Charges	24
Chapter 45 - Mortgages and Deeds of Trust	24
Chapter 45A - Good Funds Settlement Act	24
Chapter 46 - Partition	24
Chapter 47 - Probate and Registration	25
Chapter 47A - Unit Ownership	25
Chapter 47B - Real Property Marketable Title Act	25
Chapter 47C - North Carolina Condominium Act	25
Chapter 47D - Notice of Settlement Act [Expired.]	25
Chapter 47E - Residential Property Disclosure Act	25
Chapter 47F - North Carolina Planned Community Act	25
Chapter 47G - Option to Purchase Contracts	25
Chapter 47H - Contracts for Deed	25
Chapter 48 - Adoptions +	26
Chapter 48A - Minors	26
Chapter 49 - Bastardy	26
Chapter 49A - Rights of Children	26
Chapter 50 - Divorce and Alimony	26
Chapter 50A - Uniform Child-Custody Jurisdiction and	

Enforcement Act	26
Chapter 50B - Domestic Violence	26
Chapter 50C - Civil No-Contact Orders	26
Chapter 51 - Marriage	26
Chapter 52 - Powers and Liabilities of Married Persons	27
Chapter 52A - Uniform Reciprocal Enforcement of Support Act [Repealed.]	27
Chapter 52B - Uniform Premarital Agreement Act	27
Chapter 52C - Uniform Interstate Family Support Act	27
Chapter 53 - Banks	27
Chapter 53A - Business Development Corporations and North Carolina Capital Resource Corporations	28
Chapter 53B - Financial Privacy Act	28
Chapter 54 - Cooperative Organizations	28
Chapter 54A - Capital Stock Savings and Loan Associations [Repealed.]	28
Chapter 54B - Savings and Loan Associations	29
Chapter 54C - Savings Banks	29
Chapter 55 - North Carolina Business Corporation Act	30
Chapter 55A - North Carolina Nonprofit Corporation Act	31
Chapter 55B - Professional Corporation Act	31
Chapter 55C - Foreign Trade Zones	31
Chapter 55D - Filings, Names, and Registered Agents for Corporations, Nonprofit Corporations, and Partnerships	31
Chapter 56 - Electric, Telegraph and Power Companies [Repealed.]	31
Chapter 57 - Hospital, Medical and Dental Service Corporations [Recodified.]	31
Chapter 57A - Health Maintenance Organization Act [Recodified.]	31
Chapter 57B - Health Maintenance Organization Act [Recodified.]	31
Chapter 57C - North Carolina Limited Liability Company Act.	31
Chapter 58 - Insurance.	32
Chapter 58 - Insurance (Continuation)	33
Chapter 58 - Insurance (Continuation)	34
Chapter 58 - Insurance (Continuation)	35
Chapter 58 - Insurance (Continuation)	36
Chapter 58 - Insurance (Continuation)	37
Chapter 58 - Insurance (Continuation)	38
Chapter 58A - North Carolina Health Insurance Trust Commission [Recodified.]	38
Chapter 59 - Partnership.	39
Chapter 59B - Uniform Unincorporated Nonprofit Association Act.	39
Chapter 60 - Railroads and Other Carriers [Repealed and Transferred.]	39
Chapter 61 - Religious Societies	39
Chapter 62 - Public Utilities	39

Chapter 62 - Public Utilities (Continuation)	40
Chapter 62A - Public Safety Telephone Service And Wireless Telephone Service	40
Chapter 63 - Aeronautics	40
Chapter 63A - North Carolina Global TransPark Authority	40
Chapter 64 - Aliens	40
Chapter 65 – Cemeteries	40
Chapter 66 - Commerce and Business	41
Chapter 67 - Dogs	41
Chapter 68 - Fences and Stock Law	41
Chapter 69 - Fire Protection	41
Chapter 70 - Indian Antiquities, Archaeological Resources and Unmarked Human Skeletal Remains Protection	42
Chapter 71 - Indians [Repealed.]	42
Chapter 71A - Indians	42
Chapter 72 - Inns, Hotels and Restaurants	42
Chapter 73 - Mills	42
Chapter 74 - Mines and Quarries	42
Chapter 74A - Company Police [Repealed.]	42
Chapter 74B - Private Protective Services Act [Repealed.]	42
Chapter 74C - Private Protective Services	42
Chapter 74D - Alarm Systems	42
Chapter 74E - Company Police Act	42
Chapter 74F - Locksmith Licensing Act	42
Chapter 74G - Campus Police Act	42
Chapter 75 - Monopolies, Trusts and Consumer Protection	42
Chapter 75A - Boating and Water Safety	43
Chapter 75B - Discrimination in Business	43
Chapter 75C - Motion Picture Fair Competition Act	43
Chapter 75D - Racketeer Influenced and Corrupt Organizations	43
Chapter 75E - Unlawful Activities in Connection With Certain Corporate Transactions	43
Chapter 76 - Navigation	43
Chapter 76A - Navigation and Pilotage Commissions	43
Chapter 77 - Rivers, Creeks, and Coastal Waters	43
Chapter 78 - Securities Law [Repealed.]	43
Chapter 78A - North Carolina Securities Act	43
Chapter 78B - Tender Offer Disclosure Act [Repealed.]	43
Chapter 78C - Investment Advisers	43
Chapter 78D - Commodities Act	43
Chapter 79 - Strays [Repealed.]	43
Chapter 80 - Trademarks, Brands, etc.	44
Chapter 81 - Weights and Measures [Recodified.]	44
Chapter 81A - Weights and Measures Act of 1975.	44
Chapter 82 - Wrecks [Repealed.]	44
Chapter 83 - Architects [Recodified.]	44

Chapter 83A - Architects	44
Chapter 84 - Attorneys-at-Law	44
Chapter 84A - Foreign Legal Consultants	44
Chapter 85 - Auctions and Auctioneers [Repealed.]	44
Chapter 85A - Bail Bondsmen and Runners [Recodified.]	44
Chapter 85B - Auctions and Auctioneers	44
Chapter 85C - Bail Bondsmen and Runners [Recodified.]	44
Chapter 86 - Barbers [Recodified.]	44
Chapter 86A - Barbers	44
Chapter 87 - Contractors	44
Chapter 88 - Cosmetic Art [Repealed.]	44
Chapter 88A - Electrolysis Practice Act	44
Chapter 88B - Cosmetic Art	45
Chapter 89 - Engineering and Land Surveying [Recodified.]	45
Chapter 89A - Landscape Architects	45
Chapter 89B - Foresters	45
Chapter 89C - Engineering and Land Surveying	45
Chapter 89D - Landscape Contractors	45
Chapter 89E - Geologists Licensing Act	45
Chapter 89F - North Carolina Soil Scientist Licensing Act	45
Chapter 89G - Irrigation Contractors	45
Chapter 90 - Medicine and Allied Occupations	45
Chapter 90 - Medicine and Allied Occupations (Continuation)	46
Chapter 90 - Medicine and Allied Occupations (Continuation)	47
Chapter 90 - Medicine and Allied Occupations (Continuation)	48
Chapter 90A - Sanitarians and Water and Wastewater Treatment Facility Operators	48
Chapter 90B - Social Worker Certification and Licensure Act	48
Chapter 90C - North Carolina Recreational Therapy Licensure Act	48
Chapter 90D - Interpreters and Transliterators	48
Chapter 91 - Pawnbrokers [Repealed.]	48
Chapter 91A - Pawnbrokers Modernization Act of 1989	48
Chapter 92 - Photographers [Deleted.]	48
Chapter 93 - Certified Public Accountants	48
Chapter 93A - Real Estate License Law	49
Chapter 93B - Occupational Licensing Boards	49
Chapter 93C - Watchmakers [Repealed.]	49
Chapter 93D - North Carolina State Hearing Aid Dealers and Fitters Board.	49
Chapter 93E - North Carolina Appraisers Act	49
Chapter 94 - Apprenticeship	49
Chapter 95 - Department of Labor and Labor Regulations	49
Chapter 95 - Department of Labor and Labor Regulations (Continuation)	50
Chapter 96 - Employment Security	50
Chapter 97 - Workers' Compensation Act	50
Chapter 97 - Workers' Compensation Act (Continuation)	51

Chapter 98 - Burnt and Lost Records	51
Chapter 99 - Libel and Slander	51
Chapter 99A - Civil Remedies for Criminal Actions	51
Chapter 99B - Products Liability	51
Chapter 99C - Actions Relating to Winter Sports Safety and Accidents	51
Chapter 99D - Civil Rights	51
Chapter 99E - Special Liability Provisions	51
Chapter 100 - Monuments, Memorials and Parks	51
Chapter 101 - Names of Persons	51
Chapter 102 - Official Survey Base	51
Chapter 103 - Sundays, Holidays and Special Days	51
Chapter 104 - United States Lands	51
Chapter 104A - Degrees of Kinship	51
Chapter 104B - Hurricanes or Other Acts of Nature	51
Chapter 104C - Atomic Energy, Radioactivity and Ionizing Radiation [Repealed and Recodified.]	51
Chapter 104D - Southern States Energy Compact	51
Chapter 104E - North Carolina Radiation Protection Act	51
Chapter 104F - Southeast Interstate Low-Level Radioactive Waste Management Compact [Repealed]	51
Chapter 104G - North Carolina Low-Level Radioactive Waste Management Authority Act of 1987 [Repealed]	51
Chapter 105 - Taxation	51
Chapter 105 - Taxation (Continuation)	52
Chapter 105 - Taxation (Continuation)	53
Chapter 105 - Taxation (Continuation)	54
Chapter 105A - Setoff Debt Collection Act	55
Chapter 105B - Defaulted Student Loan Recovery Act	55
Chapter 106 - Agriculture	55
Chapter 106 - Agriculture (Continue)	56
Chapter 106 - Agriculture (Continue)	57
Chapter 107 - Agricultural Development Districts [Repealed.]	57
Chapter 108 - Social Services [Repealed and Recodified.]	57
Chapter 108A - Social Services	57
Chapter 108B - Community Action Programs	58
Chapter 108C Medicaid and Health Choice Provider Requirements.	58
Chapter 108D Medicaid Managed Care for Behavioral Health Services.	58
Chapter 109 - Bonds [Recodified.]	58
Chapter 110 - Child Welfare	58
Chapter 111 - Aid to the Blind	58
Chapter 112 - Confederate Homes and Pensions [Repealed.]	58
Chapter 113 - Conservation and Development	58
Chapter 113 - Conservation and Development (Continuation)	59

Chapter 113A - Pollution Control and Environment	59
Chapter 113A - Pollution Control and Environment (Continuation)	60
Chapter 113B - North Carolina Energy Policy Act of 1975	60
Chapter 114 - Department of Justice	60
Chapter 115 - Elementary and Secondary Education [Repealed.]	60
Chapter 115A - Community Colleges, Technical Institutes, and Industrial Education Centers [Repealed.]	60
Chapter 115B - Tuition and Fee Waivers	60
Chapter 115C - Elementary and Secondary Education	60
Chapter 115C - Elementary and Secondary Education (Continuation)	61
Chapter 115C - Elementary and Secondary Education (Continuation)	62
Chapter 115C - Elementary and Secondary Education (Continuation)	63
Chapter 115D - Community Colleges	63
Chapter 115E - Private Educational Facilities Finance Act [Recodified]	63
Chapter 116 - Higher Education	63
Chapter 116 - Higher Education (Continuation)	63
Chapter 116A - Escheats and Abandoned Property [Repealed.]	64
Chapter 116B - Escheats and Abandoned Property	64
Chapter 116C - Continuum of Education Programs	64
Chapter 116D - Higher Education Bonds	64
Chapter 117 - Electrification	64
Chapter 118 - Firemen's and Rescue Squad Workers' Relief and Pension Funds [Recodified.]	64
Chapter 118A - Firemen's Death Benefit Act [Repealed.]	64
Chapter 118B - Members of a Rescue Squad Death Benefit Act [Repealed.]	64
Chapter 119 - Gasoline and Oil Inspection and Regulation	64
Chapter 120 - General Assembly	65
Chapter 120 - General Assembly (Continuation)	66
Chapter 120 - General Assembly (Continuation)	67
Chapter 120C - Lobbying	67
Chapter 121 - Archives and History	67
Chapter 122 - Hospitals for the Mentally Disordered [Repealed.]	67
Chapter 122A - North Carolina Housing Finance Agency	67
Chapter 122B - North Carolina Agricultural Facilities Finance Act [Repealed.]	67
Chapter 122C - Mental Health, Developmental Disabilities, and Substance Abuse Act of 1985	67
Chapter 122C - Mental Health, Developmental Disabilities, and Substance Abuse Act of 1985 (Continuation)	68
Chapter 122D - North Carolina Agricultural Finance Act	68

Chapter 122E - North Carolina Housing Trust and Oil Overcharge Act	68
Chapter 123 - Impeachment	69
Chapter 123A - Industrial Development [Repealed.]	69
Chapter 124 - Internal Improvements	69
Chapter 125 - Libraries	69
Chapter 126 - State Personnel System	69
Chapter 127 - Militia [Repealed.]	69
Chapter 127A - Militia	69
Chapter 127B - Military Affairs	69
Chapter 127C - Advisory Commission on Military Affairs	69
Chapter 128 - Offices and Public Officers	69
Chapter 128 - Offices and Public Officers (Continuation)	70
Chapter 129 - Public Buildings and Grounds	70
Chapter 130 - Public Health [Repealed.]	70
Chapter 130A - Public Health	70
Chapter 130A - Public Health (Continuation)	71
Chapter 130A - Public Health (Continuation)	72
Chapter 130B - Hazardous Waste Management Commission [Repealed.]	72
Chapter 131 - Public Hospitals [Repealed.]	72
Chapter 131A - Health Care Facilities Finance Act	72
Chapter 131B - Licensing of Ambulatory Surgical Facilities [Repealed.]	72
Chapter 131C - Charitable Solicitation Licensure Act [Repealed.]	72
Chapter 131D - Inspection and Licensing of Facilities	72
Chapter 131E - Health Care Facilities and Services	72
Chapter 131E - Health Care Facilities and Services (Continuation)	73
Chapter 131F - Solicitation of Contributions	73
Chapter 132 - Public Records	73
Chapter 133 - Public Works	74
Chapter 134 - Youth Development [Recodified.]	74
Chapter 134A - Youth Services [Repealed.]	74
Chapter 135 - Retirement System for Teachers and State Employees; Social Security; Health Insurance Program for Children	74
Chapter 135 - Retirement System for Teachers and State Employees; Social Security; Health Insurance Program for Children	75
Chapter 136 - Transportation	75
Chapter 136 - Transportation (Continuation)	76
Chapter 137 - Rural Rehabilitation [Repealed.]	76
Chapter 138 - Salaries, Fees and Allowances	76
Chapter 138A - State Government Ethics Act	76
Chapter 139 - Soil and Water Conservation Districts	76

Chapter 140 - State Art Museum; Symphony and Art Societies	76
Chapter 140A - State Awards System	76
Chapter 141 - State Boundaries	76
Chapter 142 - State Debt	76
Chapter 143 - State Departments, Institutions, and Commissions	77
Chapter 143 - State Departments, Institutions, and Commissions (Continuation)	78
Chapter 143 - State Departments, Institutions, and Commissions (Continuation)	79
Chapter 143 - State Departments, Institutions, and Commissions (Continuation)	80
Chapter 143A - State Government Reorganization	80
Chapter 143B - Executive Organization Act of 1973	80
Chapter 143B - Executive Organization Act of 1973 (Continuation)	81
Chapter 143B - Executive Organization Act of 1973 (Continuation)	82
Chapter 143C - State Budget Act	83
Chapter 143D - The State Governmental Accountability and Internal Control Act	83
Chapter 144 - State Flag, Official Governmental Flags, Motto, and Colors	83
Chapter 145 - State Symbols and Other Official Adoptions.	83
Chapter 146 - State Lands	83
Chapter 147 - State Officers	83
Chapter 148 - State Prison System	84
Chapter 149 - State Song and Toast	84
Chapter 150 - Uniform Revocation of Licenses [Repealed.]	84
Chapter 150A - Administrative Procedure Act [Recodified.]	84
Chapter 150B - Administrative Procedure Act	84
Chapter 151 - Constables [Repealed.]	84
Chapter 152 - Coroners	84
Chapter 152A - County Medical Examiner [Repealed.]	84
Chapter 152A - County Medical Examiner [Repealed.] (Continuation)	85
Chapter 153 - Counties and County Commissioners [Repealed.]	85
Chapter 153A - Counties	85
Chapter 153B - Mountain Resources Planning Act	85
Chapter 153C - Uwharrie Regional Resources Act	85
Chapter 154 - County Surveyor [Repealed.]	85
Chapter 155 - County Treasurer [Repealed.]	85
Chapter 156 - Drainage	85
Chapter 156 – Drainage (Continuation)	86

Chapter 157 - Housing Authorities and Projects	86
Chapter 157A - Historic Properties Commissions [Transferred.]	86
Chapter 158 - Local Development	86
Chapter 159 - Local Government Finance	86
Chapter 159 - Local Government Finance (Continuation)	87
Chapter 159A - Pollution Abatement and Industrial Facilities Financing Act [Unconstitutional.]	87
Chapter 159B - Joint Municipal Electric Power and Energy Act	87
Chapter 159C - Industrial and Pollution Control Facilities Financing Act	87
Chapter 159D - The North Carolina Capital Facilities Financing Act	87
Chapter 159E - Registered Public Obligations Act	87
Chapter 159F - North Carolina Energy Development Authority [Repealed.]	87
Chapter 159G - Water Infrastructure	87
Chapter 159H - [Reserved.]	87
Chapter 159I - Solid Waste Management Loan Program and Local Government Special Obligation Bonds	87
Chapter 160 - Municipal Corporations [Repealed And Transferred.]	87
Chapter 160A - Cities and Towns	88
Chapter 160A - Cities and Towns (Continuation)	89
Chapter 160B - Consolidated City-County Act	89
Chapter 160C - Baseball Park Districts [Repealed.]	90
Chapter 161 - Register of Deeds	90
Chapter 162 - Sheriff	90
Chapter 162A - Water and Sewer Systems	90
Chapter 162B Continuity of Local Government in Emergency.	90
Chapter 163 Elections and Election Laws.	90
Chapter 163 Elections and Election Laws. (Continuation)	91
Chapter 164 Concerning the General Statutes of North Carolina.	92
Chapter 165 Veterans.	92
Chapter 166 Civil Preparedness Agencies [Repealed.]	92
Chapter 166A North Carolina Emergency Management Act.	92
Chapter 167 State Civil Air Patrol [Repealed.]	92
Chapter 168 Persons with Disabilities.	92
Chapter 168A Persons With Disabilities Protection Act.	92

§ 106-354. Local State inspectors; commissioned as quarantine inspectors; salaries, etc.

The State Veterinarian shall appoint the necessary number of local State inspectors to assist in systematic tick eradication, who shall be commissioned by the Commissioner of Agriculture as quarantine inspectors. The salaries of said inspectors shall be sufficient to insure the employment of competent men. If the service of any of said inspectors is not satisfactory to the State Veterinarian, his services shall be immediately discontinued and his commission canceled. (1923, c. 146, s. 5; C.S., s. 4895(t); 1925, c. 275, s. 6.)

§ 106-355. Enforcement of compliance with law.

If the county commissioners shall fail, refuse or neglect to comply with the provisions of G.S. 106-351 to 106-363, the State Veterinarian shall apply to any court of competent jurisdiction for a writ of mandamus, or shall institute such other proceedings as may be necessary and proper to compel such county commissioners to comply with the provisions of G.S. 106-351 to 106-363. (1923, c. 146, s. 6; C.S., s. 4895(u).)

§ 106-356. Owners of stock to have same dipped; supervision of dipping; dipping period.

Any person or persons, firms or corporations, owning or having in charge any cattle, horses or mules in any county where tick eradication shall be taken up, or is in progress under existing laws, shall, on notification by any quarantine inspector to do so, have such cattle, horses or mules dipped regularly every 14 days in a vat properly charged with arsenical solution as recommended by the United States Bureau of Animal Industry, under the supervision of said inspector at such time and place and in such manner as may be designated by the quarantine inspector. The dipping period shall be continued as long as may be required by the rules and regulations of the State Board of Agriculture, which shall be sufficient in number and length of time to completely destroy and eradicate all cattle ticks (Margaropus annulatus) in such county or counties. (1923, c. 146, s. 7; C.S., s. 4895(v).)

§ 106-357. Service of notice.

Quarantine and dipping notice for cattle, horses and mules, the owner or owners of which cannot be found, shall be served by posting copy of such notice in not less than three public places within the county, one of which shall be placed at the county courthouse. Such posting shall be due and legal notice. (1923, c. 146, s. 8; C.S., s. 4895(w).)

§ 106-358. Cattle placed in quarantine; dipping at expense of owner.

Cattle, horses or mules infested with or exposed to the cattle tick (Margaropus annulatus) the owner or owners of which, after five days' written notice from a quarantine inspector of such animals as is provided for in G.S. 106-357, shall fail or refuse to dip such animals regularly every 14 days in a vat properly charged with arsenical solution, as recommended by the United States Bureau of Animal Industry, under the supervision of a quarantine inspector, shall be placed in quarantine, dipped and cared for at the expense of the owner or owners, by the quarantine inspector. (1923, c. 146, s. 9; C.S., s. 4895(x).)

§ 106-359. Expense of dipping as lien on animals; enforcement of lien.

Any expense incurred in the enforcement of G.S. 106-358 and the cost of feeding and caring for animals while undergoing the process of tick eradication shall constitute a lien upon any animal, and should the owner or owners fail or refuse to pay said expense, after three days' notice, they shall be sold by the sheriff of the county after 20 days' advertising at the courthouse door and three other public places in the immediate neighborhood of the place at which the animal was taken up for the purpose of tick eradication. The said advertisement shall state therein the time and place of sale, which place shall be where the animal is confined. The sale shall be at public auction and to the highest bidder for cash. Out of the proceeds of the sale the sheriff shall pay the cost of publishing the notices of the tick-eradication process, including dipping, cost of feeding and caring for the animals and cost of the sale, which shall include one dollar and fifty cents ($1.50) in the case of each sale to said sheriff. The surplus, if any, shall be paid to the owner of the animal if he can be ascertained. If he cannot be ascertained within 30 days after such sale, then the sheriff shall pay such surplus to the county treasurer for the benefit of the public school fund of the county: Provided, however, that if the owner of the animal shall, within 12 months after the fund is turned over to the county treasurer, as aforesaid, prove to the satisfaction of the board of county commissioners of the county that he was the owner of such animal, then, upon the order of said board, such surplus shall be refunded to the owner. (1923, c. 146, s. 10; C.S., s. 4895(y).)

§ 106-360. Duty of sheriff.

It shall be the duty of the sheriff, in any county in which the work of tick eradication is in progress, to render all quarantine inspectors any assistance necessary in the enforcement of G.S. 106-351 to 106-363 and the regulations of the North Carolina Department of Agriculture and Consumer Services. If the sheriff of any county shall neglect, fail or refuse to render his assistance when so required, he shall be guilty of a Class 1 misdemeanor. (1923, c. 146, s. 11; C.S., s. 4895(z); 1993, c. 539, s. 771; 1994, Ex. Sess., c. 24, s. 14(c); 1997-261, s. 109.)

§ 106-361. Rules and regulations.

The Commissioner of Agriculture, by and with the consent of the State Board of Agriculture, shall have full power to promulgate and enforce such rules and regulations that may hereafter be necessary to complete tick eradication in North Carolina. (1923, c. 146, s. 12; C.S., s. 4895(aa).)

§ 106-362. Penalty for violation.

Any person, firm or corporation who shall violate any provisions set forth in G.S. 106-351 to 106-363 or any rule or regulation duly established by the State Board of Agriculture, or any officer or inspector who shall willfully fail to comply with any provision of G.S. 106-351 to 106-363 shall be guilty of a Class 1 misdemeanor. (1923, c. 146, s. 13; C.S., s. 4895(bb); 1993, c. 539, s. 772; 1994, Ex. Sess., c. 24, s. 14(c).)

§ 106-363. Damaging dipping vats a felony.

Any person or persons who shall willfully damage or destroy by any means any vat erected, or in the process of being erected, as provided for tick eradication, shall be guilty of a Class H felony. (1923, c. 146, s. 14; C.S., s. 4895(cc); 1993, c. 539, s. 1296; 1994, Ex. Sess., c. 24, s. 14(c).)

Part 7. Rabies.

§§ 106-364 through 106-387: Repealed by Session Laws 1983, c. 891, s. 8.

Part 8. Brucellosis (Bang's Disease).

§ 106-388. Animals affected with, or exposed to, brucellosis declared subject to quarantine, etc.

It is hereby declared that the disease of animals known as brucellosis, or Bang's disease, is of an infectious and contagious nature, and animals affected with, or exposed to, or suspected of being carriers of the disease, shall be subject to quarantine and the rules and regulations of the Department of Agriculture and Consumer Services. (1937, c. 175, s. 1; 1967, c. 511; 1997-261, s. 109.)

§ 106-389. Brucellosis defined; program for vaccination; sale, etc., of vaccine; cooperation with the United States Department of Agriculture.

"Brucellosis" shall mean the disease wherein an animal is infected with Brucella organisms (including Brucella Abortus, B. Melitensis and B. Suis), irrespective of the occurrence or absence of abortion or other symptoms. An animal shall be declared affected with brucellosis if it is classified as a reactor to a serological test for the disease, or if the Brucella organism has been found in the body, its secretions or discharges. The State Veterinarian is hereby authorized and empowered to set up a program for the vaccination of calves in accordance with the recommendations of the Brucellosis Committee of the United States Livestock Sanitary Association, and approved by the United States Department of Agriculture, when in his opinion vaccination is necessary for the control and eradication of brucellosis. Vaccinated animals shall be permanently identified by tattooing or other methods approved by the Commissioner of Agriculture. Above the ages designated by regulation of the Board of Agriculture, all such vaccinates classified as reactors on an official test for brucellosis, shall be considered as affected with brucellosis and shall be branded with the letter "B" in accordance with G.S. 106-390. It shall be unlawful to sell, offer for sale, distribute, or use brucellosis vaccine or any product containing live Brucella organisms, except as provided for in regulations adopted by the Board of Agriculture.

The control and eradication of brucellosis in the herds of North Carolina shall be conducted as far as available funds will permit, and in accordance with the rules and regulations made by the Board of Agriculture. The Board of Agriculture is hereby authorized to cooperate with the United States Department of Agriculture in the control and eradication of brucellosis. (1937, c. 175, s. 2; 1945, c. 462, s. 1; 1953, c. 1119; 1967, c. 511.)

§ 106-390. Blood sample testing; diseased animals to be branded and quarantined; sale; removal of identification, etc.

All blood samples for the brucellosis test shall be drawn by persons whose qualifications are set by regulation of the Board of Agriculture. Animals from which blood is collected for a brucellosis test shall be identified by numbered ear tag, tattoo, or in some other manner approved by the Commissioner of Agriculture. It shall be the duty of the person who collects the blood sample, or other designated authorized person, to brand all cattle affected with brucellosis with the letter "B" on the left hip or jaw, not less than three or more than four inches high, tag such animals with an approved brucellosis reactor ear tag, and report the same to the State Veterinarian. It shall be the duty of the person owning said cattle at the time of said testing to assist with and cooperate with the person testing said cattle. Cattle affected with brucellosis shall be quarantined and slaughtered at a State or federally inspected slaughter plant within 10 days after branding and tagging; provided the State Veterinarian, in his discretion, may grant an extension of time for said slaughter not to exceed 30 days; and provided further that the Commissioner of Agriculture may allow a branded and tagged animal having unusual breeding value to be held for a period of time determined by him under conditions of isolation and quarantine prescribed by the State Veterinarian. Animals believed by the State Veterinarian or his authorized representative to have been exposed to brucellosis, or animals classified as suspects, shall be quarantined on the owner's premises or at such other place as is mutually agreeable to the owner and the State Veterinarian until the quarantine is removed in accordance with law or until the animal is disposed of in accordance with law. No animal affected with, or exposed to, brucellosis shall be sold, traded or otherwise disposed of except for immediate slaughter, and it shall be the duty of the person disposing of such infected animals to see that they are promptly slaughtered and a written report of same made to the State Veterinarian.

All cattle, swine, sheep, goats or other animals subject to infection by Brucella organisms, sold, or offered at public sale, except for immediate slaughter, shall be subject to test requirements established by the Board of Agriculture.

No ear tag, back tag, or other mark of identification approved by the Commissioner of Agriculture for identifying animals for the purpose of brucellosis testing, including testing at slaughter plants, shall be removed from the animal without authorization from the State Veterinarian or his authorized representative. (1937, c. 175, s. 3; 1945, c. 462, s. 2; 1959, c. 1171; 1963, c. 489; 1967, c. 511; 1969, c. 465.)

§ 106-391. Civil liability of vendors.

Any person or persons who knowingly sells, or otherwise disposes of, to another, an animal affected with brucellosis shall be liable in a civil action to any person injured, and for any and all damages resulting therefrom. (1937, c. 175, s. 4; 1967, c. 511.)

§ 106-392. Sales by nonresidents.

When cattle are sold, or otherwise disposed of, in this State, by a nonresident of this State, the person or persons on whose premises the cattle are sold, or otherwise disposed of, with his knowledge and consent, shall be equally responsible for violations of G.S. 106-388 to 106-398 and the regulations of the Department of Agriculture and Consumer Services. (1937, c. 175, s. 5; 1967, c. 511; 1997-261, s. 109.)

§ 106-393. Duties of State Veterinarian; quarantine of animals; required testing.

When the State Veterinarian receives information, or has reasonable grounds to believe, that brucellosis exists in any animal, or animals, or that it has been exposed to the disease, he shall promptly cause said animal, or animals, to be quarantined on the premises of owner or such other place as is mutually agreeable to the owner and the State Veterinarian or his authorized representative. Said animals shall not be removed from premises where quarantined until quarantine has been released by State Veterinarian or his authorized representative. A permit to move such infected or exposed animals to immediate slaughter may be issued by the State Veterinarian or his authorized representative. The Board of Agriculture is empowered to make regulations to provide for compulsory testing of animals for brucellosis. (1937, c. 175, s. 6; 1967, c. 511.)

§ 106-394. Cooperation of county boards of commissioners.

The several boards of county commissioners in the State are hereby expressly authorized and empowered within their discretion to make such appropriations from the general funds of their county as will enable them to cooperate effectively with the State and United States Departments of Agriculture in the eradication of brucellosis in their respective counties. (1937, c. 175, s. 7; 1967, c. 511.)

§ 106-395. Compulsory testing.

Whenever a county board of commissioners shall cooperate with the State and the United States governments, as provided for in G.S. 106-388 to 106-398, the testing of all cattle in said county shall become compulsory, and it shall be the duty of the cattle owners to give such assistance as may be necessary for the proper testing of said cattle. (1937, c. 175, s. 8; 1967, c. 511.)

§ 106-396. Authority to promulgate and enforce rules and regulations.

The Commissioner of Agriculture, by and with the consent of the State Board of Agriculture, shall have full power to promulgate and enforce such rules and regulations as may be necessary to carry out the provisions of G.S. 106-388 to 106-398, and for the effective control and eradication of brucellosis, including the establishment of fees and charges for the collection of blood samples. (1937, c. 175, s. 10; 1967, c. 511; 1981, c. 495, s. 8.)

§ 106-397. Violation made misdemeanor.

Any person or persons who shall violate any provision set forth in G.S. 106-388 to 106-398, or any rule or regulation duly established pursuant to this Article by the State Board of Agriculture or any inspector who shall willfully fail to comply with any provisions of G.S. 106-388 to 106-398, shall be guilty of a Class 1 misdemeanor. (1937, c. 175, s. 11; 1967, c. 511; 1993, c. 539, s. 773; 1994, Ex. Sess., c. 24, s. 14(c).)

§ 106-398. Punishment for sale of animals known to be infected, or under quarantine.

Any person or persons who shall willfully and knowingly sell or otherwise dispose of any animal or animals known to be affected with brucellosis, or under quarantine because of suspected exposure to brucellosis, except as provided for in G.S. 106-388 to 106-398, shall be guilty of a Class 1 misdemeanor. (1937, c. 175, s. 12; 1967, c. 511; 1993, c. 539, s. 774; 1994, Ex. Sess., c. 24, s. 14(c).)

§ 106-399. Repealed by Session Laws 1967, c. 511.

§§ 106-399.1 through 106-399.3. Reserved for future codification purposes.

Part 9. Control of Livestock Diseases.

§ 106-399.4. Imminent threat of contagious animal disease; emergency measures and procedures.

(a) When determined by the State Veterinarian, in consultation with the Commissioner of Agriculture and with the approval of the Governor, that there is an imminent threat within the State of a contagious animal disease that has the potential for very serious and rapid spread, is of serious socioeconomic and public health consequence, or is of major importance in the international trade of animals and animal products, the State Veterinarian or an authorized representative may develop and implement any emergency measures and procedures that the State Veterinarian determines necessary to prevent and control the animal disease.

(b) Written notice of emergency procedures and measures implemented under this section, including an identification of the disease threat and a description of any potentially infected area and animal, shall be mailed or delivered to news media, farm organizations, agriculture agencies, and any other interested or affected parties as determined by the State Veterinarian. Such emergency procedures and measures may include, but are not limited to, restrictions on the transportation of any potentially infected animals, restrictions on the transportation of agriculture products and other commodities into and out of potentially infected areas, restrictions on access to potentially infected areas, quarantines under G.S. 106-401(a), emergency disinfectant and other control measures at all portals of entry into the State, including airports, ports, and other transportation corridors, and any other measures necessary to prevent and control the threat of disease infection.

(c) All State agencies and political subdivisions of the State shall cooperate with the implementation of the emergency procedures and measures developed under this section. All State agencies and political subdivisions of the State shall comply with the emergency procedures and measures developed under this section.

(d) When determined by the State Veterinarian, in consultation with the Commissioner of Agriculture and with the approval of the Governor, that there is an imminent threat within the State of a contagious animal disease that has the potential for very serious and rapid spread, is of serious socioeconomic and public health consequence, or is of major importance in the international trade of animals and animal products, the State Veterinarian or an authorized representative may enter any property in the State to examine any animal that the State Veterinarian has reasonable grounds to believe is infected with or exposed to a contagious animal disease. The owner or operator of the premises on which the animal is located shall permit entry on the premises by the State Veterinarian or an authorized representative and shall cooperate with the State Veterinarian or an authorized representative. The provisions of G.S. 106-401(a) with respect to obtaining an emergency order do not apply to this subsection. (2001-12, s. 1; 2003-6, s. 1; 2005-21, s. 1; 2009-103, s. 1.)

§ 106-399.5. Warrantless inspections.

When determined by the State Veterinarian, in consultation with the Commissioner of Agriculture and with the approval of the Governor, that there is an imminent threat within the State of a contagious animal disease that has the potential for very serious and rapid spread, is of serious socioeconomic and public health consequence, or is of major importance in the international trade of animals and animal products, the State Veterinarian or an authorized representative may stop and inspect without a warrant any individual or any motor vehicle on a public or private road that is moving:

(1) Into the State from any other country, to determine whether the individual or motor vehicle is carrying any animal or any article that is capable of introducing or spreading the animal disease.

(2) In interstate commerce, upon probable cause to believe that the individual or motor vehicle is carrying any animal or any article that is capable of introducing or spreading the animal disease.

(3) In intrastate commerce from any other portion of the State or from any premises or area quarantined under G.S. 106-401, upon probable cause to believe that the individual or motor vehicle is carrying any animal or any article that is capable of introducing or spreading the animal disease. (2001-12, s. 1; 2003-6, s. 1; 2005-21, s. 1; 2009-103, s. 1.)

§ 106-400. Sale or transportation of animals affected with disease prohibited.

No person shall sell, trade, offer for sale or trade, or transport by motor vehicle on any public road or other public place within the State any animal affected with a contagious animal disease, unless permitted by the State Veterinarian in writing and in accordance with the provisions of the permit. The State Veterinarian or an authorized representative may examine any animal that is being transported or moved, sold, traded, or offered for sale or trade on any public road or other public place within the State for the purpose of determining if the animal is affected with a contagious animal disease or is being transported or offered for sale or trade in violation of this Part. If the animal is found to be diseased or is being moved, sold, offered for sale or trade in violation of this Part, it shall be placed under quarantine under G.S. 106-401 in a place to be determined by the State Veterinarian or an authorized representative. Any animal shipped or otherwise moved into this State in violation of federal laws or regulations shall be handled in accordance with the provisions of this Part. (1939, c. 360, s. 1; 2001-12, s. 5; 2003-6, s. 1; 2005-21, s. 1; 2009-103, s. 1.)

§ 106-400.1. Swine disease testing.

In order to control or prevent the spread of swine diseases, the Board of Agriculture may adopt rules authorizing the State Veterinarian or an authorized representative to enter, at reasonable times, the premises where swine are kept and to examine the swine and obtain blood or tissue samples for testing purposes. The State Veterinarian may quarantine swine that have not been properly tested. (1987, c. 793, s. 1; 2001-12, s. 6; 2003-6, s. 1; 2005-21, s. 1; 2009-103, s. 1.)

§ 106-401. State Veterinarian authorized to quarantine.

(a) The State Veterinarian or an authorized representative may enter any property in the State or stop any motor vehicle on a public or private road to examine any animal that the State Veterinarian has reasonable grounds to believe is affected with or exposed to a contagious animal disease. If the person refuses to consent to the entry and examination after the State Veterinarian or an authorized representative has notified, in writing, the owner or person in whose custody the animal is found, of the intention to enter the property and conduct the examination, the State Veterinarian or an authorized representative may petition the district court in the county where the animal is found for an emergency order authorizing the entry and examination. The State Veterinarian or an authorized representative may quarantine any animal affected with or exposed to a contagious disease, or injected with or otherwise exposed to any material capable of producing a contagious disease and shall give public notice of the quarantine by posting or placarding with a suitable quarantine sign the entrance to any part of the premises on which the animal is held. The animal shall be maintained by the owner of the animal or the owner or operator of the premises in accordance with this Part at the expense of the owner of the animal or the owner or operator of the premises. No animal under quarantine shall be removed from the place of quarantine unless permitted by the State Veterinarian or an authorized representative in writing. The quarantine shall remain in effect until cancelled by official written notice from the State Veterinarian or an authorized representative, and the quarantine shall not be cancelled until any sick or diseased animal has been properly disposed of and the premises have been properly cleaned and disinfected.

(b) When determined by the State Veterinarian, in consultation with the Commissioner of Agriculture and with the approval of the Governor, that there is an imminent threat within the State of a contagious animal disease that has the potential for very serious and rapid spread, is of serious socioeconomic and public health consequence, or is of major importance in the international trade of animals and animal products, the State Veterinarian or an authorized representative may quarantine areas within the State. As part of the quarantine under this subsection, the State Veterinarian or an authorized representative may enter any property in the State to examine any animal, to obtain blood and tissue samples for testing for the animal disease, and for any other reason directly related to preventing or controlling the animal disease, and may stop motor vehicles on a public or private road. The provisions of subsection (a) of this section with respect to obtaining an emergency order do not apply to this subsection. Written notice of the quarantine, including a description of the area and the type of animal affected by the disease, shall be mailed or delivered to news media, farm organizations, agriculture agencies, and other entities reasonably calculated to give notice of the quarantine to affected animal owners, to the owners or operators of affected premises, and to the public. No animal subject to the quarantine shall be moved to any other premises unless permitted by the State Veterinarian or an authorized representative in writing. (1939, c. 360, s. 2; 1971, c. 724; 2001-12, s. 2; 2003-6, s. 1; 2005-21, s. 1; 2009-103, s. 1.)

§ 106-401.1. Inspection and quarantine of poultry.

The State Veterinarian or an authorized representative may enter any property in the State or stop any motor vehicle to examine any poultry that the State Veterinarian has reason to believe is affected with or exposed to a contagious animal disease. The State Veterinarian or an authorized representative may quarantine any poultry affected with or exposed to a contagious disease or injected with or otherwise exposed to any material capable of producing a contagious disease and give public notice of the quarantine by posting or placarding with a suitable quarantine sign the entrance to or any part of the premises on which the poultry is held. The poultry shall be maintained by the poultry owner or the owner or operator of the premises in accordance with this Part at the expense of the poultry owner or the owner or operator of the premises. The quarantine under this section does not apply to those diseases that are endemic in the State and for which adequate preventive and control measures are not available. No poultry under quarantine shall be moved from the place of quarantine, unless permitted by the State Veterinarian or an authorized representative in writing. The quarantine shall remain in effect until cancelled by official written notice from the State Veterinarian or an authorized representative and shall not be released or cancelled until the sick or dead poultry have been properly disposed of and the premises have been properly cleaned and disinfected. (1969, c. 693, s. 1; 2001-12, s. 7; 2003-6, s. 1; 2005-21, s. 1; 2009-103, s. 1.)

§ 106-402. Confinement and isolation of diseased animals required.

Any animal or poultry affected with or exposed to a contagious animal disease shall be confined by the owner of the animal or poultry or the owner or operator of the premises in such a manner, by penning or otherwise securing and actually isolating the animal or poultry from the approach or contact with other animals or poultry not so affected; it shall not have access to any ditch, canal, branch, creek, river, or other surface water that passes beyond the affected premises, to any public road, or to the premises of any other person. (1939, c. 360, s. 3; 1969, c. 693, s. 2; 2001-12, s. 8; 2003-6, s. 1; 2005-21, s. 1; 2009-103, s. 1.)

§ 106-402.1. Movement of animals prohibited; destruction of animals to control animal disease authorized.

(a) When determined by the State Veterinarian, in consultation with the Commissioner of Agriculture and with the approval of the Governor, that there is an imminent threat within the State of a contagious animal disease that has the potential for very serious and rapid spread, is of serious socioeconomic and public health consequence, or is of major importance in the international trade of animals and animal products or that it is necessary to control a contagious animal disease, the State Veterinarian or an authorized representative may prohibit the movement of any animal to or from any premises used for shows, sales, markets, fairs, exhibitions, processing or rendering facilities, or other public or private assembly or may prohibit commingling of animals. Written notice of the prohibition under this subsection shall be mailed, delivered, or otherwise provided to the owner or operator of the premises by any means reasonably calculated to give notice. The owner or operator of the premises shall not permit any animal to enter or remain on the premises in violation of this section.

(b) When determined by the State Veterinarian, in consultation with the Commissioner of Agriculture and with the approval of the Governor, that there is an imminent threat within the State of a contagious animal disease that has the potential for very serious and rapid spread, is of serious socioeconomic and public health consequence, or is of major importance in the international trade of animals and animal products or that it is necessary to control a contagious animal disease, the State Veterinarian may order the destruction of any animal and, after consulting with the State Health Director, the proper disposal of the animal. G.S. 106-403 does not apply to the disposal of animals under this subsection. The order shall be in writing and shall include the manner in which the destruction of the animal will be carried out. The order shall be delivered to the owner of the animal and the owner or operator of the premises on which the animal is located by certified mail or any other means reasonably calculated to give the owner of the animal and the owner or operator of the premises notice. In the event the owner of the animal and the owner or operator of the premises cannot be notified, the State Veterinarian or an authorized representative may seize and destroy the animal. The owner or operator of the premises on which the animal is located shall permit entry on the premises by the State Veterinarian or an authorized representative and shall cooperate with the State Veterinarian or an authorized representative. The provisions of G.S. 106-401(a) with respect to obtaining an emergency order do not apply to this subsection.

(c) When determined by the State Veterinarian, in consultation with the Commissioner of Agriculture and with the approval of the Governor, that there is an imminent threat within the State of a contagious animal disease that has the potential for very serious and rapid spread, is of serious socioeconomic and public health consequence, or is of major importance in the international trade of animals and animal products or that it is necessary to control a contagious animal disease, the State Veterinarian may require the Executive Director of the Wildlife Resources Commission to develop a plan to address the movement of wildlife and the destruction of wildlife. (2001-12, s. 3; 2003-6, s. 1; 2005-21, s. 1; 2009-103, s. 1.)

§ 106-403. Disposition of dead domesticated animals.

It is the duty of the owner of domesticated animals that die from any cause and the owner or operator of the premises upon which any domesticated animals die, to bury the animals to a depth of at least three feet beneath the surface of the ground within 24 hours after knowledge of the death of the domesticated animals, or to otherwise dispose of the domesticated animals in a manner approved by the State Veterinarian. It is a violation of this section to bury any dead domesticated animal closer than 300 feet to any flowing stream or public body of water. It is unlawful for any person to remove the carcasses of dead domesticated animals from the person's premises to the premises of any other person without the written permission of the person having charge of the other premises and without burying the carcasses as provided under this section. The governing body of each municipality shall designate some appropriate person whose duty it shall be to provide for the removal and disposal, according to the provisions of this section, of any dead domesticated animals located within the limits of the municipality when the owner of the animals cannot be determined. The board of commissioners of each county shall designate some appropriate person whose duty it shall be to provide for the removal and disposal under this section, of any dead domesticated animals located within the limits of the county, but without the limits of any municipality, when the owner of the animals cannot be determined. All costs incurred by a municipality or county in the removal of dead domesticated animals shall be recoverable from the owner of the animals upon admission of ownership or conviction. "Domesticated animal" as used in this section includes poultry. (1919, c. 36; C.S., s. 4488; 1927, c. 2; 1939, c. 360, s. 4; 1971, c. 567, ss. 1, 2; 2001-12, s. 9; 2003-6, s. 1; 2005-21, s. 1; 2009-103, s. 1.)

§ 106-404. Animals affected with glanders to be killed.

If the owner of any animal having the glanders or farcy omits or refuses, upon discovery or knowledge of its condition, to destroy the animal at once, that person is guilty of a Class 3 misdemeanor. (1881, c. 368, s. 8; Code, s. 2489; 1891, c. 65; Rev., s. 3296; C.S., s. 4489; 1993, c. 539, s. 775; 1994, Ex. Sess., c. 24, s. 14(c); 2001-12, s. 10; 2003-6, s. 1; 2005-21, s. 1; 2009-103, s. 1.)

§ 106-405. Prohibited acts; penalties.

(a) Except as provided in G.S. 106-404, any person who knowingly and willfully violates any provision of this Part is guilty of a Class 2 misdemeanor.

(b) It is prohibited that any person knowingly and willfully:

(1) Hide or conceal any animals that are subject to a quarantine under this Part.

(2) Fail to report the occurrence of an animal disease for which a quarantine under this Part is in effect.

(c) Any person who has committed an act that is prohibited under subsection (b) of this section shall be subject to an administrative penalty not to exceed ten thousand dollars ($10,000) per violation. Each act in violation of subsection (b) of this section is a separate violation. (1939, c. 360, s. 6; 1969, c. 693, s. 3; 1993, c. 539, s. 776; 1994, Ex. Sess., c. 24, s. 14(c); 2001-12, s. 4; 2003-6, s. 1; 2005-21, s. 1; 2009-103, s. 1.)

Part 10. Feeding Garbage to Swine.

§ 106-405.1. Definitions.

For the purpose of this Part, the following words shall have the meanings ascribed to them in this section:

(1) "Garbage" means consisting in whole or in part of animal waste resulting from handling, preparing, cooking and consuming food, including the offal from or parts thereof; provided that the Commissioner of Agriculture or his authorized

representative is empowered to exempt from this definition the waste resulting from the processing of seafood.

(2) "Person" means the State, any municipality, political subdivision, institution, public or private corporation, individual, partnership, or any other entity. (1953, c. 720, s. 1; 1967, c. 872, s. 1.)

§ 106-405.2. Permit for feeding garbage to swine.

(a) No person shall feed garbage to swine without first securing a permit therefor from the North Carolina Commissioner of Agriculture or his authorized agent. Such permits shall be issued for a period of one year and shall be renewable on the date of expiration.

(b) No permit shall be issued or renewed for garbage feeding under this Part in any county or other subdivision in which local regulations to prohibit garbage feeding are in effect.

(c) This Part shall not apply to any individual who feeds only his own household garbage to swine: Provided, that any such swine sold or disposed of shall be sold or disposed of in accordance with rules and regulations promulgated by the State Board of Agriculture.

(d) This Part shall not apply to any person who holds a valid federal permit under the Swine Health Protection Act, P.L. 96-468. (1953, c. 720, s. 2; 1971, c. 566, s. 1; 1981, c. 392.)

§ 106-405.3. Application for permit.

(a) Any person desiring to obtain a permit to feed garbage to swine shall make written application therefor to the North Carolina Commissioner of Agriculture in accordance with requirements of this Part.

(b) The Commissioner of Agriculture is hereby authorized to collect a fee of twenty-five dollars ($25.00) for each permit issued to a garbage feeder under the provisions of this Part. The fees provided for in this Part shall be used exclusively for the enforcement of this Part.

(c) No permit fee shall be collected from any federal, State, county, or municipal institution. (1953, c. 720, s. 3; 1967, c. 872, s. 2.)

§ 106-405.4. Revocation of permits.

Upon determination that any person, having a permit issued under this Part or one who has applied for a permit hereunder, has violated or failed to comply with any provisions of this Part, the North Carolina Commissioner of Agriculture may revoke such permit or refuse to issue a permit to an applicant therefor. (1953, c. 720, s. 4.)

§ 106-405.5. Sanitation.

Premises on which garbage feeding is permitted under this Part must be equipped with feeding platforms constructed of concrete, wood or other impervious material, or troughs of such material of sufficient size to accommodate the swine herd. Premises must be kept free of collections of unused garbage and waste materials. Sanitation, rat and fly control measures must be practiced as a further means of the prevention of the spread of diseases. (1953, c. 720, s. 5.)

§ 106-405.6. Cooking or other treatment.

All garbage, regardless of previous processing, shall, before being fed to swine, be thoroughly heated to at least 212 degrees F. for at least 30 minutes unless treated in some other manner which shall be approved in writing by the North Carolina Commissioner of Agriculture as being equally effective for the protection of animal and human health. (1953, c. 720, s. 6.)

§ 106-405.7. Inspection and investigation; maintenance of records.

(a) Any authorized representative of the North Carolina Commissioner of Agriculture shall have the power to enter at reasonable times upon any private or public property for the purpose of inspecting and investigating conditions relating to the proper treatment of garbage to be fed to swine, sanitation of the premises and health of the animals.

(b) Garbage feeders shall keep a complete permanent record relating to the operation of equipment and their procedure of treating garbage, and also from whom all swine are received and to whom sold for immediate slaughter. Such record is to be available to the Commissioner of Agriculture or his authorized representative.

(c) Any operator, manager or person in charge of a restaurant, cafe, boardinghouse, school, hospital, or other public or private place where food is served to persons other than members of the immediate family or nonpaying guests of such operator, manager, or person in charge, shall not allow or permit garbage to be removed from the premises thereof unless the person removing said garbage is in possession of a valid garbage-feeding permit issued by the North Carolina Department of Agriculture and Consumer Services, or unless such person removing said garbage is in possession of a document from the county department of health wherein such garbage is located stating that the person removing said garbage is authorized to dispose of such garbage in a legal manner or unless such person removing said garbage is an employee of a municipality engaged in the regular collection of garbage for said municipality. The name and address or license number of any motor vehicle of any person removing garbage other than under authorization from the county department of health, the North Carolina Department of Agriculture and Consumer Services or a municipality, shall be reported by such operator, manager or person in charge, to the State Veterinarian within five days after the first removal of such garbage is made. (1953, c. 720, s. 7; 1971, c. 566, s. 2; 1997-261, s. 109.)

§ 106-405.8. Enforcement of Part; rules and regulations.

The North Carolina Commissioner of Agriculture is hereby charged with the administration and enforcement of the provisions of this Part. The North Carolina Commissioner of Agriculture, by and with the consent of the State Board of Agriculture, shall have full power to cooperate with the United States Bureau of Animal Industry in the control and eradication of vesicular exanthema.

The Commissioner of Agriculture, by and with the consent of the State Board of Agriculture, shall have full power to promulgate and enforce such rules and regulations that may hereafter be necessary to carry out the provisions of this Part. (1953, c. 720, s. 8.)

§ 106-405.9. Penalties.

Any person, firm or corporation who shall knowingly violate any provisions set forth in this Part or any rule or regulation duly established by the State Board of Agriculture, or any officer or inspector who shall willfully fail to comply with any provisions of this Part shall be guilty of a Class 1 misdemeanor. Such person, firm, or corporation may be enjoined from continuing such violation. (1953, c. 720, s. 9; 1993, c. 539, s. 777; 1994, Ex. Sess., c. 24, s. 14(c).)

§§ 106-405.10 through 106-405.14. Reserved for future codification purposes.

Part 11. Equine Infectious Anemia.

§ 106-405.15. "Equine infectious anemia" defined.

Equine infectious anemia shall mean the disease wherein an animal is infected with the virus of equine infectious anemia, irrespective of the occurrence or absence of clinical signs of the disease. An animal shall be declared infected with equine infectious anemia if it is classified as a reactor to a serological test or other test approved by the State Veterinarian. (1973, c. 1198, s. 1.)

§ 106-405.16. Animals infected with or exposed to equine infectious anemia declared subject to quarantine.

It is hereby declared that the disease of horses, ponies, mules and asses (and other equine animals) known as equine infectious anemia is of an infectious and contagious nature and that animals infected with, exposed to, or suspected of being carriers of the disease shall be subject to quarantine and identification as required by the rules and regulations of the North Carolina Department of Agriculture and Consumer Services. (1973, c. 1198, s. 2; 1997-261, s. 109.)

§ 106-405.17. Authority to promulgate and enforce rules and regulations.

The State Board of Agriculture shall have full power to promulgate and enforce such rules and regulations as it deems necessary for the control and eradication of equine infectious anemia. This authority shall include, but not be limited to, the power to make regulations requiring the testing of horses, ponies, mules and asses for equine infectious anemia prior to sale, exhibition or assembly at public stables or other public places, and authority to require the owner, operator or person in charge of shows, sales, public stables and other public places to require proof of freedom from equine infectious anemia before any animal is permitted to remain on the premises. The Board shall also have the authority to set fees for such tests as necessary to recover the costs to the North Carolina Department of Agriculture and Consumer Services. (1973, c. 1198, s. 3; 1981, c. 495, s. 7; 1997-261, s. 109.)

§ 106-405.18. Implementation of control and eradication program.

The control and eradication of equine infectious anemia in North Carolina shall be conducted as far as available funds will permit, and in accordance with the rules and regulations made by the Board of Agriculture. The Board of Agriculture is hereby authorized to cooperate with the U.S. Department of Agriculture in the control and eradication of equine infectious anemia. (1973, c. 1198, s. 4.)

§ 106-405.19. Violation made misdemeanor.

Any person who shall willfully move, direct the movement, or allow to be moved, from the premises where quartered any animal or animals known to be infected with equine infectious anemia, or under quarantine because of suspected exposure to equine infectious anemia, or who shall violate any provision of this Part or any rule or regulation promulgated by the Board of Agriculture under this Part shall be guilty of a Class 1 misdemeanor. (1973, c. 1198, s. 5; 1993, c. 539, s. 778; 1994, Ex. Sess., c. 24, s. 14(c).)

Part 12. Penalties.

§ 106-405.20. Civil penalties.

The Commissioner may assess a civil penalty of not more than five thousand dollars ($5,000) against any person who violates a provision of this Article or any rule promulgated thereunder. In determining the amount of the penalty, the Commissioner shall consider the degree and extent of harm caused by the violation.

The clear proceeds of civil penalties assessed pursuant to this section shall be remitted to the Civil Penalty and Forfeiture Fund in accordance with G.S. 115C-457.2. (1995, c. 516, s. 8; 1998-215, s. 12.)

Article 35.

Public Livestock Markets.

§ 106-406. Permits from Commissioner of Agriculture for operation of public livestock markets; application therefor; hearing on application.

Any person, firm or corporation desiring to operate a public livestock market within the State of North Carolina shall be required to file an application with the Commissioner of Agriculture for a permit authorizing the operation of such market; provided that, those markets operating under a valid permit and in accordance with G.S. 106-406 through 106-418 at the time this Article becomes effective shall be issued a license upon payment of the annual license fee and upon satisfying the requirement for bonding as specified in G.S. 106-407. An application for a permit shall include the following information:

(1) The name and address of the applicant, name of market and a listing of the names and addresses of all persons having any financial interest in the proposed livestock market and the amount and nature of such interest, and such other information as is required to complete an application form supplied by the Commissioner; and

(2) The plans and specifications for the facilities proposed to be built, or for existing structures.

The application for a permit shall be accompanied by a permit fee of two hundred fifty dollars ($250.00), two hundred dollars ($200.00) of which shall be returned to the applicant if the application is denied, plus one hundred dollars ($100.00) annual permit fee for the first year of operation of the market, all of which shall be returned to the applicant if the application is denied. There shall be an annual renewal fee of one hundred dollars ($100.00) for each year of operation thereafter.

Upon the filing of said application, the Commissioner shall determine whether all necessary information has been furnished. If all information required has not been furnished, the Commissioner shall notify the applicant by mail of the additional information needed; it shall be furnished the Commissioner by the applicant within 10 days of such notification. Upon receipt of all required information, the Commissioner shall issue a license or fix the date of a hearing on said application, to be held in Raleigh. Notice of the time and date of the hearing shall be published in a newspaper having general circulation in the county in which the livestock market is proposed to be located; said notice shall appear at least 10 days prior to such hearing. The applicant shall be notified by mail by the Commissioner at least 20 days prior to the hearing of the time and place of said hearing. The Commissioner shall also notify by mail the members of the Public Livestock Market Advisory Board of the time and place of said hearing, at least 10 days before the date [on] which the hearing will be held.

A public hearing shall be conducted by the Commissioner on said application. If, after the hearing, at which any person may appear in support or opposition thereto, the North Carolina Public Livestock Market Advisory Board finds that the public livestock market for which a permit or license is sought fulfills the requirements of all applicable laws, it shall recommend to the Commissioner that a permit be issued to the applicant. If the Commissioner denies the application, the applicant may commence a contested case under G.S. 150B-23 by filing a petition within 10 days after receiving notice of the denial. Unless revoked by the Board of Agriculture pursuant to any applicable law or regulation, permits will be renewed each July 1 on payment of the annual renewal fee. (1941, c. 263, s. 1; 1943, c. 724, s. 1; 1967, c. 894, s. 1; 1971, c. 739, s. 1; 1973, c. 1331, s. 3; 1975, c. 69, s. 4; 1977, c. 132, ss. 1-3; 1987, c. 827, s. 32.)

§ 106-407. Bonds required of operators; exemption of certain market operations.

The Commissioner of Agriculture shall require the owner of each public livestock market issued a permit under the provisions of G.S. 106-406 to furnish a bond acceptable to the Commissioner of not less than five thousand dollars ($5,000) nor more than fifty thousand dollars ($50,000), in the discretion of the Commissioner, to secure the performance of all obligations incident to the operation of the public livestock market operation including prompt payment to the vendors of all livestock sold at said market; provided, that, at the discretion of the Commissioner of Agriculture, a bond shall not be required of a livestock market bonded under the Federal Packers and Stockyards Act.

The term "public livestock market" as used in this Article shall not be interpreted to mean any of the following:

(1)   A market where horses and mules exclusively are sold;

(2)   A market that sells only finished livestock to be used for immediate slaughter;

(3)   A dispersal sale of livestock by a farmer, dairyman, livestock breeder, or feeder when all animals offered for sale have been owned by him at least 30 days; provided that, no more than one dispersal sale shall be held by any person, firm or corporation within any period of six months.

(4)   Purebred livestock association sales and those sales where Future Farmers of America, 4-H Clubs and similar groups, State institutions, or private fairs conduct sales of livestock. (1941, c. 263, s. 2; 1967, c. 894, s. 2.)

§ 106-407.1. North Carolina Public Livestock Market Advisory Board created; appointment; membership; duties.

There is hereby created the North Carolina Public Livestock Market Advisory Board composed of eight persons, all of whom shall be residents of North Carolina, who shall be appointed and the chairman designated by the Commissioner of Agriculture on or before August 1, 1967. Two members of said Board shall be livestock producers, two shall be licensed livestock market operators, one shall be a meat packer, one shall be the State Veterinarian, one shall be a duly licensed and practicing veterinarian and one shall be an employee of the markets division of the North Carolina Department of Agriculture and Consumer Services. On the initial Board, two members shall be appointed for terms of one year, two members for terms of two years, two members for terms of three years, and two members for terms of four years. Thereafter, all members shall serve four-year terms. Any vacancy on the Board caused by death, resignation, or otherwise shall be filled by the Commissioner of Agriculture for the expiration of the term. The terms of all members of the initial and subsequent boards shall expire on June 30 of the year in which their terms expire.

It shall be the duty of the members of the Board to attend all hearings on applications for licenses to operate public livestock markets. The Board may meet once each year, or more often if directed by the Commissioner, in Raleigh or such other place in North Carolina as directed by the Commissioner for the purpose of (i) discussing problems of the livestock market industry, (ii) proposing changes in the rules and regulations of the Department of Agriculture and Consumer Services relative to public livestock markets, and (iii) making such other recommendations to the Commissioner and the Board of Agriculture as it deems in the best interest of the livestock industry of North Carolina.

Members of the Board, except members who are employees of the State, shall receive as compensation, subsistence and travel allowances, such sums as by law are provided for other commissions and boards. Compensation, subsistence and travel allowances authorized for the Board members shall be paid from fees collected pursuant to this Article. (1967, c. 894, s. 3; 1977, c. 132, s. 4; 1981, c. 337; 1997-261, s. 109.)

§ 106-407.2. Revocation of permit by Board of Agriculture; restraining order for violations.

The Board of Agriculture may revoke a permit authorizing the operation of a public livestock market for a violation of this Article or a rule adopted under this Article.

If any person, firm or corporation shall operate a public livestock market in violation of the provisions of this Article, or the rules and regulations promulgated by the North Carolina Board of Agriculture, or shall fail to comply with the provisions of this Article, or rules and regulations promulgated thereunder, a temporary or permanent restraining order may be issued by a judge of the superior court upon application by the Commissioner of Agriculture, or his authorized representative, and the judge of the superior court shall have the same power and authority as in any other injunction proceeding, and the defendant shall have the same rights including the right of appeal, as in any other injunction proceeding heard before the superior court. (1967, c. 894, s. 4; 1973, c. 1331, s. 3; 1987, c. 827, s. 33.)

§ 106-408. Marketing facilities prescribed; records of purchases and sales; time of sales; notice.

All public livestock markets operating under this Article shall have proper facilities for handling livestock and such other equipment as specified by regulation of the North Carolina Board of Agriculture. Scales approved by the North Carolina Division of Weights and Measures shall be provided at public livestock markets where animals are bought, sold or exchanged by weight. The premises, including yards, pens, alleys, and chutes shall be cleaned and disinfected in accordance with regulations promulgated by the Board of Agriculture pursuant to the authority contained in G.S. 106-416. The market shall keep a complete legible permanent record, including the use of numbered invoices, showing the name and address of the person or firm from whom all animals are received and the name and address of the person or firm to whom sold. Symbols in lieu of names shall not be used. The weight, if sold by weight, and the price paid and the price received shall be recorded on the invoice. Such records as specified in this section shall be available for inspection to the Commissioner of Agriculture or his authorized representative during regular business hours.

The sales of all livestock at livestock auction markets shall start no later than 2:00 P.M.; provided, however, the Commissioner of Agriculture shall have authority to authorize a sale to begin as late as 4:00 P.M. when the sale (i) consists solely of the sale of pigs weighing no more than 150 pounds and sold as feeder pigs, (ii) continues without interruption, and (iii) lasts no later than 5:00 P.M., or when the sale consists solely of slaughter hogs sold by teleconference. The sale of livestock shall be continuous until all are sold.

Each public livestock market operator operating under this Article shall post notice of the day(s) of sale and the starting time in a conspicuous place on the market premises. In the event of subsequent changes in day of sale or starting time, the operator shall post notice on the premises and notify the State Veterinarian in writing at least two weeks in advance of the date of change.

(1941, c. 263, s. 3; 1949, c. 997, s. 1; 1961, c. 275, s. 1; 1967, c. 894, s. 5; 1969, c. 983; 1971, c. 739, s. 2; 1987, c. 436.)

§ 106-408.1. Market operation fees.

A fee of twenty-five dollars ($25.00) shall be paid by the market operator to the North Carolina Department of Agriculture and Consumer Services for each day, or fraction thereof, a sale is held, provided that an additional maximum fee of ten dollars ($10.00) per one-half hour, or fraction thereof, shall be paid to the North Carolina Department of Agriculture and Consumer Services for operation after 6:00 P.M. Provided further, that the Board of Agriculture may at its discretion adjust both fees for market operation within the limits set in this section. A fee to be set by the Board of Agriculture may be charged to the buyer of cattle and swine required to be tested under G.S. 106-409 and 106-410, and the amount collected used to offset the twenty-five dollar ($25.00) market operation fee. All test fees charged in excess of twenty-five dollars ($25.00) shall revert to the North Carolina Department of Agriculture and Consumer Services and be payable within 24 hours following the close of a sale day. The starting and finishing time of each sale shall be recorded by the livestock inspector on his report of the sale. A copy of the report shall be given to the market operator or his representative following the sale. Failure to make the required payment within 24 hours following close of a sale day shall be cause for the Commissioner of Agriculture to prohibit, on 72 hours' notice, further sales at the market until the account is paid in full. The operation fee shall be waived when a livestock market operator employs a licensed, accredited veterinarian approved by the State Veterinarian to be present at the market from the starting time of the sale until all livestock to be admitted to the sales barn on that sale day have entered and such work in inspection, testing and vaccination as designated by the State Veterinarian has been completed. (1971, c. 739, s. 3; 1997-261, s. 109.)

§ 106-409. Removal of cattle from market for slaughter and nonslaughter purposes; identification; permit needed.

No cattle except those for immediate slaughter, shall be removed from any public livestock market except in accordance with this Article and regulations adopted by the North Carolina Board of Agriculture. All cattle removed from any public livestock market for immediate slaughter shall be identified in a manner approved by the Commissioner of Agriculture and the person removing same shall before removal sign a form in duplicate showing the number of cattle, their description, and where same are to be slaughtered or resold for slaughter. Cattle sold for slaughter shall be disposed of in one of the following ways:

(1) Moved directly to a recognized slaughtering establishment for immediate slaughter.

(2) Sold to a dealer bonded under the Packers and Stockyards Act who handles cattle for immediate slaughter.

(3) Offered for resale for slaughter through a livestock auction market holding a valid permit issued under this Article.

A "buying station" of a slaughterhouse or similar business not operating under a public livestock market permit shall not allow the removal of animals for any purpose other than that of immediate slaughter unless a written permit has been secured from the State Veterinarian or his authorized representative. This provision shall not apply to buying stations operated by feedlot operators buying animals for movement to their own feedlots.

Cattle sold for immediate slaughter shall be used for no other purpose unless prior written permission has been secured from the State Veterinarian or his authorized representative. No livestock market operator, or agent or employee thereof, shall allow the removal of any cattle from a market in violation of this section. (1941, c. 263, s. 4; 1943, c. 724, s. 2; 1949, c. 997, s. 2; 1967, c. 894, s. 6.)

§ 106-410. Removal of swine from market for slaughter and nonslaughter purposes; identification; permit needed; resale for feeding or breeding; out-of-state shipment.

No swine, except those for immediate slaughter, shall be removed from any public livestock market except in accordance with regulations adopted by the North Carolina Board of Agriculture. All swine removed from any public livestock market for immediate slaughter shall be identified in a manner prescribed by regulation adopted by the North Carolina Board of Agriculture and the person removing same shall sign a form in duplicate showing the number of hogs, their description and where they are to be slaughtered or resold for slaughter. Slaughter hogs may be disposed of in one of the following ways:

(1)   Moved directly to a recognized slaughter establishment for immediate slaughter.

(2)   Sold to a dealer, bonded under the Packers and Stockyards Act, who handles hogs for immediate slaughter.

(3)   Offered for resale for slaughter through a livestock auction market holding a valid permit issued under this Article.

Swine sold for immediate slaughter shall be used for no other purpose unless prior written permission has been secured from the State Veterinarian or his authorized representative. No market operator shall allow the removal of any swine from a market in violation of this section.

Swine for breeding or feeding purposes shall not be resold in a livestock market for other than immediate slaughter within 14 days of prior sale at a livestock market unless they are identified as having been previously sold swine at the time of resale. Such identification shall contain the date and place of the prior sale and shall be furnished in writing to the market operator by the seller of said swine.

Provided, however, that the Commissioner of Agriculture may permit swine to be shipped out of the State of North Carolina, under the same conditions as if said swine were being delivered for immediate slaughter, for immediate delivery to holding or feeding lots in any other state when he determines that said holding or feeding lots are being operated in compliance with the laws of said state and the rules and regulations promulgated thereunder. (1941, c. 263, s. 5; 1943, c. 724, s. 3; 1949, c. 997, ss. 3, 4; 1967, c. 894, s. 7; 1971, c. 739, s. 5.)

§ 106-411. Regulation of use of livestock removed from market; swine shipped out of State.

Any person or persons who shall remove, or whose agent or employee at the direction of the employer, shall remove from a public livestock market any cattle, swine, or other livestock for immediate slaughter shall use them for immediate slaughter only or resale for immediate slaughter only in compliance with this

Article and the applicable regulations of the Department of Agriculture and Consumer Services. It shall be a Class 1 misdemeanor for the owner of any cattle, swine or other livestock purchased for immediate slaughter, to order, direct or procure his agent or employee to transport said cattle, swine, or other livestock to any place other than a recognized slaughter plant or as provided in G.S. 106-409 and G.S. 106-410; and the agent or employee who transports said animal or animals shall likewise be guilty of a Class 1 misdemeanor.

Provided that, it shall not be a violation of law to ship swine out of this State to holding or feeding lots as provided for in G.S. 106-410. (1941, c. 263, s. 6; 1943, c. 724, s. 4; 1949, c. 997, s. 5; 1967, c. 894, s. 8; 1993, c. 539, s. 779; 1994, Ex. Sess., c. 24, s. 14(c); 1997-261, s. 109.)

§ 106-412. Admission of animals to markets; quarantine of diseased animals; sale restricted; regulation of trucks, etc.

No animal known to be affected with or having visible symptoms of a contagious or infectious disease shall be received or admitted into any public livestock market except upon special permit issued by the Commissioner of Agriculture or his authorized representative. All animals affected with, or exposed to, any contagious or infectious disease of animals or any animal that reacts to an official test indicating the presence of such a disease, shall be quarantined separate and apart from healthy animals and shall not be sold, traded, or otherwise disposed of except upon written permission of the Commissioner of Agriculture or his authorized representative. All animals sold for slaughter under this provision must be moved directly to a recognized slaughter establishment with State or federal meat inspection unless written permission to do otherwise is secured from the State Veterinarian or his authorized representative. The owner of the animals shall be responsible for the cost of maintaining the quarantine, the necessary treatment, and the feed and care of the animals while under quarantine and said costs shall constitute a lien against all of said animals. All trucks, trailers, and other conveyances used in transporting livestock shall be cleaned and disinfected in accordance with the regulations issued by authority of this Article. (1941, c. 263, s. 7; 1967, c. 894, s. 9.)

§ 106-413. Sale, etc., of certain diseased animals restricted; application of Article; sales by farmers.

No person or persons shall sell or offer for sale, trade or otherwise dispose of any animal or animals that are affected with a contagious or infectious disease, or that the owner or person in charge or a livestock inspector or an approved veterinarian has reason to believe are so affected or exposed; provided, however, that upon written permission of the Commissioner of Agriculture or his authorized representative it shall be lawful to sell, trade, or otherwise dispose of such animals for immediate slaughter at a plant with State or federal meat inspection. The provisions of this Article, including those regulations adopted by the North Carolina Board of Agriculture, shall apply to all animals sold or offered for sale on any public highway, right-of-way, street, or within one-half mile of any public livestock market, or other public place; provided, that the one-half mile provision shall not apply to animals raised and owned by a bona fide farmer who is a resident of the State of North Carolina and sold or offered for sale by him. (1941, c. 263, s. 8; 1943, c. 724, s. 5; 1967, c. 894, s. 10.)

§ 106-414. Transportation, sale, etc., of diseased livestock; burden of proving health; movement to laboratory; removal of identification.

No cattle, swine, or other livestock with visible symptoms of a contagious or infectious disease shall be transported or otherwise moved on any public highway or street in this State except upon written permission of the Commissioner of Agriculture or his authorized representative. The burden of proof to establish the health of any animal transported on the public highways of this State, or sold, traded, or otherwise disposed of in any public place shall be upon the vendor. Any person who shall sell, trade, or otherwise dispose of any animal affected with, or exposed to, a contagious or infectious disease, or one he has or should have reason to believe is so affected, or exposed, shall be civilly liable for all damages resulting from such sale or trade; provided that, nothing in this section shall prevent an individual who owns or has custody of sick animals from transporting sick or dead animals to a disease diagnostic laboratory operated or approved by the North Carolina Department of Agriculture and Consumer Services if reasonable and proper precautions to prevent the exposure of other animals is taken by the owner or transporter thereof.

It shall be a Class 1 misdemeanor to remove before slaughter any ear tag, back tag, or other mark of identification approved by the Commissioner of Agriculture for identifying animals for disease control purposes unless prior written authorization has been obtained from the State Veterinarian or his authorized representative. (1941, c. 263, s. 9; 1967, c. 894, s. 11; 1993, c. 539, s. 780; 1994, Ex. Sess., c. 24, s. 14(c); 1997-261, s. 109.)

§ 106-415. Cost of tests, serums, etc.

The cost of all tests, serums, vaccines and other medical supplies necessary for the enforcement of this Article and the protection of livestock against contagious and infectious diseases shall be paid for by the owner of said livestock and the cost shall constitute a lien against all said animals; provided that, the Commissioner of Agriculture, by and with the consent of the Board of Agriculture, is hereby authorized to determine reasonable charges and costs for such tests, serums, vaccines, and other medical supplies; provided further, that an animal which shows a reaction to a test for brucellosis shall be automatically "no-saled" and resold for immediate slaughter and the cost of the test paid by the original seller. (1941, c. 263, s. 10; 1949, c. 997, s. 6; 1957, c. 1269; 1967, c. 894, s. 12.)

§ 106-416. Rules and regulations.

The Commissioner of Agriculture, by and with the consent of the State Board of Agriculture, shall have full power to promulgate and enforce such rules and regulations that may be necessary to carry out the provisions of this Article. This power shall include, but not be confined to, the authority to designate a time after which livestock shall not be allowed to enter a sales barn on the day of a sale. (1941, c. 263, s. 11; 1967, c. 894, s. 13; 1971, c. 739, s. 4.)

§ 106-417. Violation made misdemeanor; responsibility for health, etc., of animals.

Any person, firm, or corporation who shall knowingly violate any provisions set forth in this Article or any rule or regulation duly established by the State Board of Agriculture, or any officer or inspector who shall willfully fail to comply with any provisions of this Article, shall be guilty of a Class 1 misdemeanor. A market operating under this Article shall not be responsible for the health or death of an animal sold through such market if the provisions of this Article have been complied with. (1941, c. 263, s. 12; 1943, c. 724, s. 6; 1967, c. 894, s. 14; 1993, c. 539, s. 781; 1994, Ex. Sess., c. 24, s. 14(c).)

§ 106-417.1. Civil penalties.

The Commissioner may assess a civil penalty of not more than five thousand dollars ($5,000) against any person who violates a provision of this Article or any rule promulgated thereunder. In determining the amount of the penalty, the Commissioner shall consider the degree and extent of harm caused by the violation.

The clear proceeds of civil penalties assessed pursuant to this section shall be remitted to the Civil Penalty and Forfeiture Fund in accordance with G.S. 115C-457.2. (1995, c. 516, s. 9; 1998-215, s. 13.)

§ 106-418. Exemption from health provisions.

The health provisions of this Article shall not apply to "no-sale" cattle offered for sale at a public livestock market by a bona fide farmer who has owned them at least 60 days. (1941, c. 263, s. 12 1/2; 1967, c. 894, s. 15.)

Article 35A.

North Carolina Livestock Prompt Pay Law.

§ 106-418.1. Short title.

This Article shall be known by the short title of "North Carolina Livestock Prompt Pay Law." (1973, c. 38, s. 2.)

§ 106-418.2. Legislative intent and purpose.

The purpose of the Article is to regulate the sale of livestock by auction at public livestock markets and to assure prompt payment for livestock sold. (1973, c. 38, s. 1.)

§ 106-418.3. Definitions.

As used in this Article, unless the context clearly requires otherwise:

(1) "Banking business day" means a day in which banks are normally open for business in North Carolina.

(2) "Commissioner" means the Commissioner of Agriculture of North Carolina or his designated agent or agents.

(3) "Custodial accounts" means custodial accounts for trust funds as explained in the Code of Federal Regulations, January 1, 1972, § 201.42.

(4) The "North Carolina Public Livestock Market Advisory Board" means the Board established under G.S. 106-407.1.

(5) "Public livestock market" means livestock sales at a market duly licensed under G.S. 106-406. (1973, c. 38, s. 3; 1975, c. 19, s. 33.)

§ 106-418.4. Duties of Commissioner.

The Commissioner shall regulate, by and with the consent of the Board of Agriculture as provided herein, the payment for livestock sold at auction. (1973, c. 38, s. 4.)

§ 106-418.5. Collection of payment.

Collection of payment for livestock purchased at auction shall be made by the public livestock market on the same date of purchase of the livestock, and the proceeds therefrom shall be deposited by the public livestock market in their custodial account not later than the next banking business day following the date of sale. Collection for livestock purchased by auction shall be made by cash, check, or draft. There shall be no loans made from the custodial account of any public livestock market to any purchaser of livestock at said sales establishment. Payment shall be made by the public livestock market to the seller of livestock at auction not later than one banking business day after the date of sale of the animal or animals. (1973, c. 38, s. 5.)

§ 106-418.6. Action upon failure of payment.

It shall be the duty and responsibility of each public livestock market to report to the Commissioner within 24 hours after having knowledge that a check or draft issued in payment for livestock has been dishonored or that a buyer of livestock at auction has not fulfilled his obligation to pay for livestock within the prescribed time in G.S. 106-418.5. It shall be the duty and responsibility of the Commissioner to notify all public livestock markets of the fact of dishonor of any such check issued or the failure to honor any draft upon presentation used in payment for livestock or due to the lack of satisfactory payment for livestock. (1973, c. 38, s. 6.)

§ 106-418.7. Authority of Board of Agriculture, North Carolina Public Livestock Market Advisory Board and the Commissioner.

The Board of Agriculture shall establish rules and regulations pertaining to the purchase and payment of livestock sold in this State at public livestock markets. The North Carolina Public Livestock Market Advisory Board shall recommend rules and regulations pertaining to the administration of this Article to the Board of Agriculture for their consideration. The Commissioner is authorized to revoke any livestock market operator's license issued or to refuse to issue a livestock market license to any person as hereinafter provided upon satisfactory proof that said person has repeatedly violated any of the provisions of this Article or any of the rules and regulations made and promulgated thereunder; provided that no license shall be revoked or refused until the person, firm or corporation shall have first been given an opportunity to appear at a hearing before the Commissioner or his agent. Any person who is refused a license, or whose license is revoked by any order of the Commissioner, may appeal within 30 days from said order to the Superior Court of Wake County or the superior court of the county of his residence. (1973, c. 38, s. 7; 1989, c. 770, s. 25.)

§ 106-418.7A. Civil penalties.

The Commissioner may assess a civil penalty of not more than five thousand dollars ($5,000) against any person who violates a provision of this Article or any rule promulgated thereunder. In determining the amount of the penalty, the Commissioner shall consider the degree and extent of harm caused by the violation.

The clear proceeds of civil penalties assessed pursuant to this section shall be remitted to the Civil Penalty and Forfeiture Fund in accordance with G.S. 115C-457.2. (1995, c. 516, s. 10; 1998-215, s. 14.)

Article 35B.

Livestock Dealer Licensing Act.

§ 106-418.8. Definitions.

When used in this Article,

(1) The term "Commissioner" means the Commissioner of Agriculture of North Carolina;

(2) The term "livestock" means cattle, sheep, goats, swine, horses and mules;

(3) The term "livestock dealer" means any person who buys livestock (i) for his own account for purposes of resale, or (ii) for the account of others; and

(4) The term "person" means an individual, partnership, corporation, association, or other legal entity. (1973, c. 196.)

§ 106-418.9. Exemptions.

The provisions of this Article shall not apply to a person who offers for sale or trade only livestock which he has raised or livestock which he owns or has had in his possession for a period of 30 days or longer or who has had the livestock grown under contract, and is not engaged in the business of buying, selling, trading, or negotiating the transfer of livestock. Neither shall this Article apply to a livestock market operator conducting sales in compliance with the Public Livestock Markets Act (General Statutes Chapter 106, Article 35). (1973, c. 196.)

§ 106-418.10. Prohibited conduct.

It shall be unlawful for any person to:

(1)   Carry on or conduct the business of a livestock dealer without a current valid license issued by the North Carolina Department of Agriculture and Consumer Services under the provisions of this Article;

(2)   Fail to keep the records required by G.S. 106-418.13. (1973, c. 196; 1997-261, s. 52.)

§ 106-418.11. Licenses.

(a)   Any person desiring to be licensed as a livestock dealer shall make application to the Commissioner. Such application shall contain the address, both business and personal, of the applicant. No financial information shall be required from the applicant.

Whenever an applicant has complied with this Article, the Commissioner shall issue to such applicant a license which shall entitle the licensee to engage in the business of livestock dealer for a period of one year, unless such license is sooner suspended, or revoked in accordance with the provisions of this Article.

The license may be renewed annually by written request to the Commissioner on a form prepared by the Department of Agriculture and Consumer Services, which form shall require only the name and current address of the licensee. No renewal fee shall be charged.

(b)   The Commissioner may suspend for a period not to exceed 120 days the license of any livestock dealer whom the Commissioner finds has violated

G.S. 106-418.10(2). For a second violation of G.S. 106-418.10(2) within a period of two years, the Commissioner may revoke a dealer's license.

(c) The Commissioner may refuse to issue a license to any person who has (i) within five years of his application therefor, been finally adjudicated as having on two or more occasions violated the provisions of G.S. 106-418.10(1) or (ii) on three or more occasions within five years of his application therefor been finally adjudicated as violating G.S. 106-418.10(2).

(d) All proceedings relative to the suspension, revocation, or refusal of a license shall be conducted pursuant to the provisions of Chapter 150B of the General Statutes. (1973, c. 196; c. 1331, s. 3; 1975, c. 19, s. 34; 1987, c. 827, s. 1; 1997-261, s. 109.)

§ 106-418.12. Hearings.

Any hearing required or permitted to be held pursuant to this Article may be conducted by the Commissioner or his delegate and his decision shall be treated for all purposes as that of the Commissioner. (1973, c. 196.)

§ 106-418.13. Maintenance of records.

Every livestock dealer shall keep complete records for at least one year of all transactions involving livestock and permit any authorized agent of the Commissioner to have access to and to copy all records relating to such transactions. Such records shall consist of the approximate age, breed and species of the livestock, the date of sale, name and address of persons from whom and to whom livestock are sold and traded. (1973, c. 196.)

§ 106-418.14. Penalties.

Any person who violates G.S. 106-418.10(1) is guilty of a Class 3 misdemeanor. For a second or subsequent violation of G.S. 106-418.10(1), a person is guilty of a Class 2 misdemeanor. (1973, c. 196; 1999-408, s. 5.)

§ 106-418.15. Short title.

This Article may be cited as the "Livestock Dealer Licensing Act." (1973, c. 196.)

§ 106-418.16. Civil penalties.

The Commissioner may assess a civil penalty of not more than five thousand dollars ($5,000) against any person who violates a provision of this Article or any rule promulgated thereunder. In determining the amount of the penalty, the Commissioner shall consider the degree and extent of harm caused by the violation.

The clear proceeds of civil penalties assessed pursuant to this section shall be remitted to the Civil Penalty and Forfeiture Fund in accordance with G.S. 115C-457.2. (1995, c. 516, s. 11; 1998-215, s. 15.)

Article 36.

Plant Pests.

§ 106-419. Plant pest defined.

A plant pest is hereby defined to mean any insect, mite, nematode, other invertebrate animal, disease, noxious weed, plant or animal parasite in any stage of development which is injurious to plants and plant products. (1957, c. 985.)

§ 106-419.1. Plants, plant products and other objects exposed to plant pests.

Any plant, plant product, object or article which has been, or which the Commissioner of Agriculture or his agents have reasonable grounds to believe has been exposed to a plant pest, may be treated as a plant pest for the purposes of this Article. (1971, c. 526.)

§ 106-420. Authority of Board of Agriculture to adopt regulations.

The Board of Agriculture is hereby authorized to adopt reasonable regulations to implement and carry out the purposes of this Article as to eradicate, repress and prevent the spread of plant pests (i) within the State, (ii) from within the State to points outside the State, and (iii) from outside the State to points within the State. The Board of Agriculture shall adopt regulations for eradicating such plant pests as it may deem capable of being economically eradicated, for repressing such as cannot be economically eradicated, and for preventing their spread within the State. Regulations may provide for quarantine of areas. It may also adopt reasonable regulations for preventing the introduction of dangerous plant pests from without the State, and for governing common carriers in transporting plants, articles or things liable to harbor such pests into, from and within the State. The Board is authorized, in order to control plant pests, to adopt regulations governing the inspection, certification and movement of nursery stock, (i) into the State from outside the State, (ii) within the State, and (iii) from within the State to points outside the State. The Board is further authorized to prescribe and collect a schedule of fees to be collected for its nursery inspection, nursery dealer certification, narcissus bulb inspection, plant pest inspection, and plant pest certification activities. (1957, c. 985; 1991, c. 442, s. 1.)

§ 106-420.1. Agreements against plant pests.

The North Carolina Board of Agriculture is authorized to enter into agreements with any agency of the United States or any agency of another state for the eradication, suppression, control and prevention of spread of plant pests. The Commissioner of Agriculture is authorized to enter into agreements with any unit of local government in this State or any organization incorporated or unincorporated who has an interest in the control of plant pests for the eradication, suppression, control and prevention of spread of plant pests. (1971, c. 526.)

§ 106-421. Permitting uncontrolled existence of plant pests; nuisance; method of abatement.

No person shall knowingly and willfully keep upon his premises any plant or plant product infested or infected by any dangerous plant pest, or permit dangerous plants or plant parasites to mature seed or otherwise multiply upon his land, except under such regulations as the Board of Agriculture may prescribe. All such infested or infected plants and premises are hereby declared public nuisances. The owner of such plants or premises shall, when notified to do so by the Commissioner of Agriculture, take such measures as may be prescribed to eradicate such pests. The notice shall be in writing and shall be mailed to the usual or last known address, or left at the ordinary place of business, of the owner or his agent. If such person fails to comply with such notice within such reasonable time as the notice prescribes, the Commissioner of Agriculture, through his duly authorized agents, shall proceed to take such measures as shall be necessary to eradicate such pests, and shall compute the actual costs of labor and materials used in eradicating such pests, and the owner of the premises in question shall pay to the Commissioner of Agriculture such assessed costs. No damages shall be awarded the owner of such premises for entering thereon and destroying or otherwise treating any infected or infested plants or soil when done by the order of the Commissioner of Agriculture. (1957, c. 985.)

§ 106-421.1. Authority of Board of Agriculture to regulate plants.

The Board of Agriculture shall have the sole authority to prohibit the planting, cultivation, harvesting, disposal, handling, or movement of plants as defined in G.S. 106-202.12. This section shall not prevent the designation of plants as noxious aquatic weeds pursuant to Article 15 of Chapter 113A of the General Statutes, nor shall it prevent the adoption or enforcement of city or county ordinances regulating the appearance of property or the handling and collection of solid waste. (2013-197, s. 1.)

§ 106-422. Agents of Board; inspection.

The Commissioner of Agriculture shall be the agent of the Board in enforcing these regulations, and shall have authority to designate such employees of the Department as may seem expedient to carry out the duties and exercise the powers provided by this Article. Persons collaborating with the Division of Entomology may also be designated by the Commissioner of Agriculture as agents for the purpose of this Article. The Commissioner of Agriculture, and any duly authorized agent of the Commissioner, shall have the authority to inspect vehicles or other means of transportation and its cargo suspected of carrying plant pests and to enter upon and inspect any premises between the hours of sunrise and sunset during every working day of the year to determine the presence or absence of injurious plant pests. Any duly authorized agent of the Commissioner shall have authority to stop or cause to be stopped on any highway or other public place, by any law-enforcement officer at the request of said authorized agent of the Commissioner, any vehicle or other means of transportation that is being used, or that the representative of the Commissioner has reasonable grounds to believe is being used, to transport or move any plant, plant product or seed in violation of the provisions of this Article. (1957, c. 985; 1967, c. 976.)

§ 106-423. Nursery inspection; nursery dealer's certificate; narcissus inspection.

The Board of Agriculture shall have the authority to define nursery stock. The Commissioner of Agriculture shall have the right to cause all plant nurseries, and narcissus bulb fields where narcissus bulbs are commercially raised, within the State to be inspected at least once each year for serious plant pests. Every person, firm or corporation buying and reselling nursery stock shall register and secure a dealer's certificate for each location from which plants are sold. (1957, c. 985.)

§ 106-423.1. Criminal penalties; violation of laws or regulations.

If anyone shall attempt to prevent inspection of his premises as provided in the preceding sections, or shall otherwise interfere with the Commissioner of Agriculture, or any of his agents, while engaged in the performance of his duties under this Article, or shall violate any provisions of this Article or any regulations of the Board of Agriculture adopted pursuant to this Article, he shall be guilty of a Class 3 misdemeanor. Each day's violation shall constitute a separate offense. (1957, c. 985; 1993, c. 539, s. 782; 1994, Ex. Sess., c. 24, s. 14(c).)

Article 37.

Cotton Grading.

§§ 106-424 through 106-429. Repealed by Session Laws 1999-44, s. 3, effective May 13, 1999.

Article 38.

Marketing Cotton and Other Agricultural Commodities.

§§ 106-429.1 through 106-434: Repealed by Session Laws 1997-74, s. 10.

§ 106-435. Fund for support of system; collection and investment.

In order to provide a sufficient indemnifying or guarantee fund to cover any loss not covered by the bonds hereinbefore mentioned, in order to provide the financial backing which is essential to make the warehouse receipt universally acceptable as collateral, and in order to provide that a State warehouse system intended to benefit all cotton growers in North Carolina shall be supported by the class it is designed to benefit, it is hereby declared: that on each bale of cotton ginned in North Carolina during the period from the ratification of this bill until June 30, 1922, twenty-five cents (25¢) shall be collected through the ginner of the bale and paid into the State treasury, to be held there as a special guarantee or indemnifying fund to safeguard the State warehouse system against any loss not otherwise covered. The State Tax Commission shall provide and enforce the machinery for the collection of this tax, which shall be held in the State treasury to the credit of the State warehouse system. Not less than ten per centum (10%) of the entire amount collected from the per bale tax shall be invested in United States government or farm loan bonds or North Carolina bonds, and the remainder may be invested in amply secured first mortgage notes or bonds to aid and encourage the establishment of warehouses operating under this system, and to aid and encourage the establishment of farm markets designed to serve the marketing, packaging, and grading needs for the sale and distribution of unprocessed farm commodities when adequate markets are not otherwise provided. Such investments shall be made by the Board of Agriculture, with the approval of the Governor and

Attorney General: Provided, such first mortgages shall be for not more than one-half the actual value of the warehouse property covered by such mortgages, and run not more than 10 years: Provided further, that the interest received from all investments shall be available for appropriation for capital projects and nonrecurring expenditures as provided in the bill making the appropriation, and for the administrative expense of carrying into effect the provisions of this law, including the employment of such persons and such means as the State Board of Agriculture in its discretion may deem necessary: Provided further, that the guarantee fund, raised under the provisions of sections 4907 to 4925 of the Consolidated Statutes of 1919, shall become to all intents and purposes a part of guarantee fund to be raised under this law and subject to all the provisions hereof. The fund created by this section may be used for loans to owners of cotton gins to make improvements to gins to comply with federal and State air quality regulations, rules, and laws. The loans shall be secured and made under terms and conditions approved by the Board of Agriculture. Income earnings, including earnings from interest, may also be used by the Department of Agriculture and Consumer Services for cotton promotion activities. (1919, c. 168, s. 5; 1921, c. 137, s. 5; Ex. Sess. 1921, c. 28; C.S., s. 4925(e); 1957, c. 1091; 1993, c. 561, s. 95(a); 1993 (Reg. Sess., 1994), c. 769, s. 26(a); 1997-261, s. 109.)

§§ 106-436 through 106-451.1: Repealed by Session Laws 1997-74, s. 11.

§§ 106-451.2 through 106-451.5. Reserved for future codification purposes.

Article 38A.

Cotton Warehouse Act.

§ 106-451.6. Short title.

The provisions of this Article may be known and designated as the "North Carolina Cotton Warehouse Act". (1987, c. 840, s. 1.)

§ 106-451.7. Definitions.

As used in the Article, unless the context otherwise requires:

(1)   "Board" means the North Carolina Board of Agriculture.

(2)   "Commissioner" means the North Carolina Commissioner of Agriculture.

(3)   "Person" means an individual, partnership, firm, corporation, association, or two or more people having a joint or common interest.

(4)   "Producer" means a farmer or grower of cotton.

(5)   "Receipt" means a warehouse receipt issued pursuant to this Article.

(6)   "Warehouse" means any building, structure or other protected enclosure in which cotton is or may be stored for hire.

(7)   "Warehouseman" means a person licensed by North Carolina Department of Agriculture and Consumer Services to engage in the business of storing cotton for hire. (1987, c. 840, s. 1; 1997-261, s. 54.)

§ 106-451.8. Board of Agriculture makes rules.

The Board is empowered to make and enforce such rules and regulations as may be necessary to make effective the provisions of this Article, including fees for inspection of warehouses. (1987, c. 840, s. 1.)

§ 106-451.9. Commissioner of Agriculture to administer and enforce Article.

The Commissioner of Agriculture shall have the following powers and duties under this Article:

(1)   To administer and enforce the provisions of this Article.

(2)   To assign and reassign the administrative and enforcement duties and functions assigned to him in this Article to one or more divisions within the Department of Agriculture and Consumer Services.

(3)   To delegate to any division head and other officer or employee of the Department of Agriculture and Consumer Services any of the powers and duties given to the Department by statute or by rules promulgated pursuant to this Article.

(4)   To investigate and determine upon application, whether the warehouse is suitable for the proper storage of cotton.

(5)   To conduct investigations of the daily operations of every State licensed warehouse.

(6)   To prescribe, within the limits of this Article, the duties of the warehousemen with respect to their care of and responsibility for cotton stored in licensed warehouses.

(7)   To issue licenses for the operation of warehouses under this Article.

(8)   To cooperate or enter into formal agreements with any other agency of this State or its subdivisions or with any agency of any other state or of the federal government for the purpose of administering or enforcing any of the provisions of this Article. (1987, c. 840, s. 1; 1997-261, s. 55.)

§ 106-451.10. Licensing of warehousemen.

(a)   The Commissioner, or his designated representative, is authorized, upon application to him, to issue to any person a license for the conduct of a cotton warehouse in accordance with this Article and such rules and regulations as may be made hereunder: Provided, that each such warehouse be found suitable for the proper storage of cotton, and that such person agree, as a condition to the granting of the license, to comply with and abide by all terms of this Article and the rules and regulations prescribed hereunder. All licenses issued pursuant to this Article shall expire on December 31 of each year. Any warehouseman may renew his license by filing a renewal application with the Commissioner on or before January 1 of each year.

(b) Each license application and license renewal application must include:

(1) A current financial statement prepared by a certified public accountant;

(2) Proof of the bond required by G.S. 106-451.11;

(3) A license fee of one hundred dollars ($100.00); and

(4) A certificate of insurance if insurance is required. (1987, c. 840, s. 1.)

§ 106-451.11. Bond required.

(a) Any person applying for a license to conduct a warehouse pursuant to this Article shall, as a condition to the granting thereof, execute and file with the Commissioner a good and sufficient bond to the State to secure the faithful performance of his obligations as a warehouseman. Said bond shall be in such form and amount, shall have such surety or sureties, subject to service of process in suits on the bond within the State and shall contain such terms and conditions as the Commissioner may prescribe to carry out the purposes of this Article. Whenever the Commissioner, or his designated representative, shall determine that a previously approved bond is, or for any cause has become, insufficient, he may require an additional bond or bonds to be given by the warehouseman concerned, conforming with the requirements of this section, and unless the same be given within the time fixed by a written demand therefor the license of such warehouseman may be suspended or revoked.

(b) The Board may require as a condition to the granting of a license that the warehouseman maintain casualty insurance on the cotton stored in a warehouse licensed under this Article. (1987, c. 840, s. 1.)

§ 106-451.12. Action on bond by person injured.

Any person injured by the breach of any obligation to secure which a bond is given, under the provisions of this Article, shall be entitled to sue on the bond in his own name in any court of competent jurisdiction to recover the damages he may have sustained by such breach. (1987, c. 840, s. 1.)

§ 106-451.13. Suspension and revocation of license.

The Commissioner, or his designated representative, may, after opportunity for hearing has been afforded to the licensee concerned, suspend or revoke any license to any warehouseman conducting a warehouse under this Article, for any violation of or failure to comply with any provision of this Article or of the rules and regulations made hereunder, or upon the ground that unreasonable or exorbitant charges have been made for services rendered. (1987, c. 840, s. 1.)

§ 106-451.14. License to classify, grade and weigh cotton stored.

The Commissioner or his designated representative, may upon presentation of satisfactory proof of competency, issue to any person a license to inspect, sample, or classify any cotton stored or to be stored in a warehouse licensed under this Article, according to condition, grade, or otherwise and to certificate the condition, grade, or other class thereof, or to weigh the same and certificate the weight thereof, or both to inspect, sample, or classify and weigh the same and to certificate the condition, grade, or other class and the weight thereof, upon condition that such person agree to comply with and abide by the terms of this Article and of the rules and regulations prescribed hereunder. (1987, c. 840, s. 1.)

§ 106-451.15. Suspension and revocation of license to classify, grade or weigh.

Any license issued to any person to inspect, sample, or classify, or to weigh cotton under this Article may be suspended or revoked by the Commissioner or his designated representative, whenever he is satisfied, after opportunity afforded to the licensee concerned for a hearing, that such licensee has failed to inspect, sample, or classify, or to weigh the cotton correctly, or has violated any of the provisions of this Article or of the rules and regulations prescribed hereunder or that he has used his license or allowed it to be used for any improper purpose whatever. (1987, c. 840, s. 1.)

§ 106-451.16. Delivery to warehouse presumed for storage.

Any cotton delivered to a warehouse under this Article shall be presumed to be delivered for storage. (1987, c. 840, s. 1.)

§ 106-451.17. Deposit of cotton deemed subject to Article.

Any producer who deposits cotton for storage in a warehouse licensed under this Article shall be deemed to have deposited the same subject to the provisions of this Article and the rules and regulations prescribed hereunder. (1987, c. 840, s. 1.)

§ 106-451.18. Receipts for cotton stored.

For all cotton stored in a warehouse licensed under this Article original receipts shall be issued by the warehouseman conducting the same, but no receipt shall be issued except for cotton actually stored in the warehouse at the time of the issuance thereof. (1987, c. 840, s. 1.)

§ 106-451.19. Contents of receipts.

Every receipt issued for cotton stored in a warehouse licensed under this Article shall contain the information required under the United States Warehouse Act, 7 U.S.C. § 214, et seq., and the regulations promulgated thereunder. (1987, c. 840, s. 1; 2006-112, s. 57.)

§ 106-451.20. Issuance of further receipt with original outstanding.

While an original receipt issued under this Article is outstanding and uncanceled by the warehouseman issuing the same no other or further receipt shall be issued for the cotton covered thereby or for any part thereof, except that in the case of a lost or destroyed receipt a new receipt, upon the same terms and subject to the same conditions and bearing on its face the number and date of the receipt in lieu of which it is issued, may be issued. (1987, c. 840, s. 1.)

§ 106-451.21. Delivery of products stored on demand; conditions to delivery.

A warehouseman conducting a warehouse licensed under this Article, in the absence of some lawful excuse, shall, without unnecessary delay, deliver the cotton stored therein upon a demand made either by the holder of a receipt for such cotton or by the depositor thereof if such demand be accompanied with (a) an offer to satisfy the warehouseman's lien; (b) an offer to surrender the receipt, if negotiable, with such endorsements as would be necessary for the negotiation of the receipt; and (c) a readiness and willingness to sign, when the cotton is delivered, an acknowledgment that it has been delivered if such signature is requested by the warehouseman. (1987, c. 840, s. 1.)

§ 106-451.22. Cancellation of receipt on delivery of cotton stored.

A warehouseman conducting a warehouse licensed under this Article shall plainly cancel upon the face thereof each receipt returned to him upon the delivery by him of the cotton for which the receipt is issued. (1987, c. 840, s. 1.)

§ 106-451.23. Records; report to Commissioner; compliance with provisions of Article, rules, and regulations.

Every warehouseman conducting a warehouse licensed under this Article shall keep in a place of safety complete and correct records of all cotton stored therein and withdrawn therefrom, of all warehouse receipts issued by him, and of the receipts returned to and canceled by him, shall make reports to the Commissioner concerning such warehouse and the condition, contents, operation, and business thereof in such form and at such times as he may require, and shall conduct said warehouse in all other respects in compliance with this Article and the rules and regulations made hereunder. (1987, c. 840, s. 1.)

§ 106-451.24. Examination of books, records, etc., of warehousemen.

The Commissioner is authorized through officials, employees, or agents of the Department of Agriculture and Consumer Services designated by him to examine all books, records, papers, and accounts of warehouses and all cotton stored in warehouses licensed under this Article and of the warehousemen conducting such warehouse relating thereof. (1987, c. 840, s. 1; 1997-261, s. 109.)

§ 106-451.25. Inspectors to be bonded.

Each inspector employed by the Commissioner for the inspection and examination of warehouses licensed under this Article shall be bonded in an amount not less than five thousand dollars ($5,000), or in such greater amount as the Commissioner deems necessary, for the faithful performance of his duties and for the proper accounting of all funds coming into his hands. The cost of the bond shall be paid by the Department of Agriculture and Consumer Services. (1987, c. 840, s. 1; 1997-261, s. 109.)

§ 106-451.26. Liability of officials and employees.

No action may be brought in any court of this State against any State official or State employee on account of any act or omission in connection with the administration of this Article unless it be shown that such official or employee acted in bad faith and with corrupt intent. (1987, c. 840, s. 1.)

§ 106-451.27. Use of income from Warehouse Fund to administer.

Income from the Warehouse Fund established under G.S. 106-435 may be used for the administration of this Article. (1987, c. 840, s. 1.)

§ 106-451.28. Violation a misdemeanor; fraudulent or deceptive acts.

Any person who shall violate any provision of this Article or who shall engage in any fraudulent or deceptive practice in the operation of a warehouse licensed under this Article shall be guilty of a Class 1 misdemeanor. (1987, c. 840, s. 1; 1993, c. 539, s. 786; 1994, Ex. Sess., c. 24, s. 14(c).)

§§ 106-451.29 through 106-451.39. Reserved for future codification purposes.

Article 38B.

Cotton Gins, Warehouses, Merchants.

§ 106-451.40. Definitions.

(1)   "Cotton gin" means any cotton gin.

(2)   "Cotton merchant" means any person who buys cotton from the producer for the purpose of resale, or acts as a broker or agent for the producer in arranging the sale of cotton. It does not include a person who buys cotton for his own use.

(3)   "Cotton warehouse" means any enclosure in which producer-owned cotton is stored or held for longer than 48 hours. (1999-412, s. 1.)

§ 106-451.41. Registration required.

No person shall engage in business as a cotton gin, cotton warehouse, or cotton merchant without first having registered with the Commissioner of Agriculture. This shall include a cotton marketing cooperative or association that performs any of these functions. (1999-412, s. 1.)

§ 106-451.42. Application; bond; display of certificate of registration.

(a)   A cotton gin, cotton warehouse, cotton merchant, or cotton marketing cooperative or association shall, on or before July 1 of each year, file an application for registration on a form provided by the Commissioner of Agriculture. A fee of twenty-five dollars ($25.00) shall be submitted with each application.

(b)   An application for registration as a cotton warehouse shall also be accompanied by a bond in the amount of three hundred thousand dollars

($300,000) issued by a company authorized to issue surety bonds in North Carolina and shall be conditioned upon fulfillment of contractual obligations related to the purchase or storage of cotton. A bond shall not be required for a person who is licensed and bonded under the U.S. Warehouse Act.

(c) The registration certificate shall be conspicuously displayed at the place of business. (1999-412, s. 1.)

§ 106-451.43. Records; receipts; other duties; denial of registration.

(a) Cotton gins, cotton warehouses, cotton merchants, and cotton cooperatives or associations shall keep records of producer-owned cotton transactions for seven years, showing the producer's name, bale number, and bale weight.

(b) Cotton gins shall, within 48 hours of ginning, make available to the person from whom cotton was received, a paper document showing the bale number and weight for each bale of cotton ginned.

(c) Cotton gins, cotton warehouses, cotton merchants, and cotton cooperatives or associations shall not market, obligate for sale, or otherwise dispose of producer-owned cotton without written consent from the producer.

(d) Cotton gins, cotton warehouses, cotton merchants, and cotton cooperatives or associations shall assist the Commissioner of Agriculture or his agents in inspecting records of producer-owned cotton transactions. Cotton gins, cotton warehouses, cotton merchants, and cotton cooperatives or associations shall assist the Commissioner or his agents in weighing or reweighing a representative sample of cotton bales stored or held at their premises, using sampling procedures approved by the Board of Agriculture.

(e) Violation of any of the requirements of this section shall be grounds for denial, suspension, or revocation of registration under G.S. 106-451.41. (1999-412, s. 1.)

§ 106-451.44. Operation without registration unlawful; injunction.

Engaging in business as a cotton gin, cotton warehouse, or cotton merchant without being registered under G.S. 106-451.41 is punishable as a Class 2 misdemeanor. In addition, the Commissioner of Agriculture may apply to any court of competent jurisdiction to obtain injunctive relief to prevent violations of this act. (1999-412, s. 1.)

§§ 106-451.45 through 106-451.49. Reserved for future codification purposes.

Article 39.

Leaf Tobacco Warehouses.

§ 106-452: Repealed by Session Laws 2006-162, s. 29, effective July 24, 2006.

§ 106-453. Oath of tobacco weigher; duty of weigher to furnish list of number and weight of baskets weighed.

All leaf tobacco sold upon the floor of any tobacco warehouse shall first be weighed by some reliable person 18 years of age or older, who shall have first sworn and subscribed to the following oath, to wit: "I do solemnly swear (or affirm) that I will correctly and accurately weigh all tobacco offered for sale at the warehouse of _____, and correctly test and keep accurate the scales upon which the tobacco so offered for sale is weighed." Such oath shall be filed in the office of the clerk of the superior court of the county in which said warehouse is situated.

Immediately upon the weighing of any lot or lots of tobacco, the tobacco weigher shall furnish, upon request, to the person delivering such tobacco to the scale for weighing a true list showing the number of baskets of tobacco weighed and the individual weight of each such basket so presented. (1895, c. 81, s. 2; Rev., s. 3043; C.S., s. 5125; 1951, c. 1105, s. 1; 1971, c. 1085, s. 2.)

§ 106-454. Warehouse proprietor, etc., to render bill of charges; penalty.

The owner, operator, or person in charge of each warehouse shall render to each seller of tobacco at the warehouse a bill plainly stating the amount charged for weighing and handling, the amount charged for auction fees, and the commission charged on such sale, and it shall be unlawful for any other charge or fees to be made or accepted. Any person, firm, corporation, or any employee thereof, violating the provisions of this section shall be guilty of a Class 3 misdemeanor for the first offense, and for the second or additional offenses a Class 2 misdemeanor. (1895, c. 81, ss. 3, 4; Rev., s. 3044; C.S., s. 5126; 1973, c. 1305; 1993, c. 539, s. 787; 1994, Ex. Sess., c. 24, s. 14(c).)

§ 106-455. Tobacco purchases to be paid for by cash or check to order.

The proprietor of each and every warehouse shall pay for all tobacco sold in said warehouse either in cash or by giving to the seller a check payable to his order in his full name or in his surname and initials and it shall be unlawful to use any other method. Every person, firm or corporation violating the provisions hereof shall, in addition to any and all civil liability which may arise by law, be guilty of a Class 3 misdemeanor. (1931, c. 101, s. 1; 1939, c. 348; 1993, c. 539, s. 788; 1994, Ex. Sess., c. 24, s. 14(c).)

Article 40.

Leaf Tobacco Sales.

§§ 106-456 through 106-460. Repealed by Session Laws 1999-44, s. 4.

Article 40.

Leaf Tobacco Sales.

§ 106-461. Nested, shingled or overhung tobacco.

It shall be unlawful for any person, firm or corporation to sell or offer to sale, upon any leaf tobacco warehouse floor, any pile or piles of tobacco, which are nested, or shingled, or overhung, or either as hereinafter defined:

(1) Nesting tobacco: That is, so arranging tobacco in the pile offered for sale that it is impossible for the buyer thereof to pull leaves from the bottom of such pile for the purpose of inspection;

(2) Shingling tobacco: That is, so arranging a pile of tobacco that a better quality of tobacco appears upon the outside and tobacco of inferior quality appears on the inside of such pile; and

(3) Overhanging tobacco: This is, so arranging a pile of tobacco that there are alternate bundles of good and sorry tobacco. (1933, c. 467, s. 1.)

§ 106-462. Sale under name other than that of true owner prohibited.

It shall be unlawful for any person, firm or corporation to sell or offer for sale or cause to be sold, or offered for sale, any leaf tobacco upon the floors of any leaf tobacco warehouse, in the name of any person, firm or corporation, other than that of the true owner or owners thereof, which true owner's name shall be registered upon the warehouse sales book in which it is being offered for sale. (1933, c. 467, s. 2.)

§ 106-463. Allowance for weight of baskets and trucks.

It shall be unlawful for any person, firm or corporation in weighing tobacco for sale to permit or allow the basket and truck upon which such tobacco is placed for the purpose of obtaining such weight to vary more than two pounds from the standard or uniform weight of such basket and truck. (1933, c. 467, s. 3.)

§ 106-464. Violation made misdemeanor.

Any person, firm or corporation violating the provisions of G.S. 106-461 to 106-463 shall be guilty of a Class 3 misdemeanor. (1933, c. 467, s. 4; 1993, c. 539, s. 789; 1994, Ex. Sess., c. 24, s. 14(c).)

§ 106-465. Organization and membership of tobacco boards of trade; rules and regulations; fire insurance and extended coverage required; price fixing prohibited.

Tobacco warehousemen and the purchasers of leaf tobacco, at auction, on warehouse floors, are hereby authorized to organize, either as nonstock corporations, or voluntary associations, tobacco boards of trade in the several towns and cities in North Carolina in which leaf tobacco is sold on warehouse floors, at auction.

Such tobacco boards of trade as may now exist, or which may hereafter be organized, are authorized to make reasonable rules and regulations for the economical and efficient handling of the sale of leaf tobacco at auction on the warehouse floors in the several towns and cities in North Carolina in which an auction market is situated.

Each tobacco board of trade organized pursuant to this section shall, on or before June 1, 1973, by regulation, require that all auction warehouse firms which are members of, or may hereafter request membership in, such board of trade for the purpose of displaying for sale and selling leaf tobacco, deposit with the board of trade prior to the market opening, a copy of a policy of fire insurance and extended coverage in a company licensed to do business in North Carolina to fully insure, as determined by the board of trade, the market value of the maximum volume of tobacco that will be weighed and left displayed for sale on said warehouse floor at any time during the marketing season. Warehouses using mechanized conveyor-line auction sales where tobacco is not displayed for sale on sales floor would be excluded from the requirement of this regulation.

In determining the market value and maximum volume of tobacco that will be weighed and placed on said warehouse floor at any one time, the board of trade shall use as criteria the prior season's official gross average price for that belt, as recorded by the North Carolina Department of Agriculture and Consumer Services and the maximum limit of daily sales, as recommended by the currently functioning flue-cured and burley tobacco marketing organizations, applied to each warehouse based on the firm's pro rata share of the market's maximum limit daily sales opportunity, multiplied times the number of days of sales that said warehouse plans to place on sales floor at any one time, including any and all tobacco weighed and deposited with the warehouse as bailee for future sale. The data relating to the official average price and the maximum limits of daily sales shall be assembled and supplied by the North

Carolina Commissioner of Agriculture or his representative to the board of trade in each tobacco market in North Carolina, at least 30 days prior to the opening of markets in each belt.

It shall be unlawful for any person, firm, or corporation to operate an auction sale in said market until said policy is so deposited with and approved by the board of trade. The board of trade shall enjoin the sale of tobacco by any warehouse firm that fails to so deposit a policy of fire insurance and extended coverage with the board.

The tobacco boards of trade in the several towns and cities in North Carolina are authorized to require as a condition to membership therein the applicants to pay a reasonable membership fee and the following schedule of maximum fees shall be deemed reasonable, to wit:

A membership fee of fifty dollars ($50.00) in those towns in which less than 3,000,000 pounds of tobacco was sold at auction between the dates of August 20, 1931, and May 1, 1932; a fee of one hundred dollars ($100.00) in those towns in which during said period of time more than 3,000,000 and less than 10,000,000 pounds of tobacco was sold; a fee of one hundred fifty dollars ($150.00) in those towns in which during said period of time more than 10,000,000 and less than 25,000,000 pounds of tobacco was sold; a fee of three hundred dollars ($300.00) in those towns in which during said period of time more than 25,000,000 pounds of tobacco was sold.

Membership, in good standing, in a local board of trade shall be deemed a reasonable requirement by such board of trade as a condition to participating in the business of operating a tobacco warehouse or the purchase of tobacco at auction therein.

Membership in the several boards of trade may be divided into two categories:

(1)   Warehousemen;

(2)   Purchasers of leaf tobacco other than warehousemen.

Purchasers of leaf tobacco may be: (i) participating or (ii) nonparticipating. The holder of a membership as a purchaser of leaf tobacco shall have the option of becoming, upon written notice to the board of trade, either a participating or a nonparticipating member. Individuals, partnerships, and/or corporations who are members of tobacco boards of trade, established under this section or coming within the provisions of this section, as nonparticipating members shall not participate in or have any voice or vote in the management, conduct, activities, allotment of sales time, and/or hours, the fixing of dates for the opening or closing of tobacco auction markets, or in any other manner or respect. Individuals, partnerships, and/or corporations who are such nonparticipating members in any of the several tobacco boards of trade shall not be responsible or liable for any of the acts, omissions or commissions of the several tobacco boards of trade.

It shall be unlawful and punishable as of a Class 1 misdemeanor for any bidder or purchaser of tobacco upon warehouse floors to refuse to take and pay for any basket or baskets so bid off from the seller when the seller has or has not accepted the price offered by the purchaser or bidder of other baskets. Any person suspended or expelled from a tobacco board of trade under the provisions of this section may appeal from such suspension to the superior court of the county in which said board of trade is located.

Nothing in this section shall authorize the organization of any association having for its purpose the control of prices or the making of rules and regulations in restraint of trade. (1933, c. 268; 1951, c. 383; 1973, c. 96; 1993, c. 539, s. 790; 1994, Ex. Sess., c. 24, s. 14(c); 1997-261, s. 109.)

Article 41.

Dealers in Scrap Tobacco.

§§ 106-466 through 106-470. Repealed by Session Laws 1999-44, s. 5, effective May 13, 1999.

Article 42.

Production, Sale, Marketing and Distribution of Tobacco.

§§ 106-471 through 106-489. Repealed by Session Laws 1955, c. 188, s. 1.

Article 43.

Combines and Power Threshers.

§§ 106-490 through 106-495. Repealed by Session Laws 1955, c. 268, s. 2.

§§ 106-495.1 through 106-495.2. Repealed by Session Laws 1975, c. 24.

Article 44.

Unfair Practices by Handlers of Fruits and Vegetables.

§ 106-496. Protection against unfair trade practices.

The Board of Agriculture is hereby authorized to make such rules and regulations as it deems necessary to protect producers of fruits and vegetables from loss caused by financial irresponsibility and unfair, harmful or unethical trade practices of handlers who incur financial liability for the purchase or production of fruits and vegetables. A "handler," as used herein, is a person, firm, corporation or other legal entity or his agent or employee who enters into a written contract for the purchase from or production by a producer of fruits and vegetables. (1941, c. 359, s. 1; 1971, c. 1064, s. 1.)

§ 106-497. Permits required.

A handler of fruits and vegetables shall not enter into a written contract with a producer until he obtains a written permit from the Commissioner of Agriculture. The Board of Agriculture may prescribe by regulation the form of the application for a permit, the information to be furnished to the Commissioner by the applicant for a permit and the date for filing the application. A permit shall not be issued until the applicant files on or before the date set by the Board a written request with the Commissioner and files with the request two copies of the applicant's proposed contract. A penalty of twenty-five dollars ($25.00) shall be paid by the applicant if the application is filed after the date established by the Board and no permit shall be issued until such penalty is paid. Any penalties collected by the Commissioner shall be used to help defray the costs of administering Article 44 of Chapter 106.

This Article shall not apply to transactions by a handler with a producer on a cash basis. "Cash" as used herein shall include bank bills, checks drawn on banks and bank notes. (1941, c. 359, s. 2; 1971, c. 1064, s. 2.)

§ 106-498. Bond required.

No permit shall be issued to a handler until such handler has furnished the Commissioner of Agriculture a bond satisfactory to the Commissioner in an amount of not less than ten thousand dollars ($10,000). The Commissioner may require a new bond or he may require the amount of any bond to be increased if he finds it necessary for the protection of the producer. Such bond shall be payable to the State and shall be conditioned upon the fulfilling of all financial obligations incurred by the handler with all producers with whom the handler contracts. Any producer alleging any injury by the fraud, deceit, willful injury or failure to comply with the terms of any written contract by a handler may bring suit on the bond against the principal and his surety in any court of competent jurisdiction and may recover the damages found to be caused by such acts complained of. (1941, c. 359, s. 3; 1967, c. 154; 1971, c. 1064, s. 3.)

§ 106-499. Contracts between handlers and producers; approval of Commissioner.

All contracts filed with the Commissioner by an applicant shall be approved by the Commissioner before a permit is issued. The Commissioner may withhold his approval in his discretion if he is of the opinion that the contract is illegal or unfair to the producer, or that the contractor is insolvent or financially irresponsible, or if for any other cause it reasonably appears to him that the contract in question might defeat the purpose of this Article. (1941, c. 359, s. 4; 1971, c. 1064, s. 4.)

§ 106-500. Additional powers of Commissioner to enforce Article.

In order to enforce this Article, the Commissioner of Agriculture, upon his own motion or upon the verified complaint of any producer, shall have the following additional powers:

(1)   To inspect or investigate transactions for the sale or delivery of fruits and vegetables to persons acting as handlers; to require verified reports and accounts of all authorized handlers; to examine books, accounts, memoranda, equipment, warehouses, storage, transportation and other facilities, fruits and vegetables and other articles connected with the business of the handlers; to inquire into failure or refusal of any handlers to accept produce under his contracts and to pay for it as agreed;

(2)   To hold hearings after due notice to interested parties and opportunity to all to be heard; to administer oaths, take testimony and issue subpoenas; to require witnesses to bring with them relevant books, papers, and other evidence; to compel testimony; to make written findings of fact and on the basis of these findings to issue orders in controversies before him, and to revoke the permits of persons disobeying the terms of this Article or of rules, regulations, and orders made by the Board or the Commissioner. Any party disobeying any order or subpoena of the Commissioner shall be guilty of contempt, and shall be certified to the superior court for punishment. Any party may appeal to the superior court from any final order of the Commissioner;

(3)   To issue all such rules and regulations, with the approval of the Board, and to appoint necessary agents and to do all other lawful things necessary to carry out the purposes of this Article.

(4)   This Article will not apply to peanuts and corn grown under contract for seed purposes. (1941, c. 359, s. 5; 1971, c. 1064, ss. 5, 6.)

§ 106-501. Violation of Article or rules made misdemeanor.

Any person who violates the provisions of this Article or the rules and regulations promulgated thereunder shall be guilty of a Class 1 misdemeanor. (1941, c. 359, s. 6; 1993, c. 539, s. 792; 1994, Ex. Sess., c. 24, s. 14(c).)

Article 45.

Agricultural Societies and Fairs.

Part 1. State Fair.

§ 106-502. Land set apart.

For the purpose of the operating of a State fair, expositions and other projects which properly represent the agricultural, manufacturing, industrial and other interests of the State of North Carolina, there is hereby dedicated and set apart 200 acres of land owned by the State or any department thereof within five miles of the State Capitol, the particular acreage to be selected, set apart, and approved by the Governor and Council of the State of North Carolina. (1927, c. 209, s. 1; 1959, c. 1186, s. 1.)

§ 106-503. Board of Agriculture to operate fair.

(a) The State fair and other projects provided for in G.S. 106-502, shall be managed, operated and conducted by the Board of Agriculture established in G.S. 106-502. To that end, said Board of Agriculture shall, at its first meeting after the ratification of this section, take over said State fair, together with all the lands, buildings, machinery, etc., located thereon, now belonging to said State fair and shall operate said State fair and other projects with all the authority and power conferred upon the former board of directors, and it shall make such rules and regulations as it may deem necessary for the holding and conducting of said fair and other projects, and/or lease said fair properties so as to provide a State fair.

(b) The Board of Agriculture may adopt regulations establishing fees or charges for admission to the State Fairgrounds and for services provided incidental to the use of the State Fairgrounds.

(c) The Board of Agriculture, subject to the provisions of Chapter 146 of the General Statutes, may establish a schedule of rental rates for fair properties and specifications for the issuance of premiums so as to provide a State fair and other projects.

(d) The Board of Agriculture shall provide and maintain recycling bins for the collection and recycling of newspaper, aluminum cans, glass containers, and recyclable plastic beverage containers at the State Fairgrounds. (1931, c. 360,

s. 3; 1959, c. 1186, s. 2; 1981, c. 495, s. 4; 1981 (Reg. Sess., 1982), c. 1359, s. 2; 1987, c. 827, s. 34; 1991, c. 336, s. 2.)

§ 106-503.1. Board authorized to construct and finance facilities and improvements for fair.

(a) Borrowing Money and Issuing Bonds. - For the purpose of building, enlarging and improving the facilities on the properties of the State fair, the State Board of Agriculture is hereby empowered and authorized to borrow a sum of money not to exceed one hundred thousand dollars ($100,000), and to issue revenue bonds therefor, payable in series at such time or times and bearing such rate of interest as may be fixed by the Governor and Council of State: Provided, that no part of the payments of the principal or interest charges on said loan shall be made out of the general revenue of the State of North Carolina, and the credit of the State of North Carolina and the State Department of Agriculture and Consumer Services or the agricultural fund, other than the revenue of the State fair funds, shall not be pledged either directly or indirectly for the payment of said principal or interest charges. The receipts, funds, and any other State fair assets may be pledged as security for the payment of any bonds that may be issued.

(b) Contracts and Leases; Pledge of Gate Receipts, etc. - For the further purpose of acquiring, constructing, operating and financing said properties and facilities on the North Carolina State fairgrounds, the Board of Agriculture may enter into such agreements, contracts and leases as may be necessary for the purpose of this section, and may pledge, appropriate, and pay such sums out of the gate receipts or other revenues coming to the State Board of Agriculture from the operation of any facilities of the State fair as may be required to secure, repay, or meet the principal and interest charges on the loan herein authorized. Prior to execution, the Board of Agriculture shall consult with the Joint Legislative Commission on Governmental Operations on all agreements, contracts, and leases authorized under this subsection. The preceding sentence applies only to agreements, contracts, and leases with an estimated revenue to the State of one hundred thousand dollars ($100,000) or more.

(c) Gifts and Endowments. - The State Board of Agriculture may receive gifts and endowments, whether real estate, moneys, goods or chattels, given or bestowed upon or conveyed to them for the benefit of the State fair, and the same shall be administered in accordance with the requirements of the donors. (1945, c. 1009; 1959, c. 1186, s. 3; 1997-261, s. 109; 2001-487, s. 71.)

§ 106-504. Lands dedicated by State may be repossessed at will of General Assembly.

Any lands which may be dedicated and set apart under the provisions of this Article may be taken possession of and repossessed by the State of North Carolina, at the will of the General Assembly. (1927, c. 209, s. 4(a).)

Part 2. County Societies.

§ 106-505. Incorporation; powers and term of existence.

Any number of resident persons, not less than 10, may associate together in any county, under written articles of association, subscribed by the members thereof, and specifying the object of the association to encourage and promote agriculture, domestic manufactures, and the mechanic arts, under such name and style as they may choose, subject to any other applicable provisions of law, and thereby become a body corporate with all the powers incident to such a body, and may take and hold such property, both real and personal, as may be needful to promote the objects of their association.

Whenever any such association is formed subsequent to April 1, 1949, a copy of the articles of incorporation shall be filed with the Secretary of State, together with any other information the Secretary of State may require. A fee of ten dollars ($10.00) shall be paid to the Secretary of State when such articles are filed. Upon receipt of such articles in proper form, and such other information as may be required, and the filing fee, the Secretary of State shall issue a charter of incorporation.

The corporate existence shall continue as long as there are 10 members, during the will and pleasure of the General Assembly. (1852, c. 2, ss. 1, 2, 3; R.C., c. 2, ss. 6, 7; Code, s. 2220; Rev., ss. 3868, 3869; C.S., s. 4941; 1949, c. 829, s. 2.)

§ 106-506. Organization; officers; new members.

Such society shall be organized by the appointment of a president, two vice-presidents, a secretary and treasurer, and such other officers as they may deem proper, who shall thereafter be chosen annually, and hold their places until others shall be appointed. And the society may from time to time, on such conditions as may be prescribed, receive other members of the corporation. (1852, c. 2, s. 3; R.C., c. 2, s. 7; Code, s. 2221; Rev., s. 3869; C.S., s. 4942.)

§ 106-507: Repealed by Session Laws 2013-316, s. 5(d), effective January 1, 2014, and applicable to admissions purchased on or after that date.

§ 106-508. Funds to be used in paying premiums.

All moneys so subscribed, as well as that received from the State treasury as herein provided, shall after paying the necessary incidental expenses of such society, be annually paid for premiums awarded by such societies, in such sums and in such way and manner as they severally, under their bylaws, rules and regulations, shall direct, on such live animals, articles of production, and agricultural implements and tools, domestic manufacturers, mechanical implements, tools and productions as are of the growth and manufacture of the county or region, and also such experiments, discoveries, or attainments in scientific or practical agriculture as are made within the county or region wherein such societies are respectively organized. (1852, c. 2, s. 7; R.C., c. 2, s. 9; Code, s. 2223; Rev., s. 3873; C.S., s. 4945; 1949, c. 829, s. 2.)

§ 106-509. Annual statements to State Treasurer.

Each agricultural society entitled to receive money from the State Treasurer shall, through its treasurer, transmit to the Treasurer of the State, in the month of December or before, a statement showing the money received from the State, the amount received from the members of the society for the preceding year, the expenditures of all such sums, and the number of the members of such society. (1852, c. 2, s. 8; R.C., c. 2, s. 10; Code, s. 2224; Rev., s. 3874; C.S., s. 4946.)

§ 106-510. Publication of statements required.

Each agricultural society receiving money from the State under this Chapter shall, in each year, publish at its own expense a full statement of its experiments and improvements, and reports of its committees, in at least one newspaper in the State; and evidence that the requirements of this Chapter have been complied with shall be furnished to the State Treasurer before he shall pay to such society the sum of fifty dollars ($50.00) for the benefit of such society for the next year. (1852, c. 2, s. 9; R.C., c. 2, s. 11; Code, s. 2225; Rev., s. 3875; C.S., s. 4947.)

§ 106-511. Records to be kept; may be read in evidence.

The secretary of such society shall keep a fair record of its proceedings in a book provided for that purpose, which may be read in evidence in suits wherein the corporation may be a party. (1852, c. 2, s. 5; R.C., c. 2, s. 12; Code, s. 2226; Rev., s. 3876; C.S., s. 4948.)

Part 3. Protection and Regulation of Fairs.

§ 106-512. Lien against licensees' property to secure charge.

All agricultural fairs which shall grant any privilege, license, or concession to any person, persons, firm, or corporation for vending wares or merchandise within any fairgrounds, or which shall rent any ground space for carrying on any kind of business in such fairgrounds, either upon stipulated price or for a certain percent of the receipts taken in by such person, persons, firm, or corporation, shall have the right to retain possession of and shall have a lien upon any or all the goods, wares, fixtures, and merchandise or other property of such person, persons, firm, or corporation until all charges for privileges, licenses, or concessions are paid, or until their contract is fully complied with. (1915, c. 242, s. 1; C.S., s. 4950.)

§ 106-513. Notice of sale to owner.

Written notice of such sale shall be served on the owner of such goods, wares, merchandise, or fixtures or other property 10 days before such sale, if he or it be a resident of the State, but if a nonresident of the State, or his or its residence be unknown, the publication of such notice for 10 days at the courthouse door and three other public places in the county shall be sufficient service of the same. (1915, c. 242, s. 2; C.S., s. 4951.)

§ 106-514. Unlawful entry on grounds a misdemeanor.

If any person, after having been expelled from the fairgrounds of any agricultural or horticultural society, shall offer to enter the same again without permission from such society; or if any person shall break over [open] the enclosing structure of said fairgrounds and enter the same, or shall enter the enclosure of said fairgrounds by means of climbing over, under or through the enclosing structure surrounding the same, or shall enter the enclosure through the gates without the permission of its gatekeeper or the proper officer of said fair association, he shall be guilty of a Class 3 misdemeanor. (1870-1, c. 184, s. 3; Code, s. 2795; 1901, c. 291; Rev., s. 3669; C.S., s. 4952; 1993, c. 539, s. 793; 1994, Ex. Sess., c. 24, s. 14(c).)

§ 106-515. Assisting unlawful entry on grounds a misdemeanor.

It shall be unlawful for any person or persons to assist any other person or persons to enter upon the grounds of any fair association when an admission fee is charged, by assisting such other person or persons to climb over or go under the fence or by pulling off a plank or to enter the enclosed grounds by any trick or device or by passing out a ticket or a pass or in any other way. Any violation of this section shall be a Class 3 misdemeanor. (1915, c. 242, ss. 3, 4; C.S., s. 4953; 1993, c. 539, s. 794; 1994, Ex. Sess., c. 24, s. 14(c).)

§ 106-516: Repealed by Session Laws 2013-316, s. 5(d), effective January 1, 2014.

§ 106-516.1. Carnivals and similar amusements not to operate without permit.

Every person, firm, or corporation engaged in the business of a carnival company or a show of like kind, including menageries, merry-go-rounds, Ferris wheels, riding devices, circus and similar amusements and enterprises operated and conducted for profit, shall, prior to exhibiting in any county annually staging an agricultural fair, apply to the sheriff of the county in which the exhibit is to be held for a permit to exhibit. The sheriff of the county shall issue a permit without charge; provided, however, that no permit shall be issued if he shall find the requested exhibition date is less than 30 days prior to a regularly advertised agricultural fair. Exhibition without a permit from the sheriff of the county in which the exhibition is to be held shall constitute a Class 1 misdemeanor: Provided, that nothing contained in this section shall prevent veterans' organizations and posts chartered by Congress or organized and operated on a statewide or nationwide basis from holding fairs or tobacco festivals on any dates which they may select if such fairs or festivals have heretofore been held as annual events. (1953, c. 854; 1963, c. 1127; 1991 (Reg. Sess., 1992), c. 1030, s. 26; 1993, c. 539, s. 795; 1994, Ex. Sess., c. 24, s. 14(c); 2005-435, s. 43.)

§§ 106-517 through 106-520: Repealed by Session Laws 2013-316, s. 5(d), effective January 1, 2014, and applicable to admissions purchased on or after that date.

Part 4. Supervision of Fairs and Animal Exhibitions.

§ 106-520.1. Definition.

As used in this Article, the word "fair" means a bona fide exhibition designed, arranged and operated to promote, encourage and improve agriculture, horticulture, livestock, poultry, dairy products, mechanical fabrics, domestic economy, and 4-H Club and Future Farmers of America activities, by offering premiums and awards for the best exhibits thereof or with respect thereto. (1949, c. 829, s. 1.)

§ 106-520.2. Use of "fair" in name of exhibition.

It shall be unlawful for any person, firm, corporation, association, club, or other group of persons to use the word "fair" in connection with any exhibition, circus, show, or other variety of exhibition unless such exhibition is a fair within the meaning of G.S. 106-520.1. (1949, c. 829, s. 1.)

§ 106-520.3. Commissioner of Agriculture to regulate.

The Commissioner of Agriculture, with the advice and approval of the State Board of Agriculture, is hereby authorized, empowered and directed to make rules and regulations with respect to classification, operation and licensing of fairs, so as to insure that such fairs shall conform to the definition set out in G.S. 106-520.1, and shall best promote the purposes of fairs as set out in such definition. Every fair, and every exhibition using the word "fair" in its name, except fairs classified by the Commissioner of Agriculture as noncommercial community fairs, must comply with the standards, rules and regulations set up and promulgated by the Commissioner of Agriculture, and must secure a license from the Commissioner of Agriculture before such exhibition or fair is staged or operated. No license shall be issued for any such exhibition or fair unless it meets the standards and complies with the rules and regulations of the Commissioner of Agriculture with respect thereto. (1949, c. 829, s. 1.)

§ 106-520.3A. Animal exhibition regulation; permit required; civil penalties.

(a) Title. - This section may be referred to as "Aedin's Law". This section provides for the regulation of animal exhibitions as they may affect the public health and safety.

(b) Definitions. - As used in this section, unless the context clearly requires otherwise:

(1) "Animal" means only those animals that may transmit infectious diseases.

(2) "Animal exhibition" means any sanctioned agricultural fair where animals are displayed on the exhibition grounds for physical contact with humans.

(c) Permit Required. - No animal exhibition may be operated for use by the general public unless the owner or operator has obtained an operation permit issued by the Commissioner. The Commissioner may issue an operation permit only after physical inspection of the animal exhibition and a determination that the animal exhibition meets the requirements of this section and rules adopted pursuant to this section. The Commissioner may deny, suspend, or revoke a permit on the basis that the exhibition does not comply with this section or rules adopted pursuant to this section.

(d) Rules. - For the protection of the public health and safety, the Commissioner of Agriculture, with the advice and approval of the State Board of Agriculture, and in consultation with the Division of Public Health of the Department of Health and Human Services, shall adopt rules concerning the operation of and issuance of permits for animal exhibitions. The rules shall include requirements for:

(1) Education and signage to inform the public of health and safety issues.

(2) Animal areas.

(3) Animal care and management.

(4) Transition and nonanimal areas.

(5) Hand-washing facilities.

(6) Other requirements necessary for the protection of the public health and safety.

(e) Educational Outreach. - The Department shall continue its consultative and educational efforts to inform agricultural fair operators, exhibitors, agritourism business operators, and the general public about the health risks associated with diseases transmitted by physical contact with animals.

(f) Civil Penalty. - In addition to the denial, suspension, or revocation of an operation permit, the Commissioner may assess a civil penalty of not more than five thousand dollars ($5,000) against any person who violates a provision of this section or a rule adopted pursuant to this section. In determining the amount of the penalty, the Commissioner shall consider the degree and extent of harm caused by the violation.

The clear proceeds of civil penalties assessed pursuant to this section shall be remitted to the Civil Penalty and Forfeiture Fund in accordance with G.S. 115C-457.2.

(g) Legal Representation by Attorney General. - It shall be the duty of the Attorney General to represent the Department of Agriculture and Consumer Services or designate a member of the Attorney General's staff to represent the Department in all actions or proceedings in connection with this section. (2005-191, s. 1(b).)

§ 106-520.4. Local supervision of fairs.

No county or regional fairs shall be licensed to be held unless such fair is operated under supervision of a local board of directors who shall employ appropriate managers, who shall be responsible for the conduct of such fair, and otherwise comply with the standards, rules and regulations promulgated by the Commissioner of Agriculture. The Commissioner of Agriculture, with the advice and approval of the State Board of Agriculture, shall make rules and regulations requiring county and regional fairs to emphasize agricultural, educational, home and industrial exhibits by providing adequate premiums. (1949, c. 829, s. 1.)

§ 106-520.5. Reports.

Every fair shall make such reports to the Commissioner of Agriculture, as said Commissioner may require. (1949, c. 829, s. 1.)

§ 106-520.6. Premiums and premium lists supplemented.

The State Board of Agriculture may supplement premiums and premium lists for county and regional fairs and the North Carolina State Fair, and improve and expand the facilities for exhibits at the North Carolina State Fair, at any time or times, out of any funds which may be available for such purposes. (1949, c. 829, s. 1.)

§ 106-520.7. Violations made misdemeanor.

Any person who violates any provision of G.S. 106-520.1 through G.S. 106-520.6 is guilty of a Class 1 misdemeanor. (1949, c. 829, s. 1; 1993, c. 539, s. 797; 1994, Ex. Sess., c. 24, s. 14(c).)

Article 46.

Erosion Equipment.

§§ 106-521 through 106-527: Repealed by Session Laws 1987, c. 244, s. 1(j).

Article 47.

State Marketing Authority.

§ 106-528. State policy and purpose of Article.

It is declared to be the policy of the State of North Carolina and the purpose of this Article to promote, encourage and develop the orderly and efficient marketing of products of the home, farm, sea and forest; to establish, maintain, supervise and control, with the cooperation of counties, cities and towns, centrally located markets for the sale and distribution of such products, so as to promote a steady flow of commodities, properly graded and labeled, into the channels of trade at the time and place to enable the producer to get the market price and the consumer to get a product in keeping with the price paid. (1941, c. 39, s. 1.)

§ 106-529. State Marketing Authority created; members and officers; commodity advisers; meetings and expenses.

To secure these aims, there is hereby created an incorporated public agency of the State, to be known as the State Marketing Authority, hereinafter referred to as the "Authority." It shall consist of the members of the State Board of Agriculture, and the Commissioner of Agriculture shall be the chairman. They shall perform the duties and exercise the powers herein set out as a part of their official duties as members of the Board of Agriculture. The Governor shall appoint from time to time commodity advisers to plan with the Authority the programs undertaken in their respective communities. The Authority shall elect and prescribe the duties of a secretary-treasurer, who shall not be a member of the Authority. He shall give bond in such amount as the Authority shall determine in some reliable surety company doing business in North Carolina, and the Authority shall pay the premiums. The Authority shall meet in regular session annually at a fixed place and date, and shall meet in special session at such other times and places as the chairman may request. The members shall receive no salary, but shall receive actual expenses plus seven dollars ($7.00) per day for actual time spent in performing their duties. (1941, c. 39, s. 2.)

§ 106-530. Powers of Authority.

The Authority shall have the following powers:

(1) To sue and be sued in its corporate name in any court or before any administrative agency of the State or of the United States, and to enter into agreements with the United States Department of Agriculture or any other legally constituted State or federal agency, or with any county, city or town in the furtherance of the purposes of this Article.

(2) To plan, build, construct, or cause to be built or constructed, or to purchase, lease or acquire the use of any warehouses or other facilities that may be necessary for the successful operation by the Authority of wholesale markets for products of the home, farm, sea and forest at chosen points in North Carolina. The Authority may make such contracts as may be needed for these purposes. In no case shall the Authority be responsible for any rent except from the income of the market in excess of other operating expenses. The Authority may select and employ for each market capable managers, who shall be familiar with the problems of the grower and the distributor, and of the marketing

of farm products, and who shall have the business ability and training to operate a market and to plan for its proper development and growth in order best to serve the interests of producers, distributors, consumers in the area, and the general public. The managers may employ assistants and agents with the approval of the Authority. The Authority may make such regulations as will promote the policy of this Article, as to the manner in which the markets shall be operated, the business conducted, and stalls sublet to dealers.

(3) To fix the terms upon which individual, cooperative or corporate wholesale merchants, warehouses or warehousemen may place their facilities or services under the supervision and regulation of the Authority. The Authority may extend to any such wholesale merchants, warehouses or warehousemen marketing benefits in the form of inspection, market informational and news service and may make regulations as to the operation of such facilities or services and as to forms, reports, handling, grades, weights, packages, labels, and other standards for the products handled by such merchants, warehouses or warehousemen.

(4) To fix rentals and charges for each type of service or facility in the markets under its control, taking into consideration the cost of such facility or service, the interest and amortization period required, a proper relationship between types of operators in the market, cost of operation, and the need for reasonable reserves for repairs, depreciation, expansion, and similar items. These rentals and charges shall not bring any profit to any agency over and above the costs of operation, necessary reserves, and debt service.

(5) To issue permits to itinerant dealers in intrastate commerce, who express a willingness to come under the program of the State Marketing Authority. Such permits shall enable the holders to solicit orders and to buy and sell produce under the rules and regulations of the Authority and in conformance with G.S. 106-185 to 106-196 and not inconsistent with the United States Perishable Agricultural Commodities Act, 1930 (46 Stat. 531).

(6) To issue bonds and other securities to obtain funds to acquire, construct, and equip warehouses to be used in carrying out the purposes of this Article. The bonds shall be entitled "North Carolina Marketing Authority Bonds" and shall be issued in such form and denominations and shall mature at such time or times, not exceeding 30 years after their date, and shall bear such interest, not exceeding five percent (5%) per annum, payable either annually or semiannually, as the Authority shall determine. They shall be signed by the chairman of the Authority, and the corporate seal affixed or impressed upon

each bond and attested by the secretary-treasurer of the Authority. The coupons shall bear the facsimile signature of the chairman officiating when the bonds are issued. Any issue of these bonds and notes may be sold publicly, or at private sale for not less than par to the Reconstruction Finance Corporation or other State or federal agency or may be given in exchange to any county, city, town or individual for the lease or purchase of property to be used by the Authority. To secure such indebtedness, the Authority may give mortgages or deeds of trust, executed in the same manner as the bonds, on the property purchased or acquired, and may pledge the revenues from the markets in excess of operating expenses, interest and insurance: Provided, that each market shall be operated on a separate financial basis, and only such revenues and properties of each separate market shall be liable for the obligations of that market. No obligations incurred by the Authority shall be obligations of the State of North Carolina or any of its political subdivisions, or a burden on the taxpayers of the State or any political subdivision. This does not prevent the State or any of its agencies, departments or institutions, or any private or public agency from making a contribution to the Authority, in money or services or otherwise.

Bonds and notes issued under this Article shall be exempt from all State, county or municipal taxes or assessments of any kind; the interest shall not be taxable as income, nor shall the notes, bonds, nor coupons be taxable as part of the surplus of any bank, trust company or other corporation.

Any resolution or resolutions authorizing any bonds shall contain provisions which shall be a part of the contract with the holders of the bonds, as to:

a. Pledging the fees, rentals, charges, dues, tolls, and inspection and sales fees, and other revenues to secure payment of the bonds;

b. The rates of the fees or tolls to be charged for the use of the facilities of the warehouse or warehouses, and the use and disposition of the revenues from its operation;

c. The setting aside of reserves or working funds, and the regulation and disposition thereof;

d. Limitations on the purposes to which the proceeds of sale of any issue of bonds may be applied;

e. Limitations on the issuance of additional bonds; and

f. The procedure, if any, by which the terms of any contract with bondholders may be amended or abrogated, the amount of bonds the holders of which must consent thereto, and the manner in which such consent may be given.

(7) To accept grants in aid or free work.

(8) To adopt, use and alter a corporate seal.

(9) To dispossess tenants for nonpayment of rent and for failure to abide by the regulations of the Authority.

(10) To hire necessary agents, engineers, and attorneys, and to do all things necessary to carry out the powers granted by this Article. (1941, c. 39, s. 3.)

§ 106-531. Discrimination prohibited; restriction on use of funds.

The Authority shall not permit:

(1) Any discrimination against the sale, on any of the markets under their control, of any farm product because of type of operator or area of production.

(2) The use of any of its funds for any purpose other than for the support, necessary expansion, and operation of this State marketing system, or the use of any of its funds to establish any retail market or to build or furnish more than one market in any town. (1941, c. 39, s. 4.)

§ 106-532. Fiscal year; annual report to Governor.

The Authority shall operate on a fiscal year, which shall be from July first to June thirtieth. The Commissioner of Agriculture shall file an annual report with the Governor containing a statement of receipts and disbursements and the purposes of such disbursements, and a complete statement of the financial condition of the Authority, and an account of its activities for the year. (1941, c. 39, s. 5.)

§ 106-533. Application of revenues from operation of warehouses.

All rentals and charges, fees, tolls, storage and sales commissions and revenues of any sort from operation of each warehouse shall be applied to the payment of the cost of operating and administering the warehouse and market facilities including interest on bonds and other evidences of indebtedness issued therefor, and the cost of insurance against loss by injury to persons or property, and the balance shall be paid to the secretary-treasurer of the Authority and be used to provide a sinking fund to pay at or before maturity all bonds and notes and other evidences of indebtedness incurred for and on behalf of the building, constructing, maintaining and operating of each warehouse. A separate sinking fund account shall be kept for each market, and no market shall be liable for the obligations of any other market. (1941, c. 39, s. 6.)

§ 106-534. Exemption from taxes and assessments.

The Authority shall be regarded as performing an essential governmental function in constructing, operating or maintaining these markets, and shall be required to pay no taxes or assessments on any property acquired or used by it for the purposes herein set out. (1941, c. 39, s. 7.)

Article 48.

Relief of Potato Farmers.

§§ 106-535 through 106-538: Repealed by Session Laws 1987, c. 244, s. 1(k).

Article 49.

Poultry; Hatcheries; Chick Dealers.

§ 106-539. National poultry improvement plan.

In order to promote the poultry industry of the State, the North Carolina Department of Agriculture and Consumer Services is hereby authorized to cooperate with the United States Department of Agriculture in the operation of the national poultry improvement plan. (1945, c. 616, s. 1; 1969, c. 464; 1983, c. 290, s. 1; 1997-261, s. 109.)

§ 106-540. Rules and regulations.

The North Carolina Board of Agriculture is hereby authorized to adopt such regulations as may be necessary to:

(1)   Carry out the provisions of the national poultry improvement plan.

(2)   Set up minimum standards for the operation of hatcheries.

(3)   Regulate hatching egg dealers, chick dealers, poult dealers, poultry dealers, ratite dealers, and jobbers.

(4)   Regulate the shipping into this State of baby chicks, turkey poults and hatching eggs.

(5)   Facilitate the control and eradication of contagious and infectious diseases of poultry.

(6)   Establish fee schedules for pullorum and other disease testing, and the performance of services such as culling and selecting by Department personnel.

(7)   Provide for compulsory testing of poultry for pullorum disease and fowl typhoid. (1945, c. 616, s. 2; 1969, c. 464; 1983, c. 290, ss. 2, 3; 1998-212, s. 13.10(a).)

§ 106-541. Definitions.

For the purpose of this Article, the following definitions apply:

(1)   "Hatchery" means any establishment that operates hatchery equipment for the production of baby chicks or poults.

(2) "Hatching egg dealer, chick dealer, or jobber" means any person, firm, or corporation that buys hatching eggs, baby chicks, or turkey poults and sells or offers them for sale.

(3) "Live poultry or ratite dealer" means a person who sells or offers for sale to the general public live poultry or ratites. Live poultry or ratite dealer does not include persons who sell on their own premises live poultry or ratites that were raised on the same premises.

(4) "Mixed chicks" or "assorted chicks" means chicks produced from eggs from purebred females of a distinct breed mated to a purebred male of a distinct breed.

(5) "Poultry" means live chickens, doves, ducks, geese, grouse, guinea fowl, partridges, pea fowl, pheasants, pigeons, quail, swans, or turkeys other than chicks or poults.

(6) "Ratite" has the same meaning as in G.S. 106-549.15. (1945, c. 616, s. 3; 1969, c. 464; 1998-212, s. 13.10(b).)

§ 106-542. Hatcheries, chick dealers and others to obtain license to operate.

(a) It shall be unlawful for any person, firm or corporation to operate a hatchery within this State without first obtaining a hatchery license from the Department of Agriculture and Consumer Services for a fee of twenty-five dollars ($25.00) per year.

(b) It shall be unlawful for any person, firm or corporation to operate as a hatching egg dealer, chick dealer or jobber within this State without first obtaining a license from the Department of Agriculture and Consumer Services for a fee of ten dollars ($10.00) per year.

(b1) It shall be unlawful for any person, firm, or corporation to operate as a live poultry or ratite dealer without first registering with the Department of Agriculture and Consumer Services.

(b2) It shall be unlawful for a specialty market operator, as defined in G.S. 66-250, to knowingly and willfully permit an unregistered poultry or ratite dealer to operate on the premises of the specialty market, as defined in G.S. 66-250, more than 10 days after being notified in writing by the Department of Agriculture and Consumer Services that the dealer is not registered.

(c) The Department of Agriculture and Consumer Services may deny, suspend, revoke or refuse to renew the license of any person, firm or corporation for violation of this Article or any rule or regulation promulgated thereunder. (1945, c. 616, s. 4; 1969, c. 464; 1983, c. 290, s. 4; 1997-261, s. 56; 1998-212, s. 13.10(c).)

§ 106-543. Requirements of national poultry improvement plan must be met.

All baby chicks, turkey poults and hatching eggs produced, sold or offered for sale shall originate in flocks that meet the requirements of the national poultry improvement plan as administered by the North Carolina Department of Agriculture and Consumer Services and the regulations issued by authority of this Article for the control of pullorum disease and other infectious diseases provided that nothing in this Article shall require any hatchery to adopt the national poultry improvement plan. (1945, c. 616, s. 5; 1969, c. 464; 1983, c. 290, s. 5; 1997-261, s. 109.)

§ 106-544. Shipments from out of State.

All baby chicks, turkey poults and hatching eggs shipped or otherwise brought into this State shall originate in flocks that meet the minimum requirements of pullorum and typhoid disease control provided for in this Article and the regulations issued by authority of this Article, and shall be accompanied by a certificate approved by the official state agency or the livestock sanitary officials of the state of origin certifying same. (1945, c. 616, s. 6; 1969, c. 464.)

§ 106-545. False advertising.

No hatchery, hatchery dealer, chick dealer or jobber shall use false or misleading advertising in the sale of their products. (1945, c. 616, s. 7; 1969, c. 464.)

§ 106-546. Notice describing grade of chicks to be posted.

All hatcheries, chick dealers or jobbers offering chicks for sale to the public shall post in a conspicuous manner in their place of business a poster furnished by the North Carolina Department of Agriculture and Consumer Services describing the grade of chicks approved by the North Carolina Department of Agriculture and Consumer Services. (1945, c. 616, s. 8; 1969, c. 464; 1997-261, s. 109.)

§ 106-547. Records to be kept.

Every hatchery, hatching egg dealer, chick dealer, poultry dealer, ratite dealer, or jobber shall keep such records of operation as the regulations of the Department of Agriculture and Consumer Services may require for the proper inspection of said hatchery, dealer, or jobber. (1945, c. 616, s. 9; 1969, c. 464; 1997-261, s. 109; 1998-212, s. 13.10(d).)

§ 106-548. Quarantine.

When the State Veterinarian receives information or has reason to believe that pullorum disease or fowl typhoid exists in any poultry or that they have been exposed to one of these diseases, he shall promptly cause said poultry to be quarantined on the premises where located. Said poultry or hatching eggs shall not be removed from the premises where quarantined until quarantine has been released by the State Veterinarian or his authorized representative. A permit to move such infected or exposed poultry to immediate slaughter, or to another premise under quarantine, may be issued by the State Veterinarian or his authorized representative. (1945, c. 616, s. 10; 1969, c. 464; 1983, c. 290, s. 6.)

§ 106-549. Violation a misdemeanor.

Any person, firm or corporation who shall willfully violate any provision of this Article or any rule or regulation duly established by authority of this Article, shall be guilty of a Class 2 misdemeanor. (1945, c. 616, s. 11; 1969, c. 464; 1993, c. 539, s. 798; 1994, Ex. Sess., c. 24, s. 14(c).)

§ 106-549.01. Civil penalties.

The Department of Agriculture and Consumer Services may assess a civil penalty of not more than five thousand dollars ($5,000) against any person who violates a provision of this Article or any rule promulgated thereunder. In determining the amount of the penalty, the Department shall consider the degree and extent of harm caused by the violation.

The clear proceeds of civil penalties assessed pursuant to this section shall be remitted to the Civil Penalty and Forfeiture Fund in accordance with G.S. 115C-457.2. (1995, c. 516, s. 12; 1997-261, s. 57; 1998-215, s. 16.)

Article 49A.

Voluntary Inspection of Poultry.

§§ 106-549.1 through 106-549.14: Repealed by Session Laws 1981, c. 284.

Article 49B.

Meat Inspection Requirements; Adulteration and Misbranding.

§ 106-549.15. Definitions.

As used in this Article, except as otherwise specified, the following terms shall have the meanings stated below:

(1) "Adulterated" shall apply to any carcass, part thereof, meat or meat food product under one or more of the following circumstances:

a. If it bears or contains any poisonous or deleterious substance which may render it injurious to health; but in case the substance is not an added substance, such article shall not be considered adulterated under this clause if the quantity of such substance in or on such article does not ordinarily render it injurious to health;

b. 1. If it bears or contains (by reason of administration of any substance to the live animal or otherwise) any added poisonous or added deleterious substance (other than one which is (i) a pesticide chemical in or on a raw agricultural commodity; (ii) a food additive; or (iii) a color additive) which may, in the judgment of the Commissioner, make such article unfit for human food;

2. If it is, in whole or in part, a raw agricultural commodity and such commodity bears or contains a pesticide chemical which is unsafe within the meaning of section 408 of the Federal Food, Drug, and Cosmetic Act;

3. If it bears or contains any food additive which is unsafe within the meaning of section 409 of the Federal Food, Drug, and Cosmetic Act;

4. If it bears or contains any color additive which is unsafe within the meaning of section 706 of the Federal Food, Drug, and Cosmetic Act: Provided, that an article which is not adulterated under clause 2, 3, or 4 shall nevertheless be deemed adulterated if use of the pesticide chemical, food additive or color additive in or on such article is prohibited by order of the Commissioner in establishments at which inspection is maintained under this Article;

c. If it consists in whole or in part of any filthy, putrid, or decomposed substance or is for any other reason unsound, unhealthful, unwholesome, or otherwise unfit for human food;

d. If it has been prepared, packed, or held under insanitary conditions whereby it may have become contaminated with filth, or whereby it may have been rendered injurious to health;

e. If it is, in whole or in part, the product of an animal which has died otherwise than by slaughter;

f. If its container is composed, in whole or in part, of any poisonous or deleterious substance which may render the contents injurious to health;

g. If it has been intentionally subjected to radiation, unless the use of the radiation was in conformity with a regulation or exemption in effect pursuant to section 409 of the Federal Food, Drug, and Cosmetic Act;

h. If any valuable constituent has been in whole or in part omitted or abstracted therefrom; or if any substance has been substituted, wholly or in part therefor; or if damage or inferiority has been concealed in any manner; or if any substance has been added thereto or mixed or packed therewith so as to increase its bulk or weight, or reduce its quality or strength, or make it appear better or of greater value than it is; or

i. If it is margarine containing animal fat and any of the raw material used therein consist in whole or in part of any filthy, putrid, or decomposed substance.

(2) "Animal food manufacturer" means any person, firm, or corporation engaged in the business of manufacturing or processing animal food derived wholly or in part from carcasses, or parts or products of the carcasses, of cattle, sheep, swine, goats, horses, mules, or other equines.

(3) "Authorized representative" means the Director of the Meat and Poultry Inspection Service of the North Carolina Department of Agriculture and Consumer Services.

(4) "Board" means the North Carolina Board of Agriculture.

(5) "Capable of use as human food" shall apply to any carcass, or part or product of a carcass, of any animal, unless it is denatured or otherwise identified as required by regulations prescribed by the Board to deter its use as human food, or it is naturally inedible by humans.

(6) "Commissioner" means the North Carolina Commissioner of Agriculture or his authorized representative.

(7) "Federal Food, Drug, and Cosmetic Act" means the act so entitled, approved June 25, 1938 (52 Stat. 1040), and acts amendatory thereof or supplementary thereto.

(8) "Federal Meat Inspection Act" means the act so entitled approved March 4, 1907 (34 Stat. 1260), as amended by the Wholesome Meat Act (81 Stat. 584).

(9) "Firm" means any partnership, association, or other unincorporated business organization.

(10) "Intrastate commerce" means commerce within this State.

(11) "Label" means a display of written, printed, or graphic matter upon the immediate container (not including package liners) of any article.

(12) "Labeling" means all labels and other written, printed, or graphic matter (i) upon any article or any of its containers or wrappers, or (ii) accompanying such article.

(13) "Meat broker" means any person, firm, corporation engaged in the business of buying or selling carcasses, parts of carcasses, meat, or meat food products of cattle, sheep, swine, goats, bison, horses, mules, or other equines on commission, or otherwise negotiating purchases or sales of such articles other than for his own account or as an employee of another person, firm, or corporation.

(14) "Meat food product" means any product capable of use as human food that is made wholly or in part from any meat or other portion of the carcass of any cattle, sheep, swine, goats, bison, fallow deer, or red deer, excepting products that contain meat or other portions of such carcasses only in a relatively small proportion or historically have not been considered by consumers as products of the meat food industry, and that are exempted from definition as a meat food product by the Board under such conditions as it may prescribe to assure that the meat or other portions of such carcasses contained in such product are not adulterated and that such products are not represented as meat food products. This term as applied to food products of equines shall have a meaning comparable to that provided in this subdivision with respect to cattle, sheep, swine, goats, and bison.

(15) "Misbranded" shall apply to any carcass, part thereof, meat or meat food product under one or more of the following circumstances:

a. If its labeling is false or misleading in any particular;

b. If it is offered for sale under the name of another food;

c. If it is imitation of another food, unless its label bears, in type of uniform size and prominence, the word "imitation" and immediately thereafter, the name of the food imitated;

d. If its container is so made, formed, or filled as to be misleading;

e. If in a package or other container unless it bears a label showing (i) the name and place of business of the manufacturer, packer, or distributor; and (ii) an accurate statement of the quantity of the contents in terms of weight, measure, or numerical count; provided, that under clause (ii) of this paragraph e, reasonable variations may be permitted, and exemptions as to small packages may be established, by regulations prescribed by the Board;

f. If any word, statement, or other information required by or under authority of this or the subsequent Article to appear on the label or other labeling is not prominently placed thereon with such conspicuousness (as compared with other words, statements, designs, or devices, in the labeling) and in such terms as to render it likely to be read and understood by the ordinary individual under customary conditions of purchase and use;

g. If it purports to be or is represented as a food for which a definition and standard of identity or composition has been prescribed by regulations of the Board under G.S. 106-549.21 unless (i) it conforms to such definition and standard, and (ii) its label bears the name of the food specified in the definition and standard and, insofar as may be required by such regulations, the common names of optional ingredients (other than spices, flavoring, and coloring) present in such food;

h. If it purports to be or is represented as a food for which a standard or standards of fill of container have been prescribed by regulations of the Board under G.S. 106-549.21, and it falls below the standard of fill of container applicable thereto, unless its label bears, in such manner and form as such regulations specify, a statement that it falls below such standard;

i. If it is not subject to the provisions of paragraph g, unless its label bears (i) the common or usual name of the food, if any there be, and (ii) in case it is fabricated from two or more ingredients, the common or usual name of each such ingredient; except that spices, flavorings, and colorings may, when authorized by the Commissioner, be designated as spices, flavorings, and colorings without naming each: Provided, that, to the extent that compliance with the requirements of clause (ii) of this paragraph i is impracticable, or results in deception or unfair competition, exemptions shall be established by regulations promulgated by the Board;

j. If it purports to be or is represented for special dietary uses, unless its label bears such information concerning its vitamin, mineral, and other dietary properties as the Board determines to be, and by regulations prescribes as, necessary in order fully to inform purchasers as to its value for such uses;

k.   If it bears or contains any artificial flavoring, artificial coloring, or chemical preservatives, unless it bears labeling stating that fact: Provided, that, to the extent that compliance with the requirements of this paragraph k is impracticable, exemptions shall be established by regulations promulgated by the Board; or

l.   If it fails to bear, directly thereon or on its container, as the Board may by regulations prescribe, the inspection legend and, unrestricted by any of the foregoing, such other information as the Board may require in such regulations to assure that it will not have false or misleading labeling and that the public will be informed of the manner of handling required to maintain the article in a wholesome condition.

(16)   "Official certificate" means any certificate prescribed by regulations of the Board for issuance by an inspector or other person performing official functions under this or the subsequent Article.

(17)   "Official device" means any device prescribed or authorized by the Board for use in applying any official mark.

(18)   "Official inspection legend" means any symbol prescribed by regulations of the Board showing that an article was inspected and passed in accordance with this or the subsequent Article.

(19)   "Official mark" means the official inspection legend or any other symbol prescribed by regulations of the Board to identify the status of any article or animal under this or the subsequent Article.

(20)   "Pesticide chemical," "food additive," "color additive," and "raw agricultural commodity" shall have the same meanings for purposes of this Article as under the Federal Food, Drug, and Cosmetic Act.

(21)   "Prepared" means slaughtered, canned, salted, smoked, rendered, boned, cut up, or otherwise manufactured or processed.

(21a)   "Ratite" means a bird whose breastbone is smooth so that flight muscles cannot attach, such as an ostrich, an emu, and a rhea. These birds are subject to the provisions of this Article and Article 49C to the same extent as any other meat food product.

(22) "Renderer" means any person, firm, or corporation engaged in the business of rendering carcasses, or parts or products of the carcasses, of cattle, sheep, swine, goats, fallow deer, red deer, horses, mules, or other equines, except rendering conducted under inspection under this Article. (1969, c. 893, s. 1; 1991, c. 317, ss. 4, 5; 1993, c. 311, s. 1; 1995, c. 194, ss. 1, 2; 1997-142, ss. 4, 5; 1997-261, s. 58.)

§ 106-549.16. Statement of purpose.

Meat and meat food products are an important source of the nation's total supply of food. It is essential in the public interest that the health and welfare of consumers be protected by assuring that meat and meat food products distributed to them are wholesome, not adulterated, and properly marked, labeled, and packaged. Unwholesome, adulterated, or misbranded meat or meat food products are injurious to the public welfare, destroy markets for wholesome, not adulterated, and properly labeled and packaged meat and meat food products, and results in sundry losses to livestock producers and processors of meat and meat food products, as well as injury to consumers. The unwholesome, adulterated, mislabeled, or deceptively packaged articles can be sold at lower prices and compete unfairly with the wholesome, not adulterated, and properly labeled and packaged articles, to the detriment of consumers and the public generally. It is hereby found that regulation by the Board and cooperation by North Carolina and the United States as contemplated by this and the subsequent Article are appropriate to protect the health and welfare of consumers and otherwise effectuate the purposes of this and the subsequent Article. (1969, c. 893, s. 2; 1971, c. 54, s. 3.)

§ 106-549.17. Inspection of animals before slaughter; humane methods of slaughtering.

(a) For the purpose of preventing the use in intrastate commerce, as hereinafter provided, of meat and meat food products which are adulterated, the Commissioner shall cause to be made, by inspectors appointed for that purpose, an examination and inspection of all cattle, sheep, swine, goats, fallow deer, red deer, bison, horses, mules, and other equines before they shall be allowed to enter into any slaughtering, packing, meat-canning, rendering, or similar establishment in this State in which slaughtering and preparation of meat and meat food products of such animals are conducted for intrastate commerce; and all cattle, sheep, swine, goats, fallow deer, red deer, bison, horses, mules, and other equines found on such inspection to show symptoms of disease shall be set apart and slaughtered separately from all other cattle, sheep, swine, goats, fallow deer, red deer, bison, horses, mules, or other equines, and when so slaughtered, the carcasses of said cattle, sheep, swine, goats, fallow deer, red deer, bison, horses, mules, or other equines shall be subject to a careful examination and inspection, all as provided by the rules and regulations to be prescribed by the Board as herein provided for.

(b)   For the purpose of preventing the inhumane slaughtering of livestock, the Commissioner shall cause to be made, by inspectors appointed for that purpose, an examination and inspection of the method by which cattle, sheep, swine, goats, fallow deer, red deer, bison, horses, mules, and other equines are slaughtered and handled in connection with slaughter in the slaughtering establishments inspected under this law. The Commissioner may refuse to provide inspection to a new slaughtering establishment or may cause inspection to be temporarily suspended at a slaughtering establishment if the Commissioner finds that any cattle, sheep, swine, goats, fallow deer, red deer, bison, horses, mules, or other equines have been slaughtered or handled in connection with slaughter at such establishment by any method not in accordance with subsection (c) of this section until the establishment furnishes assurances satisfactory to the Commissioner that all slaughtering and handling in connection with slaughter of livestock shall be in accordance with such a method.

(c)   Either of the following two methods of slaughtering of livestock and handling of livestock in connection with slaughter are found to be humane:

(1)   In the case of cattle, calves, fallow deer, red deer, bison, horses, mules, sheep, swine, and other livestock, all animals are rendered insensible to pain by a single blow or gunshot or an electrical, chemical, or other means that is rapid and effective, before being shackled, hoisted, thrown, cast, or cut; or

(2)   By slaughtering in accordance with the ritual requirements of the Jewish faith or any other religious faith that prescribes a method of slaughter whereby the animal suffers loss of consciousness by anemia of the brain caused by the simultaneous and instantaneous severance of the carotid arteries with a sharp

instrument and handling in connection with such slaughtering. (1969, c. 893, s. 3; 1981, c. 376, s. 1; 1991, c. 317, s. 6; 1995, c. 194, s. 3; 1997-142, s. 6.)

§ 106-549.18. Inspection; stamping carcass.

For the purposes hereinbefore set forth the Commissioner shall cause to be made by inspectors appointed for that purpose, as hereinafter provided, a post mortem examination and inspection of the carcasses and parts thereof of all cattle, sheep, swine, goats, fallow deer, red deer, bison, horses, mules, and other equines, capable of use as human food, to be prepared at any slaughtering, meat-canning, salting, packing, rendering, or similar establishment in this State in which such articles are prepared for intrastate commerce; and the carcasses and parts thereof of all such animals found to be not adulterated shall be marked, stamped, tagged, or labeled, as "Inspected and Passed"; and said inspectors shall label, mark, stamp, or tag as "Inspected and Condemned," all carcasses and parts thereof of animals found to be adulterated; and all carcasses and parts thereof thus inspected and condemned shall be destroyed for food purposes by the said establishment in the presence of an inspector, and the Commissioner or his authorized representative may remove inspectors from any such establishment which fails to so destroy any such condemned carcass or part thereof, and said inspectors, after said first inspection shall, when they deem it necessary, reinspect said carcasses or parts thereof to determine whether since the first inspection the same have become adulterated and if any carcass or any part thereof shall, upon examination and inspection subsequent to the first examination and inspection, be found to be adulterated, it shall be destroyed for food purposes by the said establishment in the presence of an inspector, and the Commissioner or his authorized representative may remove inspectors from any establishment which fails to so destroy any such condemned carcass or part thereof. (1969, c. 893, s. 4; 1991, c. 317, s. 7; 1995, c. 194, s. 4; 1997-142, s. 7.)

§ 106-549.19. Application of Article; place of inspection.

The foregoing provisions shall apply to all carcasses or parts of carcasses of cattle, sheep, swine, goats, fallow deer, red deer, bison, horses, mules, and other equines or the meat or meat products thereof, capable of use as human food, which may be brought into any slaughtering, meat-canning, salting, packing, rendering, or similar establishment, where inspection under this Article is maintained, and such examination and inspection shall be had before the said carcasses or parts thereof shall be allowed to enter into any department wherein the same are to be treated and prepared for meat food products; and the foregoing provisions shall also apply to all such products which, after having been issued from any such slaughtering, meat-canning, salting, packing, rendering, or similar establishment, shall be returned to the same or to any similar establishment where such inspection is maintained. The Commissioner or his authorized representative may limit the entry of carcasses, part of carcasses, meat and meat food products, and other materials into any establishment at which inspection under this Article is maintained, under such conditions as he may prescribe to assure that allowing the entry of such articles into such inspected establishments will be consistent with the purposes of this and the subsequent Article. (1969, c. 893, s. 5; 1991, c. 317, s. 8; 1995, c. 194, s. 5; 1997-142, s. 8.)

§ 106-549.20. Inspectors' access to businesses.

For the purposes hereinbefore set forth the Commissioner or his authorized representative shall cause to be made by inspectors appointed for that purpose an examination and inspection of all meat food products prepared in any slaughtering, meat-canning, salting, packing, rendering, or similar establishment, where such articles are prepared for intrastate commerce and for the purposes of any examination and inspection said inspectors shall have access at all times during regular business hours to every part of said establishment; and said inspectors shall mark, stamp, tag, or label as "North Carolina Department of Agriculture and Consumer Services Inspected and Passed" all such products found to be not adulterated; and said inspectors shall label, mark, stamp, or tag as "North Carolina Department of Agriculture and Consumer Services Inspected and Condemned" all such products found adulterated, and all such condemned meat food products shall be destroyed for food purposes, as hereinbefore provided, and the Commissioner or his authorized representative may remove inspectors from any establishment which fails to so destroy such condemned meat food products. (1969, c. 893, s. 6; 1997-261, s. 109.)

§ 106-549.21. Stamping container or covering; regulation of container.

(a) When any meat or meat food product prepared for intrastate commerce which has been inspected as hereinbefore provided and marked "North Carolina Department of Agriculture and Consumer Services Inspected and Passed" shall be placed or packed in any can, pot, tin, canvas, or other receptacle or covering in any establishment where inspection under the provisions of this Article is maintained, the person, firm, or corporation preparing said product shall cause a label to be attached to said can, pot, tin, canvas, or other receptacle or covering, under supervision of an inspector, which label shall state that the contents thereof have been "North Carolina Department of Agriculture and Consumer Services Inspected and Passed" under the provisions of this Article, and no inspection and examination of meat or meat food products deposited or inclosed in cans, tins, pots, canvas, or other receptacle or covering in any establishment where inspection under the provisions of this Article is maintained shall be deemed to be complete until such meat or meat food products have been sealed or inclosed in said can, tin, pot, canvas, or other receptacle or covering under the supervision of an inspector.

(b) All carcasses, parts of carcasses, meat and meat food products inspected at any establishment under the authority of this Article and found to be not adulterated shall at the time they leave the establishment bear, in distinctly legible form, directly thereon or on their containers, as the Commissioner or authorized representative may require, the information required under subdivision (15) of G.S. 106-549.15.

(c) The Board whenever it determines such action is necessary for the protection of the public, may prescribe:

(1) The styles and sizes of type to be used with respect to material required to be incorporated in labeling to avoid false or misleading labeling of any articles or animals subject to this and the subsequent Article;

(2) Definitions and standards of identity or composition for articles subject to this Article and standards of fill of container for such articles not inconsistent with any such standards established under the Federal Food, Drug, and Cosmetic Act, or under the Federal Meat Inspection Act, and there shall be consultation between the Commissioner or his authorized representative and the Secretary of Agriculture of the United States prior to the issuance of such standards to avoid inconsistency between such standards and the federal standards.

(d) No article subject to this title shall be sold or offered for sale by any person, firm, or corporation, in intrastate commerce, under any name or other marking or labeling which is false or misleading, or in any container of a misleading form or size, but established trade names and other marking and labeling and containers which are not false or misleading, and which are approved by the Commissioner or his authorized representative, are permitted.

(e) If the Commissioner or his authorized representative has reason to believe that any marking or labeling or the size or form of any container in use or proposed for use with respect to any article subject to this title is false or misleading in any particular, he may direct that such use be withheld unless the marking, labeling, or container is modified in such manner as he may prescribe so that it will not be false or misleading. If the person, firm, or corporation using or proposing to use the marking, labeling or container does not accept the determination of the Commissioner or his authorized representative, such person, firm, or corporation may request a hearing, but the use of the marking, labeling, or container shall, if the Commissioner so directs, be withheld pending hearing and final determination by the Commissioner. A person who uses or proposes to use the marking, labeling, or container and who does not accept the determination of the Commissioner may commence a contested case under G.S. 150B-23. If directed by the Commissioner, the marking, labeling, or container may not be used pending a final decision. (1969, c. 893, s. 7; 1973, c. 1331, s. 3; 1987, c. 827, s. 35; 1997-261, s. 109.)

§ 106-549.22. Rules and regulations of Board.

The Commissioner or his authorized representative shall cause to be made, by experts in sanitation, or by other competent inspectors, such inspection of all slaughtering, meat-canning, salting, packing, rendering, or similar establishments in which cattle, sheep, swine, goats, fallow deer, red deer, bison, horses, mules, and other equines are slaughtered and the meat and meat food products thereof are prepared for intrastate commerce as may be necessary to inform himself concerning the sanitary conditions of the same, and the Board shall prescribe the rules and regulations of sanitation under which such establishments shall be maintained; and where the sanitary conditions of any such establishment are such that the meat or meat food products are rendered adulterated, the Commissioner or his authorized representative shall refuse to allow said meat or meat food products to be labeled, marked, stamped, or tagged as "North Carolina Department of Agriculture and Consumer Services

Inspected and Passed." (1969, c. 893, s. 8; 1991, c. 317, s. 9; 1995, c. 194, s. 6; 1997-142, s. 9; 1997-261, s. 109.)

§ 106-549.23. Prohibited slaughter, sale and transportation.

No person, firm, or corporation shall, with respect to any cattle, sheep, swine, goats, fallow deer, red deer, bison, horses, mules, or other equines, or any carcasses, parts of carcasses, meat or meat food products of any such animals:

(1) Slaughter any of these animals or prepare any of these articles which are capable of use as human food, at any establishment preparing any such articles for intrastate commerce except in compliance with the requirements of this and the subsequent Article;

(2) Slaughter, or handle in connection with slaughter, any such animals in any manner not in accordance with G.S. 106-549.17(c) of this Article;

(3) Sell, transport, offer for sale or transportation, or receive for transportation, in intrastate commerce:

a. Any of these articles which (i) are capable of use as human food and (ii) are adulterated or misbranded at the time of sale, transportation, offer for sale or transportation, or receipt for transportation; or

b. Any articles required to be inspected under this Article unless they have been so inspected and passed; or

(4) Do, with respect to any of these articles which are capable of use as human food, any act while they are being transported in intrastate commerce or held for sale after such transportation, which is intended to cause or has the effect of causing the articles to be adulterated or misbranded. (1969, c. 893, s. 9; 1981, c. 376, s. 2; 1991, c. 317, s. 10; 1995, c. 194, s. 7; 1997-142, s. 10.)

§ 106-549.24. Prohibited acts regarding certificate.

(a) No brand manufacturer, printer, or other person, firm, or corporation shall cast, print, lithograph, or otherwise make any device containing any official mark or simulation thereof, or any label bearing any such mark or simulation, or any form of official certificate or simulation thereof, except as authorized by the Commissioner or his authorized representative.

(b) No person, firm, or corporation shall

(1) Forge any official device, mark or certificate;

(2) Without authorization from the Commissioner or his authorized representative use any official device, mark, or certificate, or simulation thereof, or alter, detach, deface, or destroy any official device, mark, or certificate;

(3) Contrary to the regulations prescribed by the Board, fail to use, or to detach, deface, or destroy any official device, mark, or certificate;

(4) Knowingly possess, without promptly notifying the Commissioner or his authorized representative, any official device or any counterfeit, simulated, forged, or improperly altered official certificate or any device or label or any carcass of any animal, or part or product thereof, bearing any counterfeit, simulated, forged, or improperly altered official mark;

(5) Knowingly make any false statement in any shipper's certificate or other nonofficial or official certificate provided for in the regulations prescribed by the Board;

(6) Knowingly represent that any article has been inspected and passed, or exempted, under this Article when, in fact, it has, respectively, not been so inspected and passed, or exempted. (1969, c. 893, s. 10.)

§ 106-549.25. Slaughter, sale and transportation of equine carcasses.

No person, firm, or corporation shall sell, transport, offer for sale or transportation, or receive for transportation, in intrastate commerce, any carcasses of horses, mules, or other equines or parts of such carcasses, or the meat or meat food products thereof, unless they are plainly and conspicuously marked or labeled or otherwise identified as required by regulations prescribed by the Board to show the kinds of animals from which they were derived. When required by the Commissioner or his authorized representative, with respect to establishments at which inspection is maintained under this Article, such animals and their carcasses, parts thereof, meat and meat food products shall be prepared in establishments separate from those in which cattle, sheep, swine, fallow deer, red deer, bison, or goats are slaughtered or their carcasses, parts thereof, meats or meat food products are prepared. (1969, c. 893, s. 11; 1991, c. 317, s. 11; 1995, c. 194, s. 8; 1997-142, s. 11.)

§ 106-549.26. Inspection of establishment; bribery of or malfeasance of inspector.

The Commissioner or his authorized representative shall appoint from time to time inspectors to make examination and inspection of all cattle, sheep, swine, goats, fallow deer, red deer, bison, horses, mules, and other equines the inspection of which is hereby provided for, and of all carcasses and parts thereof, and of all meats and meat food products thereof, and of the sanitary conditions of all establishments in which such meat and meat food products hereinbefore described are prepared; and said inspectors shall refuse to stamp, mark, tag or label any carcass or any part thereof, or meat food product therefrom, prepared in any establishment hereinbefore mentioned, until the same shall have actually been inspected and found to be not adulterated; and shall perform such other duties as are provided by this and the subsequent Article and by the rules and regulations to be prescribed by said Board and said Board shall, from time to time, make such rules and regulations as are necessary for the efficient execution of the provisions of this and the subsequent Article, and all inspections and examinations made under this Article shall be such and made in such manner as described in the rules and regulations prescribed by said Board not inconsistent with the provisions of this Article and as directed by the Commissioner or his authorized representative. Any person, firm, or corporation, or any agent or employee of any person, firm, or corporation, who shall give, pay, or offer, directly or indirectly, to any inspector, or any other officer or employee of this State authorized to perform any of the duties prescribed by this and the subsequent Article or by the rules and regulations of the Board or by the Commissioner or his authorized representative any money or other thing of value, with intent to influence said inspector, or other officer or employee of this State in the discharge of any duty herein provided for, shall be deemed guilty of a Class I felony which may include a fine not less than five hundred dollars ($500.00) nor more than ten thousand dollars ($10,000); and any inspector, or other officer or employee of this State authorized to perform any of the duties prescribed by this Article who shall accept any money, gift, or other thing of value from any person, firm, or corporation, or officers, agents, or employees thereof, given with intent to influence his official action, or who shall receive or accept from any person, firm, or corporation engaged in intrastate commerce any gift, money, or other thing of value given with any purpose or intent whatsoever, shall be deemed guilty of a Class I felony and shall, upon conviction thereof, be summarily discharged from office and may be punished by a fine not less than five hundred dollars ($500.00) nor more than ten thousand dollars ($10,000). (1969, c. 893, s. 12; 1991, c. 317, s. 12; 1993, c. 539, s. 1298; 1994, Ex. Sess., c. 24, s. 14(c); 1995, c. 194, s. 9; 1997-142, s. 12.)

§ 106-549.27. Exemptions from Article.

(a) The provisions of this Article requiring inspection of the slaughter of animals and the preparation of the carcasses, parts thereof, meat and meat food products at establishments conducting such operations shall not

(1) Apply to the slaughtering by any person of animals of his own raising, and the preparation by him and transportation in intrastate commerce of the carcasses, parts thereof, meat and meat food products of such animals exclusively for use by him and members of his household and his nonpaying guests and employees; nor

(2) To the custom slaughter by any person, firm, or corporation of cattle, sheep, swine, fallow deer, red deer, bison, or goats delivered by the owner thereof for such slaughter, and the preparation by such slaughterer and transportation in intrastate commerce of the carcasses, parts thereof, meat and meat food products of such animals, exclusively for use, in the household of such owner, by him, and members of his household and his nonpaying guests and employees: Provided, that all carcasses, parts thereof, meat and meat food products derived from custom slaughter shall be identified as required by the Commissioner, during all phases of slaughtering, chilling, cooling, freezing, packing, meat canning, rendering, preparation, storage and transportation; provided further, that the custom slaughterer does not engage in the business of buying or selling any carcasses, parts thereof, meat or meat food products of any cattle, sheep, swine, goats, fallow deer, red deer, bison, or equines, capable of use as human food, unless the carcasses, parts thereof, meat or meat food products have been inspected and passed and are identified as having been inspected and passed by the Commissioner or the United States Department of Agriculture.

(b) The provisions of this Article requiring inspection of the slaughter of animals and the preparation of carcasses, parts thereof, meat and meat food products shall not apply to operations of types traditionally and usually conducted at retail stores and restaurants, when conducted at any retail store or restaurant or similar retail-type establishment for sale in normal retail quantities or service of such articles to consumers at such establishments. Meat food products coming under this subsection may be stored, processed, or prepared at any freezer locker plant provided such meat food products are identified and kept separate and apart from other meat food products bearing the official mark of inspection while in the freezer locker plant.

(c) In order to accomplish the objectives of this Article, the Commissioner shall exempt any other operations which the Commissioner shall determine would best be exempted to further the purposes of this Article, to the extent such exemptions conform to the Federal Meat Inspection Act and the regulations thereunder.

(d) The slaughter of animals and preparation of articles referred to in paragraphs (a)(2) and (b) of this section shall be conducted in accordance with such sanitary conditions as the Board may by regulations prescribe. Willful violation of any such regulation is a Class 2 misdemeanor.

(e) The adulteration and misbranding provisions of this title, other than the requirement of the inspection legend, shall apply to articles which are not required to be inspected under this section. (1969, c. 893, s. 13; 1971, c. 54, ss. 1, 2; 1991, c. 317, s. 13; 1993, c. 539, s. 799; 1994, Ex. Sess., c. 24, s. 14(c); 1995, c. 194, s. 10; 1997-142, s. 13.)

§ 106-549.28. Regulation of storage of meat.

The Board may by regulations prescribe conditions under which carcasses, parts of carcasses, meat, and meat food products of cattle, sheep, swine, goats, fallow deer, red deer, bison, horses, mules, or other equines, capable of use as human food, shall be stored or otherwise handled by any person, firm, or corporation engaged in the business of buying, selling, freezing, storing, or transporting, in or for intrastate commerce, such articles, whenever the Board deems such action necessary to assure that such articles will not be adulterated or misbranded when delivered to the consumer. Willful violation of any such regulation is a Class 2 misdemeanor. (1969, c. 893, s. 14; 1991, c. 317, s. 14;

1993, c. 539, s. 800; 1994, Ex. Sess., c. 24, s. 14(c); 1995, c. 194, s. 11; 1997-142, s. 14.)

Article 49C.

Federal and State Cooperation as to Meat Inspection; Implementation of Inspection.

§ 106-549.29. North Carolina Department of Agriculture and Consumer Services responsible for cooperation.

(a) The North Carolina Department of Agriculture and Consumer Services is hereby designated as the State agency which shall be responsible for cooperating with the Secretary of Agriculture of the United States under the provisions of section 301 of the Federal Meat Inspection Act and such agency is directed to cooperate with the Secretary of Agriculture of the United States in developing and administering the meat inspection program of this State under this and the previous Article in such a manner as will effectuate the purposes of this and the previous Article.

(b) In such cooperative efforts, the North Carolina Department of Agriculture and Consumer Services is authorized to accept from said Secretary advisory assistance in planning and otherwise developing the State program, technical and laboratory assistance and training (including necessary curricular and instructional materials and equipment), and financial and other aid for administration of such a program.

(c) The North Carolina Department of Agriculture and Consumer Services is further authorized to recommend to the said Secretary of Agriculture such officials or employees of this State as the Commissioner shall designate, for appointment to the advisory committees provided for in Section 301 of the Federal Meat Inspection Act; and the Commissioner or his authorized representative shall serve as the representative of the Governor for consultation with said Secretary under paragraph (c) of Section 301 of said act. (1969, c. 893, s. 15; 1985 (Reg. Sess., 1986), c. 1014, s. 155(a); 1997-261, s. 59.)

§ 106-549.29:1. Repealed by Session Laws 1969, c. 893, s. 26.

§ 106-549.30. Refusal of Commissioner to inspect and certify meat.

The Commissioner may (for such period, or indefinitely, as he deems necessary to effectuate the purposes of this and the previous Article) refuse to provide, or withdraw, inspection service under Article 49B with respect to any establishment if he determines, after opportunity for a hearing is accorded to the applicant for, or recipient of, such service, that such applicant or recipient is unfit to engage in any business requiring inspection under Article 49B because the applicant or recipient, or anyone responsibly connected with the applicant or recipient, has been convicted, in any federal or state court, of (i) any felony, or (ii) more than one violation of any law, other than a felony, based upon the acquiring, handling, or distributing of unwholesome, mislabeled, or deceptively packaged food or upon fraud in connection with transactions in food. This section shall not affect in any way other provisions of this or the previous Article for withdrawal of inspection services under Article 49B from establishments failing to maintain sanitary conditions or to destroy condemned carcasses, parts, meat or meat food products.

For the purpose of this section a person shall be deemed to be responsibly connected with the business if he was a partner, officer, director, holder, or owner of ten per centum (10%) or more of its voting stock or employee in a managerial or executive capacity. The determination and order of the Commissioner with respect thereto under this section shall be final and conclusive unless the affected applicant for, or recipient of, inspection service files application for judicial review within 30 days after the effective date of such order in the appropriate court as provided in G.S. 106-549.33. (1969, c. 893, s. 16.)

§ 106-549.31. Enforcement against uninspected meat.

Whenever any carcass, part of a carcass, meat or meat food product of cattle, sheep, swine, goats, horses, mules, or other equines, or any product exempted from the definition of a meat food product, or any dead, dying, disabled, or diseased cattle, sheep, swine, goat, or equine is found by any inspector of the Meat and Poultry Inspection Service of the North Carolina Department of Agriculture and Consumer Services upon any premises where it is held for purposes of, or during or after distribution in intrastate commerce, and there is reason to believe that any such article is adulterated or misbranded and is capable of use as human food, or that is has not been inspected, in violation of the provisions of Article 49B or of the Federal Meat Inspection Act or the Federal Food, Drug and Cosmetic Act, or that such article or animal has been or is intended to be distributed in violation of any such provisions, it may be detained by such inspector, upon approval of his supervisor, for a period not to exceed 20 days, pending action under G.S. 106-549.33, and shall not be moved by any person, firm, or corporation from the place at which it is located when so detained, until released by the area supervisor of the Meat and Poultry Inspection Service. All official marks may be required by such inspector to be removed from such article or animal before it is released unless it appears to the satisfaction of the area supervisor that the article or animal is eligible to retain such marks. (1969, c. 893, s. 17; 1997-261, s. 109.)

§ 106-549.32. Enforcement against condemned meat; appeal.

(a) Any carcass, part of a carcass, meat or meat food product of cattle, sheep, swine, goats, horses, mules or other equines, or any dead, dying, disabled, or diseased cattle, sheep, swine, goat, or equine, that is being transported in intrastate commerce, or is held for sale in this State after such transportation, and that (i) is or has been prepared, sold, transported or otherwise distributed or offered or received for distribution in violation of this or the previous Article, or (ii) is capable of use as human food and is adulterated or misbranded, or (iii) in any other way is in violation of this or the previous Article, shall be liable to be proceeded against and seized and condemned, at any time, on a complaint in any proper court as provided in G.S. 106-549.33 within the jurisdiction of which the article or animal is found. If the article or animal is condemned it shall, after entry of the order be disposed of by destruction or sale as the court may direct and the proceeds, if sold, less the court costs and fees, and storage and other proper expenses, shall be paid into the general fund of this State, but the article or animals shall not be sold contrary to the provisions of this or the previous Article. Provided, that upon the execution and delivery of a good and sufficient bond conditioned that the article or animal shall not be sold or otherwise disposed of contrary to the provisions of this or the previous Article, the court may direct that such article or animal be delivered to the owner thereof subject to such supervision by the authorized representative of the Commissioner as is necessary to insure compliance with the applicable laws. When an order of condemnation is entered against the article or animal and it is released under bond, or destroyed, court costs and fees, and storage and other proper expenses shall be awarded against the person, if any, intervening as claimant of the article or animal. The proceedings in such cases shall be heard by the superior court without a jury, with the right of the aggrieved party to appeal to the Court of Appeals, and all such proceedings shall be at the suit of and in the name of this State. No appeal shall lie from the Court of Appeals.

(b)   The provisions of this section shall in no way derogate from authority for condemnation or seizure conferred by other provisions of this or the previous Article, or other laws. (1969, c. 893, s. 18.)

§ 106-549.33. Jurisdiction of superior court.

The superior court is vested with jurisdiction specifically to enforce, and to prevent and restrain violations of this and the previous Article, and shall have jurisdiction in all other kinds of cases arising under this and the previous Article, provided however, all prosecutions for criminal violations under this and the previous Article shall be in any court having jurisdiction over said violation. (1969, c. 893, s. 19.)

§ 106-549.34. Interference with inspector.

Any person who willfully assaults, resists, opposes, impedes, intimidates, or interferes with any person while engaged in or on account of the performance of his official duties under this or the previous Article shall be guilty of a Class 2 misdemeanor. For the purposes of this section, "impede," "oppose," and "intimidate," or "interfere" shall include, but not be limited to, the use of profane and indecent language, or any act or gesture, verbal or nonverbal, which tends to cast disrespect on an inspector or the Meat and Poultry Inspection Service. Whoever, in the commission of any such acts, uses a deadly weapon, shall be guilty of a Class 1 misdemeanor. (1969, c. 893, s. 20; 1993, c. 539, s. 801; 1994, Ex. Sess., c. 24, s. 14(c).)

§ 106-549.35. Punishment for violation.

(a)   Any person, firm, or corporation who violates any provision of this or the previous Article or any regulation of the Board for which no other criminal penalty is provided by this or the previous Article is guilty of a Class 2 misdemeanor; but if such violation involves intent to defraud, or any distribution or attempted distribution of an article that is adulterated (except as defined in G.S. 106-549.15(1)h, such person, firm or corporation is guilty of a Class H felony which may include a fine of not more than ten thousand dollars ($10,000). Provided, that no person, firm, or corporation shall be subject to penalties under this section for receiving for transportation any article or animal in violation of this or the previous Article if such receipt was made in good faith, unless such person, firm, or corporation refuses to furnish on request of a representative of the Meat and Poultry Inspection Service the name and address of the person from whom he received such article or animal, and copies of all documents, if any there be, pertaining to the delivery of the article or animal to him.

(b) Nothing in this Article shall be construed as requiring the Commissioner or his authorized representative to report for prosecution or for the institution of condemnation or injunction proceedings, minor violations of this Article whenever he believes that the public interest will be adequately served by a suitable written notice of warning.

(c) The Commissioner may assess a civil penalty of not more than five thousand dollars ($5,000) against any person who violates a provision of this Article or Article 49B, or any rule promulgated thereunder. In determining the amount of the penalty, the Commissioner shall consider the degree and extent of harm caused by the violation.

The clear proceeds of civil penalties assessed pursuant to this subsection shall be remitted to the Civil Penalty and Forfeiture Fund in accordance with G.S. 115C-457.2. (1969, c. 893, s. 21; 1995, c. 516, s. 5; 1998-215, s. 17; 1999-408, s. 6.)

§ 106-549.36. Gathering information; reports required; use of subpoena.

(a) The Commissioner shall also have power -

(1) To gather and compile information concerning and, to investigate from time to time the organization, business, conduct, practices, and management of any person, firm, or corporation engaged in intrastate commerce, and the relation thereof to other persons, firms, or corporations;

(2) To require, by general or special orders, persons, firms, and corporations engaged in intrastate commerce, or any class of them, or any of them to file with the Commissioner, in such form as the Commissioner may prescribe, annual or special, or both annual and special, reports or answers in writing to specific questions, furnishing to the Commissioner such information as he may require as to the organization, business, conduct, practices, management, and relation to other persons, firms, and corporations, of the person, firm, or corporation filing such reports or answers in writing. Such reports and answers shall be made under oath, or otherwise, as the Commissioner may prescribe, and shall be filed with the Commissioner within such reasonable period as the Commissioner may prescribe, unless additional time be granted in any case by the Commissioner.

(b) For the purposes of this and the previous Article the Commissioner shall at all reasonable times have access to, for the purpose of examination, and the right to copy any documentary evidence of any person, firm, or corporation being investigated or proceeded against, and may require by subpoena the attendance and testimony of witnesses and the production of all documentary evidence of any person, firm, or corporation relating to any matter under investigation. The Commissioner may sign subpoenas and may administer oaths and affirmations, examine witnesses, and receive evidence.

(1) Such attendance of witnesses, and the production of such documentary evidence, may be required at any designated place of hearing. In case of disobedience to a subpoena the Commissioner may invoke the aid of any court designated in G.S. 106-549.33 in requiring the attendance and testimony of witnesses and the production of documentary evidence.

(2) Any of the courts designated in G.S. 106-549.33 within the jurisdiction of which such inquiry is carried on may, in case of contumacy or refusal to obey a subpoena issued to any person, firm, or corporation, issue an order requiring such person, firm, or corporation, to appear before the Commissioner or to produce documentary evidence if so ordered, or to give evidence touching the matter in question; and any failure to obey such order of the court may be punished by such court as a contempt thereof.

(3) Upon the application of the Attorney General of this State at the request of the Commissioner, the superior court shall have jurisdiction to issue writs of mandamus commanding any person, firm, or corporation to comply with the provisions of this or the previous Article or any order of the Commissioner made in pursuance thereof.

(4) The Commissioner may order testimony to be taken by deposition in any proceeding or investigation pending under this Article at any stage of such proceeding or investigation. Such depositions may be taken before any person designated by the Commissioner and having power to administer oaths. Such testimony shall be reduced to writing by the person taking the deposition, or under his direction and shall then be subscribed by the deponent. Any person may be compelled to appear and depose and to produce documentary evidence in the same manner as witnesses may be compelled to appear and testify and produce documentary evidence before the Commissioner as hereinbefore provided.

(5) Witnesses summoned before the Commissioner shall be paid the same fees and mileage that are paid witnesses in the courts of this State, and witnesses whose depositions are taken and the persons taking the same shall severally be entitled to the same fees as are paid for like services in such courts.

(6) No person, firm, or corporation shall be excused from attending and testifying or from producing books, papers, schedules of charges, contracts, agreements, or other documentary evidence before the Commissioner or in obedience to the subpoena of the Commissioner whether such subpoena be signed or issued by him or his delegate, or in any cause or proceedings, criminal or otherwise, based upon or growing out of any alleged violation of this or the previous Article, or of any amendments thereto, on the ground or for the reason that the testimony or evidence, documentary or otherwise, required of him or it may tend to incriminate him or it or subject him or it to a penalty or forfeiture; but no person shall be prosecuted or subjected to any penalty or forfeiture for or on account of any transaction, matter, or thing concerning which he is compelled, after having claimed his privilege against self-incrimination, to testify or produce evidence, documentary or otherwise, except that any person so testifying shall not be exempt from prosecution and punishment for perjury committed in so testifying.

(c) Any person, firm, or corporation that shall neglect or refuse to attend and testify or to answer any lawful inquiry, or to produce documentary evidence, if in his or its power to do so, in obedience to the subpoena or lawful requirement of the Commissioner shall be guilty of a Class 2 misdemeanor.

(1) Any person, firm, or corporation that shall willfully make, or cause to be made, any false entry or statement of fact in any report required to be made under this Article, or that shall willfully make, or cause to be made, any false

entry in any account, record, or memorandum kept by any person, firm, or corporation subject to this Article or that shall willfully neglect or fail to make, or to cause to be made, full, true, and correct entries in such accounts, records, or memoranda, of all facts and transactions appertaining to the business of such person, firm, or corporation, or that shall willfully remove out of the jurisdiction of this State, or willfully mutilate, alter, or by any other means falsify any documentary evidence of any such person, firm, or corporation or that shall willfully refuse to submit to the Commissioner or to any of his authorized agents, for the purpose of inspection and taking copies, any documentary evidence of any such person, firm, or corporation in his possession or within his control, shall be deemed guilty of a Class 2 misdemeanor.

(2) If any person, firm, or corporation required by this Article to file any annual or special report shall fail so to do within the time fixed by the Commissioner for filing the same, and such failure shall continue for 30 days after notice of such default, such person, firm, or corporation shall forfeit to this State the sum of one hundred dollars ($100.00) for each and every day of the continuance of such failure, which forfeiture shall be payable into the general fund of this State, and shall be recoverable in a civil suit in the name of the State brought in the superior court where the person, firm, or corporation has his or its principal office or in Wake County. It shall be the duty of the Attorney General of this State, to prosecute for the recovery of such forfeitures. The costs and expenses of such prosecution shall be paid out of the amount recovered in such action.

(3) Any officer or employee of this State who shall make public any information obtained by the Commissioner without his authority, unless directed by a court, shall be deemed guilty of a Class 2 misdemeanor. (1969, c. 893, s. 22; 1993, c. 539, s. 802; 1994, Ex. Sess., c. 24, s. 14(c).)

§ 106-549.37. Jurisdiction coterminous with federal law.

The requirements of this Article shall apply to persons, firms, corporation establishments, animals, and articles regulated under the Federal Meat Inspection Act only to the extent provided for in section 408 of said federal act. (1969, c. 893, s. 23.)

§ 106-549.38. Rules and regulations of State Department of Agriculture and Consumer Services.

All rules and regulations of the Department of Agriculture and Consumer Services not inconsistent with the provisions of this Article shall remain in full force and effect until amended or repealed by the Board. (1969, c. 893, s. 27; 1997-261, s. 60.)

§ 106-549.39. Hours of inspection; overtime work; fees.

(a) Overtime Fees. - The Commissioner is not required to furnish meat inspection services during the following times unless the establishment under inspection pays the Department for the services:

(1) More than eight hours in a day.

(2) More than 40 hours in a calendar week.

(3) On a Sunday.

(4) On a legal holiday.

The Commissioner may establish a fee at an hourly rate to be paid by an establishment inspected during the times listed above. The fee shall be credited to the Department as a departmental receipt and applied to the cost of inspecting the establishment.

(b) Inspection Fees. - The Commissioner may establish a fee at an hourly rate to be paid by an establishment preparing an animal listed in this subsection as a meat food product. The fee shall be credited to the Department as a departmental receipt and applied to the cost of inspecting these animals to be used for food. The animals whose inspection is subject to the fee imposed under this subsection are:

(1) Bison.

(2) Repealed by Session Laws 2009-102, s. 1, effective June 15, 2009. (1969, c. 893, s. 27(a); 1993, c. 311, s. 2; 1995, c. 194, s. 12; 2009-102, s. 1.)

§§ 106-549.40 through 106-549.48. Repealed by Session Laws 1969, c. 893, s. 26.

Article 49D.

Poultry Products Inspection Act.

§ 106-549.49. Short title.

This Article shall be designated as the North Carolina Poultry Products Inspection Act. (1971, c. 677, s. 1.)

§ 106-549.50. Purpose and policy.

(a) Poultry and poultry products are an important source of the nation's total supply of food. It is essential in the public interest that the health and welfare of consumers be protected by assuring that slaughtered poultry and poultry products distributed to them are wholesome, not adulterated, and properly marked, labeled, and packaged. Unwholesome, adulterated, or misbranded poultry or poultry products are injurious to the public welfare, destroy markets for wholesome, not adulterated, and properly labeled and packaged poultry and poultry products, and result in sundry losses to poultry producers and processors of poultry and poultry products, as well as injury to consumers. The unwholesome, adulterated, mislabeled, or deceptively packaged articles can be sold at lower prices and compete unfairly with the wholesome, not adulterated, and properly labeled and packaged articles, to the detriment of consumers and the public generally. It is hereby found that regulation by the Board and cooperation by this State and the United States as contemplated by this Article are appropriate to protect the health and welfare of consumers and otherwise effectuate the purposes of this Article.

(b) It is hereby declared to be the policy of the General Assembly to provide for the inspection of poultry and poultry products and otherwise regulate the processing and distribution of such articles as hereinafter prescribed to prevent the movement or sale in intrastate commerce of poultry and poultry products which are adulterated or misbranded. It is the intent of the General Assembly that when poultry and poultry products are condemned because of disease, the reason for condemnation in such instances shall be supported by scientific fact, information, or criteria, and such condemnation under this Article shall be achieved through uniform inspection standards and uniform application thereof. (1971, c. 677, ss. 2, 3.)

§ 106-549.51. Definitions.

For purposes of this Article, the following terms shall have the meanings stated below:

(1) "Adulterated" shall apply to any poultry product under one or more of the following circumstances:

a. If it bears or contains any poisonous or deleterious substance which may render it injurious to health; but in case the substance is not an added substance, such article shall not be considered adulterated under this clause if the quantity of such substance in or on such article does not ordinarily render it injurious to health;

b. 1. If it bears or contains (by reason of administration of any substance to the live poultry or otherwise) any added poisonous or added deleterious substance (other than one which is a pesticide chemical in or on a raw agricultural commodity; a food additive; or a color additive) which may, in the judgment of the Commissioner, make such article unfit for human food;

2. If it is, in whole or in part, a raw agricultural commodity and such commodity bears or contains a pesticide chemical which is unsafe within the meaning of section 408 of the Federal Food, Drug, and Cosmetic Act;

3. If it bears or contains any food additive which is unsafe within the meaning of section 409 of the Federal Food, Drug, and Cosmetic Act;

4. If it bears or contains any color additive which is unsafe within the meaning of section 706 of the Federal Food, Drug, and Cosmetic Act: Provided, that an article which is not otherwise deemed adulterated under paragraphs 2, 3, or 4 shall nevertheless be deemed adulterated if use of the pesticide chemical, food additive, or color additive in or on such article is prohibited by regulations of the Board in official establishments;

c. If it consists in whole or in part of any filthy, putrid, or decomposed substance or is for any other reason unsound, unhealthful, unwholesome, or otherwise unfit for human food;

d. If it has been prepared, packed, or held under insanitary conditions whereby it may have become contaminated with filth, or whereby it may have been rendered injurious to health;

e. If it is, in whole or in part, the product of any poultry which has died otherwise than by slaughter;

f. If its container is composed, in whole or in part, of any poisonous or deleterious substance which may render the contents injurious to health;

g. If it has been intentionally subjected to radiation, unless the use of the radiation was in conformity with a regulation or exemption in effect pursuant to section 409 of the Federal Food, Drug, and Cosmetic Act; or

h. If any valuable constituent has been in whole or in part omitted or abstracted therefrom; or if any substance has been substituted, wholly or in part therefor; or if damage or inferiority has been concealed in any manner; or if any substance has been added thereto or mixed or packed therewith so as to increase its bulk or weight, or reduce its quality or strength, or make it appear better or of greater value than it is.

(2) "Animal food manufacturer" means any person engaged in the business of manufacturing or processing animal food derived wholly or in part from carcasses, or parts or products of the carcasses, of poultry.

(3) "Board" means the North Carolina Board of Agriculture.

(4) "Capable of use of human food" shall apply to any carcass, or part or product of a carcass, of any poultry, unless it is denatured or otherwise identified as required by regulations prescribed by the Board to deter its use as human food, or it is naturally inedible by humans.

(5) "Color additive" shall have the same meaning for purposes of this Article as under the Federal Food, Drug, and Cosmetic Act.

(6) "Commissioner" means the North Carolina Commissioner of Agriculture or his authorized representative.

(7) "Container" or "package" includes any box, can, tin, cloth, plastic, or other receptacle, wrapper, or cover.

(8) "Federal Food, Drug, and Cosmetic Act" means the act so entitled, approved June 25, 1938 (52 Stat. 1040), and acts amendatory thereof or supplementary thereto.

(9) "Federal Poultry Products Inspection Act" means the act so entitled, approved August 28, 1957 (71 Stat. 441), as amended by the Wholesome Poultry Products Act (82 Stat. 791).

(10) "Food additive" shall have the same meaning for purposes of this Article as under the Federal Food, Drug, and Cosmetic Act.

(11) "Immediate container" includes any consumer package; or any other container in which poultry products, not consumer packaged, are packed.

(12) "Inspection service" means the official government service within the Department of Agriculture and Consumer Services designated by the Commissioner as having the responsibility for carrying out the provisions of this Article.

(13) "Inspector" means an employee or official of the Department of Agriculture and Consumer Services authorized by the Commissioner to inspect poultry and poultry products under the authority of this Article, or any employee or official of the government of any county or other governmental subdivision of this State authorized by the Commissioner to inspect poultry and poultry products under authority of this Article, under an agreement entered into between the Department and such governmental subdivision.

(14) "Intrastate commerce" means commerce within this State.

(15) "Label" means a display of written, printed, or graphic matter upon any article or the immediate container (not including package liners) of any article.

(16) "Labeling" means all labels and other written, printed, or graphic matter

a. Upon any article or any of its containers or wrappers, or

b. Accompanying such article.

(17) "Misbranded" shall apply to any poultry product under one or more of the following circumstances:

a. If its labeling is false or misleading in any particular;

b. If it is offered for sale under the name of another food;

c. If it is an imitation of another food, unless its label bears, in type of uniform size and prominence, the word "imitation" and immediately thereafter, the name of the food imitated;

d. If its container is so made, formed, or filled as to be misleading;

e. Unless it bears a label showing

1. The name and place of business of the manufacturer, packer, or distributor; and

2. An accurate statement of the quantity of the product in terms of weight, measure, or numerical count;

Provided, that under paragraph 2 of this subsubdivision e, reasonable variations may be permitted, and exemptions as to small packages or articles not in packages or other containers may be established, by regulations prescribed by the Board;

f. If any word, statement, or other information required by or under authority of this Article to appear on the label or other labeling is not prominently placed thereon with such conspicuousness (as compared with other words, statements, designs, or devices, in the labeling) and in such terms as to render it likely to be read and understood by the ordinary individual under customary conditions of purchase and use;

g. If it purports to be or is represented as a food for which a definition and standard of identity or composition has been prescribed by regulations of the Board under G.S. 106-549.55 unless

1. It conforms to such definition and standard, and

2. Its label bears the name of the food specified in the definition and standard and, insofar as may be required by such regulations, the common

names of optional ingredients (other than spices, flavoring, and coloring) present in such food;

h.   If it purports to be or is represented as a food for which a standard or standards of fill of container have been prescribed by regulations of the Board under G.S. 106-549.55, and it falls below the standard of fill of container applicable thereto, unless its label bears, in such manner and form as such regulations specify, a statement that it falls below such standard;

i.   If it is not subject to the provisions of subsubdivision g, unless its label bears

1.   The common or usual name of the food, if any there be, and

2.   In case it is fabricated from two or more ingredients, the common or usual name of each such ingredient; except that spices, flavorings, and colorings may, when authorized by the Commissioner be designated as spices, flavorings, and colorings without naming each: Provided, that, to the extent that compliance with the requirements of clause 2 of this subsubdivision i is impracticable, or results in deception or unfair competition, exemptions shall be established by regulations promulgated by the Board;

j.   If it purports to be or is represented for special dietary uses, unless its label bears such information concerning its vitamin, mineral, and other dietary properties as the Board, after consultation with the Secretary of Agriculture of the United States, determines to be, and by regulations prescribes as, necessary in order fully to inform purchasers as to its value for such uses;

k.   If it bears or contains any artificial flavoring, artificial coloring, or chemical preservative, unless it bears labeling stating that fact: Provided, that, to the extent that compliance with the requirements of this subsubdivision k is impracticable, exemptions shall be established by regulations promulgated by the Board; or

l.   If it fails to bear on its containers, and in the case of nonconsumer packaged carcasses (if the Commissioner so requires) directly thereon, as the Board may by regulations prescribe, the official inspection legend and official establishment number of the establishment where the article was processed, and, unrestricted by any of the foregoing, such other information as the Board may require in such regulations to assure that it will not have false or misleading labeling and that the public will be informed of the manner of handling required to maintain the article in a wholesome condition.

(18) "Official certificate" means any certificate prescribed by regulation of the Board for issuance by an inspector or other person performing official functions under this Article.

(19) "Official device" means any device prescribed or authorized by the Board for use in applying any official mark.

(20) "Official establishment" means any establishment as determined by the Commissioner at which inspection of the slaughter of poultry, or the processing of poultry products, is maintained under the authority of this Article.

(21) "Official inspection legend" means any symbol prescribed by regulation of the Board showing that an article was inspected for wholesomeness in accordance with this Article.

(22) "Official mark" means the official inspection legend or any other symbol prescribed by regulation of the Board to identify the status of any article or poultry under this Article.

(23) "Person" means any individual, partnership, corporation, association, or other business entity.

(24) "Pesticide chemical" shall have the same meaning for purposes of this Article as under the Federal Food, Drug, and Cosmetic Act.

(25) "Poultry" means any domesticated bird, whether live or dead.

(25a) "Poultry composting facility" means a structure or enclosure in which whole, unprocessed poultry carcasses are decomposed by a natural process into an organic, biologically safe by-product that can be used for plant food.

(26) "Poultry product" means any poultry carcass, or part thereof; or any product which is made wholly or in part from any poultry carcass or part thereof, excepting products which contain poultry ingredients only in a relatively small proportion or historically have not been considered by consumers as products of the poultry food industry, and which are exempted by the Board from definition as a poultry product under such conditions as the Board may prescribe to

assure that the poultry ingredients in such products are not adulterated and that such products are not represented as poultry products.

(27) "Poultry products broker" means any person engaged in the business of buying or selling poultry products on commission, or otherwise negotiating purchases or sales of such articles other than for his own account or as an employee of another person.

(28) "Processed" means slaughtered, canned, salted, stuffed, rendered, boned, cut up, or otherwise manufactured or processed.

(29) "Raw agricultural commodity" shall have the same meaning for purposes of this Article as under the Federal Food, Drug, and Cosmetic Act.

(30) "Renderer" means any person engaged in the business of rendering carcasses, or parts or products of the carcasses, or poultry, except rendering conducted under inspection or exemption under this Article.

(31) "Shipping container" means any container used or intended for use in packaging the product packed in an immediate container. (1971, c. 677, s. 4; 1995, c. 543, s. 3; 1997-261, s. 61.)

§ 106-549.51A: Repealed by Session Laws 2009-102, s. 2, effective June 15, 2009.

§ 106-549.52. State and federal cooperation.

(a) The Department of Agriculture and Consumer Services is hereby designated as the State agency which shall be responsible for cooperating with the Secretary of Agriculture of the United States under the provisions of section 5 of the Federal Poultry Products Inspection Act and such agency is directed to cooperate with the Secretary of Agriculture of the United States in developing and administering the poultry products inspection program of this State under this Article and in developing and administering the program of this State under G.S. 106-549.58 in such a manner as will effectuate the purposes of this Article and said federal act.

(b)   In such cooperative efforts, the Department is authorized to accept from said Secretary advisory assistance in planning and otherwise developing the State program, technical and laboratory assistance and training (including necessary curricular and instructional materials and equipment), and financial and other aid for administration of such a program.

(c)   The Department is further authorized to recommend to the Secretary of Agriculture such officials or employees of this State as the Commissioner shall designate, for appointment to the advisory committees provided for in section 5 of the Federal Poultry Products Inspection Act; and the Commissioner shall serve as the representative of the Governor for consultation with said Secretary under subsection (c) of section 5 of said act. (1971, c. 677, s. 5; 1985 (Reg. Sess., 1986), c. 1014, s. 155(b); 1997-261, s. 62.)

§ 106-549.53. Inspection; condemnation of adulterated poultry.

(a)   For the purpose of preventing the entry into or flow or movement in intrastate commerce of any poultry product which is capable of use as human food and is adulterated, the Commissioner shall, where and to the extent considered by him necessary, cause to be made by inspectors antemortem inspection of poultry in each official establishment engaged in processing poultry or poultry products solely for intrastate commerce.

(b)   The Commissioner, whenever processing operations are being conducted, shall cause to be made by inspectors postmortem inspection of the carcass of each bird processed, and at any time such quarantine, segregation and reinspection as he deems necessary of poultry and poultry products capable of use as human food in each official establishment engaged in processing such poultry or poultry products solely for intrastate commerce.

(c)   All poultry carcasses and parts thereof and other poultry products found to be adulterated shall be condemned and shall, if no appeal be taken from such determination of condemnation, be destroyed for human food purposes under the supervision of an inspector: Provided, that carcasses, parts, and products, which may by reprocessing be made not adulterated, need not be so condemned and destroyed if so reprocessed under the supervision of an inspector and thereafter found to be not adulterated. If an appeal be taken from such determination, the carcasses, parts, or products shall be appropriately marked and segregated pending completion of an appeal inspection, which appeal shall be at the cost of the appellant if the Commissioner determines that the appeal is frivolous. If the determination of condemnation is sustained the carcasses, parts, and products shall be destroyed for food purposes under the supervision of an inspector. (1971, c. 677, s. 6.)

§ 106-549.54. Sanitation of premises; regulations.

(a)   Each official establishment slaughtering poultry or processing poultry products solely for intrastate commerce shall have such premises, facilities, and equipment, and be operated in accordance with such sanitary practices, as are required by regulations promulgated by the Board for the purpose of preventing the entry into or flow or movement in intrastate commerce of poultry products which are adulterated.

(b)   The Commissioner shall refuse to render inspection to any establishment whose premises, facilities, or equipment, or the operation thereof, fail to meet the requirements of this section. (1971, c. 677, s. 7.)

§ 106-549.55. Labeling standards; false and misleading labels.

(a)   All poultry products inspected at any official establishment under the authority of this Article and found to be not adulterated, shall at the time they leave the establishment bear, in distinctly legible form, on their shipping containers and immediate containers as the Commissioner may require, the information required under subdivision (17) of G.S. 106-549.51. In addition, the Commissioner whenever he determines such action is practicable and necessary for the protection of the public, may require nonconsumer packaged carcasses at the time they leave the establishment to bear directly thereon in distinctly legible form any information required under such subdivision (17).

(b)   The Board, whenever it determines such action is necessary for the protection of the public, may prescribe:

(1)   The styles and sizes of type to be used with respect to material required to be incorporated in labeling to avoid false or misleading labeling in marking or otherwise labeling any articles or poultry subject to this Article;

(2) Definitions and standards of identity or composition for articles subject to this Article and standards of fill of container for such articles not inconsistent with any such standards established under the Federal Food, Drug and Cosmetic Act, or under the Federal Poultry Products Inspection Act, and there shall be consultation between the Commissioner or his authorized representative and the Secretary of Agriculture of the United States prior to the issuance of such standards to avoid inconsistency between such standards and the federal standards.

(c) No article subject to this Article shall be sold or offered for sale by any person in intrastate commerce, under any name or other marking or labeling which is false or misleading, or in any container of a misleading form or size, but established trade names and other marking and labeling and containers which are not false or misleading and which are approved by the Commissioner, are permitted.

(d) If the Commissioner has reason to believe that any marking or labeling or the size or form of any container in use or proposed for use with respect to any article subject to this Article is false or misleading in any particular, he may direct that such use be withheld unless the marking, labeling, or container is modified in such manner as he may prescribe so that it will not be false or misleading. A person who uses or proposes to use the marking, labeling, or container and who does not accept the determination of the Commissioner may commence a contested case under G.S. 150B-23. If directed by the Commissioner, the marking, labeling, or container may not be used pending a final decision. (1971, c. 677, s. 8; 1973, c. 1331, s. 3; 1987, c. 827, s. 36; 1989, c. 770, s. 26.)

§ 106-549.56. Prohibited acts.

(a) No person shall:

(1) Slaughter any poultry or process any poultry products which are capable of use as human food at any establishment processing any such articles solely for intrastate commerce, except in compliance with the requirements of this Article;

(2) Sell, transport, offer for sale or transportation, or receive for transportation, in intrastate commerce,

a. Any poultry products which are capable of use as human food and are adulterated or misbranded at the time of such sale, transportation, offer for sale or transportation, or receipt for transportation; or

b. Any poultry products required to be inspected under this Article unless they have been so inspected and passed;

(3) Do, with respect to any poultry products which are capable of use as human food, any act while they are being transported in intrastate commerce or held for sale after such transportation, which is intended to cause or has the effect of causing such products to be adulterated or misbranded;

(4) Sell, transport, offer for sale or transportation, or receive for transportation, in intrastate commerce or from an official establishment, any slaughtered poultry from which the blood, feathers, feet, head, or viscera have not been removed in accordance with regulations promulgated by the Board, except as may be authorized by regulations of the Board;

(5) Use to his own advantage, or reveal other than to the authorized representatives of the State government or any other government in their official capacity, or as ordered by a court in any judicial proceedings, any information acquired under the authority of this Article concerning any matter which is entitled to protection as a trade secret.

(b) No brand manufacturer, printer, or other person shall cast, print, lithograph, or otherwise make any device containing any official mark or simulation thereof, or any label bearing any such mark or simulation, or any form of official certificate or simulation thereof, except as authorized by the Commissioner.

(c) No person shall:

(1) Forge any official device, mark or certificate;

(2) Without authorization from the Commissioner use any official device, mark, or certificate, or simulation thereof, or alter, detach, deface, or destroy any official device, mark, or certificate;

(3) Contrary to the regulations prescribed by the Board, fail to use, or to detach, deface, or destroy any official device, mark, or certificate;

(4) Knowingly possess, without promptly notifying the Commissioner, any official device or any counterfeit, simulated, forged, or improperly altered official certificate or any device or label or any carcass of any poultry, or part or product thereof, bearing any counterfeit, simulated, forged, or improperly altered official mark;

(5) Knowingly make any false statement in any shipper's certificate or other nonofficial or official certificate provided for in the regulations prescribed by the Board; or

(6) Knowingly represent that any article has been inspected and passed, or exempted, under this Article when, in fact, it has, respectively, not been so inspected and passed, or exempted. (1971, c. 677, s. 9.)

§ 106-549.57. No poultry in violation of Article processed.

No establishment processing poultry or poultry products solely for intrastate commerce shall process any poultry or poultry product capable of use as human food except in compliance with the requirements of this Article. (1971, c. 677, s. 10.)

§ 106-549.58. Poultry not for human consumption; records; registration.

(a) Inspection shall not be provided under this Article at any establishment for the slaughter of poultry or the processing of any carcasses or parts or products of poultry, which are not intended for use as human food, but such articles shall, prior to their offer for sale or transportation in intrastate commerce, unless naturally inedible by humans, be denatured or otherwise identified as prescribed by regulations of the Board to deter their use for human food. No person shall buy, sell, transport, or offer for sale or transportation, or receive for transportation, in intrastate commerce, any poultry carcasses or parts or products thereof which are not intended for use as human food unless they are denatured or otherwise identified as required by the regulations of the Board or are naturally inedible by humans.

(b) The following classes of persons shall, for such period of time as the Board may by regulations prescribe, not to exceed two years unless otherwise directed by the Commissioner for good cause shown, keep such records as are properly necessary for the effective enforcement of this Article in order to insure against adulterated or misbranded poultry products for the American consumer; and all persons subject to such requirements shall, at all reasonable times, upon notice by a duly authorized representative of the Department of Agriculture and Consumer Services, afford such representative access to their places of business and opportunity to examine the facilities, inventory, and records thereof, to copy all such records, and to take reasonable samples of their inventory upon payment of the fair market value therefor:

(1) Any person that engages in the business of slaughtering any poultry or processing, freezing, packaging, or labeling any carcasses, or parts or products of carcasses, of any poultry, for intrastate commerce, for use as human food or animal food;

(2) Any person that engages in the business of buying or selling (as poultry products brokers; wholesalers or otherwise), or transporting, in intrastate commerce, or storing in or for intrastate commerce, any carcasses, or parts or products of carcasses, of any poultry;

(3) Any person that engages in business, in or for intrastate commerce, as a renderer, or engages in the business of buying, selling, or transporting, in intrastate commerce, any dead, dying, disabled, or diseased poultry or parts of the carcasses of any poultry that died otherwise than by slaughter.

(c) No person shall engage in business, in or for intrastate commerce, as a poultry products broker, renderer, or animal food manufacturer, or engage in business in intrastate commerce as a wholesaler of any carcasses, or parts or products of the carcasses, of any poultry, whether intended for human food or other purposes, or engage in business as a public warehouseman storing any such articles in or for intrastate commerce, or engage in the business of buying, selling, or transporting in intrastate commerce any dead, dying, disabled, or diseased poultry, or parts of the carcasses of any poultry that died otherwise than by slaughter, unless, when required by regulations of the Board, he has registered with the Commissioner his name, and the address of each place of business at which, and all trade names under which, he conducts such business.

(d) No person engaged in the business of buying, selling, or transporting in intrastate commerce, dead, dying, disabled, or diseased poultry, or any parts of the carcasses of any poultry that died otherwise than by slaughter, shall buy, sell, transport, offer for sale or transportation, or receive for transportation in intrastate commerce, any dead, dying, disabled, or diseased poultry or parts of the carcasses of any poultry that died otherwise than by slaughter, unless such transaction or transportation is made in accordance with such regulations as the Board may prescribe to assure that such poultry, or the unwholesome parts or products thereof, will be prevented from being used for human food. (1971, c. 677, s. 11; 1997-261, s. 109.)

§ 106-549.59. Punishment for violations; carriers exempt; interference with enforcement.

(a) Any person who violates the provisions of G.S. 106-549.56, 106-549.57, 106-549.58 or 106-549.61 is guilty of a Class 1 misdemeanor; but if such violation involves intent to defraud, or any distribution or attempted distribution of an article that is adulterated (except as defined in G.S. 106-549.51(1)h), such person is guilty of a Class H felony which may include a fine of not more than ten thousand dollars ($10,000). When construing or enforcing the provisions of said sections the act, omission, or failure of any person acting for or employed by any individual, partnership, corporation, or association within the scope of his employment or office shall in every case be deemed the act, omission, or failure of such individual, partnership, corporation, or association, as well as of such person.

(a1) The Commissioner may assess a civil penalty of not more than five thousand dollars ($5,000) against any person who violates a provision of this Article or any rule adopted under this Article. In determining the amount of the penalty, the Commissioner shall consider the degree and extent of harm caused by the violation. The clear proceeds of civil penalties assessed pursuant to this subsection shall be remitted to the Civil Penalty and Forfeiture Fund in accordance with G.S. 115C-457.2.

(b) No carrier shall be subject to the penalties of this Article, other than the penalties for violation of G.S. 106-549.58, by reason of his receipt, carriage, holding, or delivery, in the usual course of business, as a carrier, of poultry or poultry products, owned by another person unless the carrier has knowledge, or is in possession of facts which would cause a reasonable person to believe that such poultry or poultry products were not inspected or marked in accordance with the provisions of this Article or were otherwise not eligible for transportation under this Article or unless the carrier refuses to furnish on request of a representative of the Department of Agriculture and Consumer Services the name and address of the person from whom he received such poultry or poultry products, and copies of all documents, if any there be, pertaining to the delivery of the poultry or poultry products to such carrier.

(c) Any person who forcibly assaults, resists, opposes, impedes, intimidates, or interferes with any person while engaged in or on account of the performance of his official duties under this Article is guilty of a Class 2 misdemeanor which may include a fine of not more than five thousand dollars ($5,000). Whoever, in the commission of any such acts, uses a deadly or dangerous weapon, is guilty of a Class A1 misdemeanor which may include a fine of not more than ten thousand dollars ($10,000). (1971, c. 677, s. 12; 1997-261, s. 109; 1999-408, s. 7; 2007-361, s. 1.)

§ 106-549.60. Notice of violation.

Before any violation of this Article is reported by the Commissioner to any North Carolina district attorney for institution of a criminal proceeding, the person against whom such proceeding is contemplated shall be given reasonable notice of the alleged violation and opportunity to present his views orally or in writing with regard to such contemplated proceeding. Nothing in this Article shall be construed as requiring the Commissioner or his authorized representative to report for criminal prosecution of this Article whenever he believes that the public interest will be adequately served and compliance with the Article obtained by a suitable written notice or warning. (1971, c. 677, s. 13; 1973, c. 47, s. 2.)

§ 106-549.61. Regulations authorized.

(a) The Commissioner may by regulations prescribe conditions under which poultry products capable of use as human food shall be stored or otherwise handled by any person engaged in the business of buying, selling, freezing, storing, or transporting, in or for intrastate commerce, such articles, whenever the Commissioner deems such action necessary to assure that such articles will not be adulterated or misbranded when delivered to the consumer. Violation of any such regulation is prohibited.

(b) The Board shall promulgate such other rules and regulations as are necessary to carry out the provisions of this Article.

(c) When opportunity is afforded for submission of comments by interested persons on proposed rules or regulations under this Article, it shall include opportunity for oral presentation of views. (1971, c. 677, s. 14.)

§ 106-549.62. Intrastate operations exemptions.

(a) The Board shall, by regulation and under such conditions, including requirements, as to sanitary standards, practices, and procedures as it may prescribe, exempt from specific provisions of this Article with respect to processing of poultry or poultry products solely for intrastate commerce and distribution of poultry or poultry products only in such commerce:

(1) Retail dealers with respect to poultry products sold directly to consumers in individual retail stores, if the only processing operation performed by such retail dealers is the cutting up of poultry products on the premises where such sales to consumers are made;

(2) For such period of time as the Commissioner determines that it would be impracticable to provide inspection and the exemption will aid in the effective administration of this Article, any person engaged in the processing of poultry or poultry products and the poultry or poultry products processed by such person: Provided, however, that no such exemption shall continue in effect more than 120 days after enactment of this Article;

(3) Persons slaughtering, processing, or otherwise handling poultry or poultry products which have been or are to be processed as required by recognized religious dietary laws, to the extent that the Commissioner determines necessary to avoid conflict with such requirements while still effectuating the purposes of this Article;

(4) The slaughtering by any person of poultry of his own raising, and the processing by him and transportation of the poultry products exclusively for use by him and members of his household and his nonpaying guests and employees;

(5) The custom slaughter by any person of poultry delivered by the owner thereof for such slaughter, and the processing by such slaughterer and transportation of the poultry products exclusively for use, in the household of such owner, by him and members of his household and his nonpaying guests and employees: Provided, that such custom slaughterer does not engage in the business of buying or selling any poultry products capable of use as human food;

(6) The slaughtering and processing of poultry products by any poultry producer on his own premises with respect to sound and healthy poultry raised on his premises and the distribution by any person of the poultry products derived from such operations, if, in lieu of other labeling requirements, such poultry products are identified with the name and address of such poultry producer, and if they are not otherwise misbranded, and are sound, clean, and fit for human food when so distributed; and

(7) The slaughtering of sound and healthy poultry or the processing of poultry products of such poultry by any poultry producer or other person for distribution by him directly to household consumers, restaurants, hotels, and boardinghouses, for use in their own dining rooms, or in the preparation of meals for sales direct to consumers, if, in lieu of other labeling requirements, such poultry products are identified with the name and address of the processor, and if they are not otherwise misbranded and are sound, clean, and fit for human food when distributed by such processor.

(b) In addition to the specific exemptions authorized in subsection (a), the Board shall, when it determines that the protection of consumers from adulterated or misbranded poultry products will not be impaired by such action, provide by regulation, consistent with subsection (c) for the exemption of the operation and products of small enterprises (including poultry producers), not exempted under subsection (a), which are engaged in slaughtering and/or cutting up poultry for distribution as carcasses or parts thereof, solely for distribution within this State, from such provisions of this Article as it deems appropriate, while still protecting the public from adulterated or misbranded products, under such conditions, including sanitary requirements, as it shall prescribe to effectuate the purposes of this Article.

(c) The exemptions provided for in subdivisions (a)(6) and (7) above shall not apply if the poultry producer or other person engages in the current calendar year in the business of buying or selling any poultry or poultry products other than as specified in such subdivisions. No exemption under subdivisions (a)(6) or (7) or subsection (b) shall apply to any poultry producer or other person who slaughters or processes the products of more than 20,000 birds of all species during the calendar year for which this exemption is being applied.

(d)   The provisions of this Article requiring inspection shall not apply to operations of types traditionally and usually conducted at retail stores and restaurants, when conducted at any retail store or restaurant or similar retail-type establishment for sale in normal retail quantities or service of such articles to consumers at such establishments, if no poultry or poultry products are processed at the establishment for distribution outside this State or otherwise subject to inspection under the Federal Poultry Products Inspection Act.

(e)   The provisions of this Article shall not apply to poultry producers with respect to poultry of their own raising on their own farms if (i) such producers slaughter not more than 1,000 birds of all species during the calendar year for which this exemption is being determined; (ii) such poultry producers do not engage in buying or selling poultry products other than those produced from poultry raised on their own farms; and (iii) such poultry moves only in intrastate commerce.

(f)   The adulteration and misbranding provisions of this Article, other than the requirement of the inspection legend, shall apply to articles which are exempted from inspection under this section, except as otherwise specified under subsections (a), (b), or (e).

(g)   The Commissioner may by order suspend or terminate any exemption under subsections (a) or (b) of this section with respect to any person whenever he finds that such action will aid in effectuating the purposes of this Article. (1971, c. 677, s. 15; 2009-102, ss. 3, 4.)

§ 106-549.63. Commissioner may limit entry of products to establishments.

The Commissioner may limit the entry of poultry products and other materials into any official establishment, under such conditions as he may prescribe to assure that allowing the entry of such articles into such inspected establishments will be consistent with the purposes of this Article. (1971, c. 677, s. 16.)

§ 106-549.64. Refusal of inspection services; hearing; appeal.

(a) The Commissioner may (for such period, or indefinitely, as he deems necessary to effectuate the purposes of this Article) refuse to provide, or withdraw, inspection service under this Article with respect to any establishment if he determines that such applicant or recipient is unfit to engage in any business requiring inspection upon this Article because the applicant or recipient or anyone responsibly connected with the applicant or recipient, has been convicted, in any federal or State court, within the previous 10 years of

(1) Any felony or more than one misdemeanor under any law based upon the acquiring, handling, or distributing of adulterated, mislabeled, or deceptively packaged food or fraud in connection with transactions in food; or

(2) Any felony, involving fraud, bribery, extortion, or any other act or circumstances indicating a lack of the integrity needed for the conduct of operations affecting the public health. For the purpose of this subsection a person shall be deemed to be responsibly connected with the business if he was a partner, officer, director, holder, or owner of ten per centum (10%) or more of its voting stock or employee in a managerial or executive capacity.

(b) Proceedings concerning the refusal or withdrawal of inspection services shall be conducted in accordance with Chapter 150B of the General Statutes. A refusal or withdrawal of inspection services by the Commissioner shall continue in effect pending a final decision in a contested case unless the Commissioner orders otherwise.

(c) Repealed by Session Laws 1987, c. 827, s. 37. (1971, c. 677, s. 17; 1973, c. 1331, s. 3; 1987, c. 827, s. 37.)

§ 106-549.65. Product detained if in violation.

Whenever any poultry product, or any product exempted from the definition of a poultry product, or any dead, dying, disabled, or diseased poultry is found by any inspector of the Meat and Poultry Inspection Service of the Department of Agriculture and Consumer Services upon any premises where it is held for purposes of, or during or after distribution in intrastate commerce, and there is reason to believe that any such article is adulterated or misbranded and is capable of use as human food, or that it has not been inspected, in violation of the provisions of this Article or of any other State or federal law or that it has been or is intended to be, distributed in violation of any such provisions, it may be detained by such representative for a period not to exceed 20 days, pending action under G.S. 106-549.66 or notification of any federal, State, or other governmental authorities having jurisdiction over such article or poultry, and shall not be moved by any person, from the place at which it is located when so detained, until released by such representative. All official marks may be required by such representative to be removed from such article or poultry before it is released unless it appears to the satisfaction of the area supervisor of the Department of Agriculture and Consumer Services Poultry Inspection Service that the article or poultry is eligible to retain such marks. (1971, c. 677, s. 18; 1997-261, s. 109.)

§ 106-549.66. Seizure or condemnation proceedings.

(a)   Any poultry product, or any dead, dying, or disabled, or diseased poultry, that is being transported in intrastate commerce, subject to this Article, or is held for sale in this State after such transportation, and that

(1)   Is or has been processed, sold, transported, or otherwise distributed or offered or received for distribution in violation of this Article, or

(2)   Is capable of use as human food and is adulterated or misbranded, or

(3)   In any other way is in violation of this Article, shall be liable to be proceeded against and seized and condemned, at any time, on an affidavit filed in any superior court within the jurisdiction of which the article or poultry is found. If the article or poultry is condemned it shall, after entry of the judgment, be disposed of by destruction or sale as the court may direct and the proceeds, if sold, less the court costs and fees, and storage and other proper expenses, shall be paid into the general fund of this State, but the article or poultry shall not be sold contrary to the provisions of this Article, or the Federal Poultry Products Inspection Act or the Federal Food, Drug, and Cosmetic Act: Provided, that upon the execution and delivery of a good and sufficient bond conditioned that the article or poultry shall not be sold or otherwise disposed of contrary to the provisions of this Article or the laws of the United States, the court may direct that such article or poultry be delivered to the owner thereof subject to such supervision by authorized representatives of the Commissioner as is necessary to insure compliance with the applicable laws. When an order of

condemnation is entered against the article or poultry and it is released under bond, or destroyed, court costs and fees, and storage and other proper expenses shall be awarded against the person, if any, intervening as claimant of the article or poultry. The proceedings in such cases shall conform, as nearly as may be, to civil actions and either party may demand trial by jury of any issue of fact joined in any case, and all such proceedings shall be at the suit of and in the name of the State.

(b) The provisions of this section shall in no way derogate from authority for condemnation or seizure conferred by other provisions of this Article, or other laws. (1971, c. 677, s. 19.)

§ 106-549.67. Superior court jurisdiction; proceedings in name of State.

The superior court is vested with jurisdiction specifically to enforce, and to prevent and restrain violations of this Article, and shall have jurisdiction in all other kinds of cases arising under this Article. All proceedings for the enforcement or to restrain violations of this Article shall be by and in the name of this State. (1971, c. 677, s. 20.)

§ 106-549.68. Powers of Commissioner; subpoenas; mandamus; self-incrimination; penalties.

(a) The Commissioner shall also have power:

(1) To gather and compile information concerning and, to investigate from time to time the organization, business, conduct, practices, and management of any person engaged in intrastate commerce, and the relation thereof to other persons;

(2) To require, by general or special orders, persons engaged in intrastate commerce, or any class of them, or any of them to file with the Commissioner, in such form as the Commissioner may prescribe, annual or special, or both annual and special, reports or answers in writing to specific questions, furnishing to the Commissioner such information as he may require as to the organization, business, conduct, practices, management, and relation to other persons of the person filing such reports or answers in writing. Such reports and answers shall be made under oath, or otherwise, as the Commissioner may prescribe, and shall be filed with the Commissioner within such reasonable

period as the Commissioner may prescribe, unless additional time be granted in any case by the Commissioner.

(b)   (1)   For the purposes of this Article the Commissioner shall at all reasonable times have access to, for the purpose of examination, and the right to copy, any documentary evidence of any person being investigated or proceeded against, and may require by subpoena the attendance and testimony of witnesses and the production of all documentary evidence of any person relating to any matter under investigation. The Commissioner may sign subpoenas and may administer oaths and affirmations, examine witnesses, and receive evidence.

(2)   Such attendance of witnesses, and the production of such documentary evidence, may be required at any designated place of hearing. In case of disobedience to a subpoena the Commissioner may invoke the aid of any court designated in G.S. 106-549.67 in requiring the attendance and testimony of witnesses and the production of documentary evidence.

(3)   Any of the courts designated in G.S. 106-549.67 within the jurisdiction of which such inquiry is carried on may, in case of contumacy or refusal to obey a subpoena issued to any person, issue an order requiring such person to appear before the Commissioner or to produce documentary evidence if so ordered, or to give evidence touching the matter in question; and any failure to obey such order of the court may be punished by such court as a contempt thereof.

(4)   Upon the application of the Attorney General of this State at the request of the Commissioner, the superior court shall have jurisdiction to issue writs or [of] mandamus commanding any person to comply with the provisions of this Article or any order of the Commissioner made in pursuance thereof.

(5)   The Commissioner may order testimony to be taken by deposition in any proceeding or investigation pending under this Article at any stage of such proceeding or investigation. Such depositions may be taken before any person designated by the Commissioner and having power to administer oaths. Such testimony shall be reduced to writing by the person taking the deposition, or under his direction and shall then be subscribed by the deponent. Any person may be compelled to appear and depose and to produce documentary evidence in the same manner as witnesses may be compelled to appear and testify and produce documentary evidence before the Commissioner as hereinbefore provided.

(6) Witnesses summoned before the Commissioner shall be paid the same fees and mileage that are paid witnesses in the courts of this State, and witnesses whose depositions are taken and the persons taking the same shall severally be entitled to the same fees as are paid for like services in such courts.

(7) No person shall be excused from attending and testifying or from producing books, papers, schedules of charges, contracts, agreements, or other documentary evidence before the Commissioner or in obedience to the subpoena of the Commissioner whether such subpoena be signed or issued by him or his delegate, or in any cause or proceeding, criminal or otherwise, based upon or growing out of any alleged violation of this Article, or of any amendments thereto, on the ground or for the reason that the testimony or evidence, documentary or otherwise, required of him or it may tend to incriminate him or it or subject him or it to a penalty or forfeiture; but no individual shall be prosecuted or subjected to any penalty or forfeiture for or on account of any transaction, matter, or thing concerning which he is compelled, after having claimed his privilege against self-incrimination, to testify or produce evidence, documentary or otherwise, except that any individual so testifying shall not be exempt from prosecution and punishment for perjury committed in so testifying.

(c) (1) Any person that shall neglect or refuse to attend and testify or to answer any lawful inquiry, or to produce documentary evidence, if in his or its power to do so, in obedience to the subpoena or lawful requirement of the Commissioner shall be guilty of a Class 1 misdemeanor.

(2) Any person that shall willfully make, or cause to be made, any false entry or statement of fact in any report required to be made under this Article, or that shall willfully make, or cause to be made, any false entry in any account, record, or memorandum kept by any person subject to this Article or that shall willfully neglect or fail to make, or to cause to be made, full, true, and correct entries in such accounts, records, or memoranda, of all facts and transactions appertaining to the business of any person subject to this Article or that shall willfully remove out of the jurisdiction of this State, or willfully mutilate, alter, or by any other means falsify any documentary evidence of any such person, or that shall willfully refuse to submit to the Commissioner or to any of his authorized agents, for the purpose of inspection and taking copies, any documentary evidence of any person subject to this Article in his or its possession or within his or its control, shall be deemed guilty of a Class 1 misdemeanor.

(3) If any person required by this Article to file any annual or special report shall fail so to do within the time fixed by the Commissioner for filing the same, and such failure shall continue for 30 days after notice of such default, such person shall forfeit to this State the sum of one hundred dollars ($100.00) for each and every day of the continuance of such failure, which forfeiture shall be payable into the general fund of this State, and shall be recoverable in a civil suit in the name of the State brought in the superior court where the person has his or its principal office or in any county in which he or it shall do business. It shall be the duty of the Attorney General of this State, to prosecute for the recovery of such forfeitures. The costs and expenses of such prosecution shall be paid out of the amount recovered in such action.

(4) Any officer or employee of this State who shall make public any information obtained by the Commissioner without his authority, unless directed by a court, shall be deemed guilty of a Class 1 misdemeanor. (1971, c. 677, s. 21; 1993, c. 539, ss. 803-805; 1994, Ex. Sess., c. 14, s. 55; c. 24, s. 14(c).)

§ 106-549.68A. Article applicable to those regulated by federal act.

The requirements of this Article shall apply to persons, establishments, poultry, poultry products and other articles regulated under the Federal Poultry Products Inspection Act only to the extent provided for in section 23 of said federal act. (1971, c. 677, s. 22.)

§ 106-549.69. Inspection costs.

The cost of inspection rendered under the requirements of this Article, shall be borne by this State, except as provided in G.S. 106-549.52 and except that the cost of overtime and holiday work performed in establishments subject to the provisions of this Article, at such rates as the Commissioner may determine shall be borne by such establishments. Sums received by the Department of Agriculture and Consumer Services in reimbursement for sums paid out for such premium pay work shall be available without fiscal year limitation to carry out the purposes of this section. (1971, c. 677, s. 23; 1997-261, s. 109.)

Article 49E.

Disposal of Dead Diseased Poultry at Commercial Farms.

§ 106-549.70. Disposal pit, incinerator, or poultry composting facility required.

Every person, firm or corporation engaged in raising or producing poultry for commercial purposes shall provide and maintain a disposal pit, incinerator, or poultry composting facility of a size and design, approved by the Department of Agriculture and Consumer Services, in which all dead poultry carcasses are disposed. This section does not apply to poultry producers with flocks of 200 or less. The definitions provided in Article 49D of this Chapter apply in this Article. (1961, c. 1197, s. 1; 1995, c. 543, s. 2; 1997-261, s. 109.)

§ 106-549.71. Penalty for violation.

Any person, firm or corporation violating the provisions of this Article is guilty of a Class 1 misdemeanor. (1961, c. 1197, s. 2; 1999-408, s. 8.)

§ 106-549.72. Civil penalties.

The Commissioner may assess a civil penalty of not more than five thousand dollars ($5,000) against any person who violates a provision of this Article or any rule promulgated thereunder. In determining the amount of the penalty, the Commissioner shall consider the degree and extent of harm caused by the violation.

The clear proceeds of civil penalties assessed pursuant to this section shall be remitted to the Civil Penalty and Forfeiture Fund in accordance with G.S. 115C-457.2. (1995, c. 516, s. 13; 1998-215, s. 18.)

§§ 106-549.73 through 106-549.80. Reserved for future codification purposes.

Article 49F.

Biological Residues in Animals.

§ 106-549.81. Definitions.

For the purpose of this Article, the following terms shall have the meanings ascribed to them in this section:

(1)   "Animal" means any member of the animal kingdom except man.

(2)   "Animal feed" means any meat, grain, forage, or other food of any plant, animal or mineral origin, or any combination thereof, which is normally fed to any animal.

(3)   "Animal produce" means any product derived from any animal, whether suitable or not for human consumption.

(4)   "Biological residue" means any substance, including metabolites, remaining in or on any animal prior to or at the time of slaughter or in any of its tissues after slaughter, or in or on any animal product or animal feed, as the result of treatment with, or exposure, of the animal, animal product, or animal feed to any pesticide, hormone, hormone-like substance, growth promoter, antibiotic, anthelmintic, tranquilizer, or other therapeutic or prophylactic agent.

(5)   "Board" means the North Carolina Board of Agriculture.

(6)   "Commissioner" means the North Carolina Commissioner of Agriculture or his authorized delegate.

(7)   "Person" means any individual, partnership, corporation, association, cooperative or other legal entity.

(8)   "State" means the State of North Carolina. (1971, c. 1183, s. 1.)

§ 106-549.82. Detention or quarantine; lifting quarantine; burden of proof.

Any animal, animal product, or animal feed which the Commissioner has reasonable cause to believe contains or bears any biological residue may be immediately detained or quarantined by written order of the Commissioner until it can be determined in a manner acceptable to the Commissioner that the animal, animal feed, or animal product does not contain or bear a biological residue, or that the biological residue therein is within tolerances which are established by, or approved by, the Board, and the detention or quarantine is removed; or the animal, animal product or animal feed is destroyed or otherwise disposed of in a manner acceptable to the Commissioner; or in the case of a live animal, it has been treated in a manner acceptable to the Commissioner to reduce the level of any biological residue to a level acceptable to the Commissioner. The burden of proof under this section shall be on the owner or custodian of such animal, animal feed or animal product. (1971, c. 1183, s. 2.)

§ 106-549.83. Appellate review; order pending appeal; bond.

Any order or [of] quarantine or detention made by the Commissioner may be appealed by the aggrieved party to the superior court of the county wherein such animal, animal product or animal feed is quarantined or detained. The superior court judge, on at least 24 hours' notice, may hear said appeal in or out of term, in court or in chambers and may affirm, reverse or modify the order of quarantine or detention imposing such conditions as he may deem just and proper. Any party may appeal from the superior court to the Court of Appeals. Pending an appeal from the Commissioner or the superior court, any regular or special superior court judge residing in or holding court in the district may enter such orders as he deems necessary for the preservation or disposition of the animal, animal product or feed, and may require the posting of a bond for the faithful performance of such order. (1971, c. 1183, s. 3.)

§ 106-549.84. Movement of contaminated animals forbidden.

(a)   No person shall ship, transport, or otherwise move, or deliver, or receive for movement, any animal, animal product, or animal feed under detention or quarantine pursuant to G.S. 106-549.82, except under written permit of the Commissioner and in accordance with the conditions stated in such written permission, or until the detention or quarantine order has been revoked by written order of the Commissioner.

(b) No person shall ship, transport, or otherwise move, or deliver or receive for movement any animal, animal product, or animal feed which he knows, or by the exercise of reasonable care would know, contains or bears a biological residue which exceeds the tolerances established or approved by the Board. (1971, c. 1183, s. 4.)

§ 106-549.85. Inspection of animals, records, etc.

The Commissioner may enter any place within the State at all reasonable times where any animal, animal product or animal feed is kept to examine the facilities, inventory and/or copy the records thereof, and to take reasonable samples of any such animal, animal product or animal feed after giving notice in writing to the owner or custodian of the premises to be entered. If such person shall refuse to consent to such entry, the Commissioner may apply to any district court judge and such judge may order, without notice, that the owner or custodian of any place where any animal, animal product or animal feed is kept to permit the Commissioner to enter such place for the purposes herein stated and failure by any person to obey such order may be punished as for contempt. (1971, c. 1183, s. 5.)

§ 106-549.86. Investigation to discover violation.

The Commissioner shall make such investigations or inspections as he deems necessary to determine whether any person has violated, or is violating, any provision of this Article or any regulation promulgated thereunder, and when any biological residue is found in or on any animal, animal product, or animal feed, the Commissioner may make such investigation or inspection as he deems necessary to determine the source of the substance which resulted in the biological residue. (1971, c. 1183, s. 6.)

§ 106-549.87. Promulgation of regulation.

The North Carolina Board of Agriculture is hereby authorized to promulgate regulations as it may deem necessary to effectuate the purposes of this Article, including but not limited to, tolerances for biological residues. It shall be unlawful for any person to violate any provision of this Article or any regulation promulgated by the Board under authority of this Article. (1971, c. 1183, s. 7.)

§ 106-549.88. Penalties.

Any person who violates any provisions of this Article or any regulations thereunder is guilty of a Class 2 misdemeanor. (1971, c. 1183, s. 8; 1999-408, s. 9.)

§ 106-549.89. Civil penalties.

The Commissioner may assess a civil penalty of not more than five thousand dollars ($5,000) against any person who violates a provision of this Article or any rule promulgated thereunder. In determining the amount of the penalty, the Commissioner shall consider the degree and extent of harm caused by the violation.

The clear proceeds of civil penalties assessed pursuant to this section shall be remitted to the Civil Penalty and Forfeiture Fund in accordance with G.S. 115C-457.2. (1995, c. 516, s. 14; 1998-215, s. 19.)

§§ 106-549.90 through 106-549.93. Reserved for future codification purposes.

Article 49G.

Production and Sale of Pen-Raised Quail.

§ 106-549.94. Regulation of pen-raised quail by Department of Agriculture and Consumer Services; certain authority of North Carolina Wildlife Resources Commission not affected.

(a) The Department of Agriculture and Consumer Services is given exclusive authority to regulate the production and sale of pen-raised quail for food purposes. The Board of Agriculture shall promulgate rules and regulations for the production and sale of pen-raised quail for food purposes in such a manner as to provide for close supervision of any person, firm, or corporation producing and selling pen-raised quail for food purposes.

(b) The North Carolina Wildlife Resources Commission shall retain its authority to regulate the possession and transportation of live pen-raised quail. (1971, c. 515, ss. 1-4; c. 1114; 1973, c. 1262, s. 18; 1977, c. 905, ss. 1, 2; 1979, c. 830, s. 15; 1997-261, ss. 63, 109.)

§ 106-549.95. Reserved for future codification purposes.

§ 106-549.96. Reserved for future codification purposes.

Article 49H.

Production and Sale of Fallow Deer and Red Deer.

§ 106-549.97. Regulation by Department of Agriculture and Consumer Services of certain cervids produced and sold for commercial purposes; certain authority of North Carolina Wildlife Resources Commission not affected; definitions.

(a) The Department of Agriculture and Consumer Services shall regulate the production and sale of farmed cervids. The Board of Agriculture shall adopt rules for the production and sale of farmed cervids in such a manner as to provide for close supervision of any person, firm, or corporation producing and selling farmed cervids and shall notify any such person, firm, or corporation that the activity is subject to compliance with Wildlife Resources Commission rules pursuant to G.S. 113-272.6.

(b) The North Carolina Wildlife Resources Commission shall regulate the possession and transportation, including importation and exportation, of cervids pursuant to G.S. 113-272.6.

(c) The following definitions apply in this Article:

(1) Repealed by Session Laws 2003-344, s. 11, effective July 27, 2003.

(2) Repealed by Session Laws 2003-344, s. 11, effective July 27, 2003.

(3) Cervid or Cervidae. - All animals in the Family Cervidae (elk and deer).

(4) Farmed Cervid. - Any member of the Cervidae family, other than white-tailed deer, elk, mule deer, or black-tailed deer, that is bought and sold for commercial purposes.

(5) White-tailed deer. - A member of the species Odocoileus virginianus. (1991, c. 317, s. 1; 1997-142, s. 1; 1997-261, s. 109; 2003-344, s. 11.)

§ 106-549.98. Inspection fees.

The Commissioner may establish a fee at an hourly rate to be paid by the owner, proprietor, or operator of each slaughtering, meat-canning, salting, packing, rendering, or similar establishment for the purpose of defraying the expenses incurred in the inspection of fallow deer as required by Article 49B of Chapter 106 of the General Statutes. The Commissioner may establish a fee at an hourly rate to be paid by the owner, proprietor, or operator of each slaughtering, meat-canning, salting, packing, rendering, or similar establishment for the purpose of defraying the expenses incurred in the inspection of red deer as required by Article 49B of Chapter 106 of the General Statutes. (1991, c. 317, s. 1; 1997-142, s. 1.)

Article 50.

Promotion of Use and Sale of Agricultural Products.

§ 106-550. Policy as to promotion of use of, and markets for, farm products.

It is declared to be in the interest of the public welfare that the North Carolina farmers who are producers of livestock, poultry, field crops and other agricultural products, including cattle, sheep, broilers, turkeys, commercial eggs, peanuts, cotton, potatoes, sweet potatoes, peaches, apples, berries, vegetables and other fruits of all kinds, as well as bulbs and flowers and other agricultural products having a domestic or foreign market, shall be permitted and encouraged to act jointly and in cooperation with growers, handlers, dealers and processors of such products in promoting and stimulating, by advertising and other methods, the increased production, use and sale, domestic and foreign, of any and all of such agricultural commodities. The provisions of this Article, however, shall not include the agricultural products of tobacco, strawberries, strawberry plants, porcine animals, or equines, with respect to which separate provisions have been made. (1947, c. 1018, s. 1; 1951, c. 1172, s. 1; 1957, cc. 260, 1352; 1989 (Reg. Sess., 1990), c. 1027, s. 1.1; 1991, c. 605, s. 2; 1995, c. 521, s. 1; 1998-154, s. 2.)

§ 106-551. Federal Agricultural Marketing Act.

The passage by the Seventy-Ninth Congress of a law designated as Public Law 733, and more particularly Title II of that act, cited as "Agricultural Marketing Act of 1946," makes it all the more important for producers, handlers, processors and others of specific agricultural commodities to associate themselves in action programs, separately and with public and private agencies, to obtain the greatest and most immediate benefits under the provisions of such law, in respect to research, studies and problems of marketing, transportation and distribution. (1947, c. 1018, s. 2.)

§ 106-552. Associations, activity, etc., deemed not in restraint of trade.

No association, meeting or activity undertaken in pursuance of the provisions of this Article and intended to benefit all of the producers, handlers and processors of a particular commodity shall be deemed or considered illegal or in restraint of trade. (1947, c. 1018, s. 3.)

§ 106-553. Policy as to referenda, assessments, etc., for promoting use and sale of farm products.

It is hereby further declared to be in the public interest and highly advantageous to the agricultural economy of the State that farmers, producers and growers commercially producing the commodities herein referred to shall be permitted by referendum to be held among the respective groups and subject to the provisions of this Article, to levy upon themselves an assessment on such respective commodities or upon the acreage used in the production of the same and provide for the collection of the same, for the purpose of financing or contributing towards the financing of a program of advertising and other methods designed to increase the consumption of and the domestic as well as foreign markets for such agricultural products. Such assessments may also be used for the purpose of financing or contributing toward the financing of a program of production, use and sale of any and all such agricultural commodities. (1947, c. 1018, s. 4; 1951, c. 1172, s. 2.)

§ 106-554. Application to Board of Agriculture for authorization of referendum.

Any existing commission, council, board or other agency fairly representative of the growers and producers of any agricultural commodity herein referred to, and any such commission, council, board or other agency hereafter created for and fairly representative of the growers or producers of any such agricultural commodity herein referred to, may at any time after the passage and ratification of this Article make application to the Board of Agriculture of the State of North Carolina for certification and approval for the purpose of conducting a referendum among the growers or producers of such particular agricultural commodity, for commercial purposes, upon the question of levying an assessment under the provisions of this Article, collecting and utilizing the same for the purposes stated in such referendum. (1947, c. 1018, s. 5.)

§ 106-555. Action by Board on application.

Upon the filing with the Board of Agriculture of such application on the part of any commission, council, board or other agency, the said Board of Agriculture shall within 30 days thereafter meet and consider such application; and if upon such consideration the said Board of Agriculture shall find that the commission, council, board or other agency making such application is fairly representative of and has been duly chosen and delegated as representative of the growers producing such commodity, and shall otherwise find and determine that such application is in conformity with the provisions of this Article and the purposes herein stated, then and in such an event it shall be the duty of the Board of Agriculture to certify such commission, council, board or other agency as the duly delegated and authorized group or agency representative of the commercial growers and producers of such agricultural commodity, and shall likewise certify that such agency is duly authorized to conduct among the growers and producers of such commodity a referendum for the purposes herein stated. (1947, c. 1018, s. 6.)

§ 106-555.1. Official State board for federal assessment programs; no subsequent referenda required.

For the purpose of any federal commodity assessment program, the producers' agency certified by the Board of Agriculture pursuant to G.S. 106-555 shall be deemed to be the official State board for such commodity. No subsequent referenda shall be required under this Article in order for such producers' agency to maintain its status as the official State board for the purposes of such federal commodity assessment program. (1991, c. 99.)

§ 106-556. Conduct of referendum among growers and producers on question of assessments.

Upon being so certified by the said Board of Agriculture in the manner hereinbefore set forth, such commission, council, board or other agency shall thereupon be fully authorized and empowered to hold and conduct on the part of the producers and growers of such particular agricultural commodity a referendum on the question of whether or not such growers and producers shall levy upon themselves an assessment under and subject to and for the purposes stated in this Article. Such referendum may be conducted either on a statewide or area basis. (1947, c. 1018, s. 7.)

§ 106-557. Notice of referendum; statement of amount, basis and purpose of assessment; maximum assessment.

With respect to any referendum conducted under the provisions of this Article, the duly certified commission, council, board or other agency shall, before calling and announcing such referendum, fix, determine and publicly announce at least 30 days before the date determined upon for such referendum, the date, hours and polling places for voting in such referendum, the amount and basis of the assessment proposed to be collected, the means by which such assessment shall be collected if authorized by the growers, and the general purposes to which said amount so collected shall be applied; no annual assessment levied under the provisions of this Article shall exceed one half of one percent (½ of 1%) of the value of the year's production of such agricultural commodity grown by any farmer, producer or grower included in the group to which such referendum is submitted. Provided, that the assessment for the research and promotion programs of the American Dairy Association of North Carolina may be fixed on the volume of milk sold not to exceed one percent (1%) of the statewide blend price paid to all North Carolina producers during the previous calendar year for three and one-half percent (3.5%) milk as computed by the United States Department of Agriculture. Provided further, that the assessment authorized by this Article and collected by the Commissioner of Agriculture to be paid to the North Carolina Yam Commission, Inc., or other duly certified agencies entitled thereto for research, marketing and promotional programs related to yams or sweet potatoes may be levied at a rate not to exceed two percent (2%) of the value of the year's production of that agricultural commodity grown by any farmer, producer or grower included in the group to which the referendum is submitted, and when authorized by two-thirds or more of the farmers, producers or growers in the area in which the referendum is conducted, the rate of the assessment may remain in effect for the length of time provided in the referendum. Provided further, that the assessment authorized by this Article on peanuts may not exceed two percent (2%) of the price paid to the producer. (1947, c. 1018, s. 8; 1967, c. 774, s. 1; c. 1268; 1981, c. 216, s. 1; 1983, c. 246, s. 1; 1997-371, s. 1; 2004-199, s. 27(e); 2006-264, s. 24.)

§ 106-557.1. Ballot by mail.

(a)   As an alternative method of conducting a referendum under the provisions of this Article, the certified agency in its discretion may conduct the referendum by a mail ballot as herein provided. In the event that a certified agency determines in its discretion to conduct a mail ballot, public notice of said mail ballot shall be made at least 30 days before the date of said referendum. Said notice shall contain the same information required by G.S. 106-557, except that the notice will also state that the ballot is to be conducted by mail rather than at polling places. The notice shall also state that official ballots are being mailed on a date specified in the notice to all persons known by the certified agency to be eligible to vote and that any person not receiving by mail an official ballot by a date specified in the notice will have 10 days thereafter to apply for an official ballot at the office of the certified agency. The notice shall state the deadline for the receipt of all ballots and the address of the certified agency.

Official ballots shall be prepared by the certified agency and mailed by first-class mail to the last known address of all persons known by the certified agency to be eligible to vote. As announced in the public notice, said ballots shall be made available for a period of not less than 10 days, to those who are eligible to vote in said referendum and did not receive a ballot by mail.

Before any person shall receive an official ballot, he shall furnish such proof as the certified agency may require of his eligibility to vote in said referendum. The certified agency shall keep a list of those persons who receive official ballots. No person may receive more than one official ballot unless he satisfies the certified agency that his ballot has been lost or destroyed.

No votes shall be counted which are not on official ballots. To be eligible to be counted, ballots must be received by the certified agency at the place and by the deadline previously announced in the public notice of said referendum.

(b) The provisions of this section shall not apply to the North Carolina Potato Association and the North Carolina Soybean Association. (1969, c. 111.)

§ 106-558. Management of referendum; expenses.

The arrangements for and management of any referendum conducted under the provisions of this Article shall be under the direction of the commission, council, board or other agency duly certified and authorized to conduct the same, and any and all expenses in connection therewith shall be borne by such commission, council, board or agency. (1947, c. 1018, s. 9.)

§ 106-559. Basis of referendum; eligibility for participation; question submitted; special provisions for North Carolina Cotton Promotion Association.

Any referendum conducted under the provisions of this Article may be held either on an area or statewide basis, as may be determined by the certified agency before such referendum is called; and such referendum, either on an area or statewide basis, may be participated in by all farmers engaged in the production of such agricultural commodity on a commercial basis, including owners of farms on which such commodity is produced, tenants and sharecroppers. In such referendum, such individuals so eligible for participation shall vote upon the question of whether or not there shall be levied an annual assessment for a period of three years in the amount set forth in the call for such referendum on the agricultural product covered by such referendum. Provided, that notwithstanding any other provision of this Chapter, the North Carolina Cotton Promotion Association, Inc., in 1967 shall hold a referendum, pursuant to law, for the years 1969 and 1970, or for the years 1969 through 1973, in its discretion. Thereafter, the North Carolina Cotton Promotion Association, Inc. shall conduct either triennial or sexennial referendums as provided by law. (1947, c. 1018, s. 10; 1967, cc. 213, 561.)

§ 106-559.1. Basis of vote on milk product assessment.

Notwithstanding any other provision of this Article, any milk product assessment referendum shall be conducted on the basis of one vote per base holder. (1981, c. 216, s. 2.)

§ 106-560. Effect of more than one-third vote against assessment.

If in such referendum with respect to any agricultural commodity herein referred to more than one third of the farmers and producers in the area in which such referendum is conducted, eligible to participate and voting therein shall vote in the negative and against the levying or collection of such assessment, then in such an event no assessment shall be levied or collected. (1947, c. 1018, s. 11.)

§ 106-561. Effect of two-thirds vote for assessment.

If in such referendum called under the provisions of this Article two thirds or more of the farmers or producers in the area in which such referendum is conducted, eligible to participate and voting therein shall vote in the affirmative and in favor of the levying and collection of such assessment proposed in such referendum on the agricultural commodity covered thereby, then such assessment shall be collected in the manner determined and announced by the agency conducting such referendum. (1947, c. 1018, s. 12.)

§ 106-562. Regulations as to referendum; notice to farm organizations and county agents.

The hours, voting places, rules and regulations and the area within which such referendum herein authorized with respect to any of the agricultural commodities herein referred to shall be established and determined by the agency of the commercial growers and producers of such agricultural commodity duly certified by the Board of Agriculture as hereinbefore provided; the said referendum date, area, hours, voting places, rules and regulations with respect to the holding of such referendum shall be published by such agency conducting the same through the medium of the public press in the State of North Carolina at least 30 days before the holding of such referendum, and direct written notice thereof shall likewise be given to all farm organizations within the State of North Carolina and to each county agent in any county in which such agricultural product is grown. Such notice shall likewise contain a statement of the amount of annual assessment proposed to be levied - which assessment in any event shall not exceed one half of one percent (1/2 of 1%) of the value of the year's production of such agricultural commodity or such other assessment as shall be authorized by law, grown by any farmer, producer or grower included in the group to which such referendum is submitted - and shall likewise state the method by which such assessment shall be collected and how the proceeds thereof shall be administered and the purposes to which the same shall be applied, which purposes shall be in keeping with the provisions of this Article. (1947, c. 1018, s. 13; 1967, c. 774, s. 2; 1983, c. 246, s. 2.)

§ 106-563. Distribution of ballots; arrangements for holding referendum; declaration of results.

The duly certified agency of the producers of any agricultural product among whom a referendum shall be conducted under the provisions of this Article shall likewise prepare and distribute in advance of such referendum all necessary ballots for the purposes thereof, and shall, under rules and regulations promulgated by said agency, arrange for the necessary poll holders for conducting the said referendum; and following such referendum and within 10 days thereafter the said agency shall canvass and publicly declare the result of such referendum. (1947, c. 1018, s. 14.)

§ 106-563.1. Supervision of referendum on milk product assessment.

Notwithstanding any other provision of this Article, any milk product assessment referendum shall be conducted under the supervision of the County Extension Chairman in each county in which the referendum is held. (1981, c. 216, s. 3.)

§ 106-564. Collection of assessments; custody and use of funds.

In the event two thirds or more of the farmers eligible for participation in such referendum and voting therein shall vote in favor of such assessment, then the said assessment shall be collected annually or at regular intervals during the year established by the rules and regulations of the duly certified commission, council, board or other agency for the number of years set forth in the call for such referendum, and the collection of such assessment shall be under such method, rules and regulations as may be determined by the agency conducting the same; and the said assessment so collected shall be paid into the treasury of the agency conducting such referendum, to be used together with other funds from other sources, including donations from individuals, concerns or corporations, and grants from State or governmental agencies, for the purpose of promoting and stimulating, by advertising and other methods, the increased use and sale, domestic and foreign, of the agricultural commodity covered by such referendum. Such assessments may also be used for the purpose of financing or contributing toward the financing of a program of production, use and sale of any and all such agricultural commodities. (1947, c. 1018, s. 15; 1951, c. 1172, s. 3; 1965, c. 1046, s. 1; 1975, c. 708, s. 1.)

§ 106-564.1. Alternate method for collection of assessments.

As an alternate method for the collection of assessments provided for in G.S. 106-564, and upon the request of the duly certified agency of the producers of any agricultural products referred to in G.S. 106-550, the Commissioner of Agriculture shall notify, by registered letter, all persons, firms and corporations engaged in the business of purchasing any such agricultural products in this State, that on and after the date specified in the letter the assessments shall be deducted by the purchaser, or his agent or representative, from the purchase price of any such agricultural products. The assessment so deducted, shall, on or before the first day of June of each year following such deduction or at regular intervals during the year following such deductions, be remitted by such purchaser to the Commissioner of Agriculture of North Carolina who shall thereupon pay the amount of the assessments to the duly certified agency of the producers entitled thereto. The books and records of all such purchasers of agricultural products shall at all times during regular business hours be open for inspection by the Commissioner of Agriculture or his duly authorized agents.

For the purposes of this Article the Commissioner may designate the duly certified agency of the producers as his agent to conduct inspections or audits of the books of the purchaser of such agricultural products. If it is discovered, as the result of such inspection or audit, that such purchaser has willfully failed to remit assessments when due, then such purchaser shall be liable to the duly certified producers agency for the reasonable costs of such inspection or audit. Such costs may be recovered by the agency by an action against the purchaser in a court of competent jurisdiction. The agency shall also be entitled to recover from such purchaser a penalty of five percent (5%) of the amount due for each month it remains unpaid, not to exceed twenty percent (20%) of the total amount due.

Any packer, processor or other purchaser who originally purchases from the grower, apples grown in North Carolina, shall collect from the grower thereof any marketing assessment due under the provisions of Article 50 of Chapter 106 and shall remit the same to the North Carolina Department of Agriculture and Consumer Services. Upon failure of said packer, processor or other purchaser to collect and remit said assessment then the amount of the assessment shall become the obligation of the packer, processor or other purchaser who originally purchased the apples from the grower and he shall become liable therefor to the North Carolina Department of Agriculture and Consumer Services. Failure of the packer, processor or other purchaser to comply with the provisions of this section shall constitute a bar to engaging in said business in this State upon proper notice from the Board of Agriculture. The Board of Agriculture shall have authority to promulgate such rules and regulations as shall be necessary to carry out the purpose and intent of this section. (1953, c. 917; 1969, c. 605, s. 3; 1975, c. 708, s. 2; 1983, c. 395; 1997-261, s. 109.)

§ 106-564.2. Further alternative method for collection of assessments.

As an alternate method for the collection of assessments provided for in G.S. 106-564, the duly certified agency representing the producers of peaches, apples or other tree fruits, is hereby authorized to establish the names, addresses and number of trees or acres of trees and certify same to the Commissioner of Agriculture. The Commissioner of Agriculture shall then notify by registered letter such certified producers that on or before the date specified by the duly certified agency, the assessments shall be paid to the Commissioner of Agriculture by the producers. The date of collections of such assessments may be established by the duly certified agency representing the producers of any agricultural product referred to in G.S. 106-550. (1955, c. 374.)

§ 106-564.3. Alternative method for collection of assessments relating to cattle.

As an alternative method for the collection of assessments provided for in Article 50 of Chapter 106 of the General Statutes, as amended, and as the same relates to all cattle, including those cattle sold for slaughter, upon the request of the duly certified agency of the producers of all cattle, including those which are to be sold for slaughter, the Commissioner of Agriculture shall notify, by registered letter, all livestock auction markets, slaughterhouses, abattoirs, packinghouses, and any and all persons, firms and corporations, engaged in the buying, selling or handling of cattle in this State, and on and after the date specified in the letter, the assessments approved and in force under said referendum shall be deducted by the purchaser, or his agent or representative, from the purchase price of all cattle bought, acquired or sold. It shall be unlawful for any livestock auction market, slaughterhouse, abattoir, packinghouse or the administrators or managers or agents of same or for any person, firm or corporation to acquire, buy or sell any cattle, including cattle for slaughter, without deducting the assessments previously authorized by said referendum. The assessment or assessments for any month so deducted, shall, on or before the twentieth day of the following month, be remitted by such purchaser as above described, to the Commissioner of Agriculture of North Carolina, who shall thereupon pay the amount of the assessments to the duly certified agency of the producers of all such cattle entitled thereto. The books and records of all such livestock auction markets, slaughterhouses, abattoirs, packinghouses, or persons, firms or corporations engaged in buying, acquiring or selling all cattle shall at all times during regular business hours be open for inspection by the Commissioner of Agriculture or his duly authorized agents. Provided, however, that if any livestock auction market, slaughterhouse, abattoir, packinghouse, or any person, firm or corporation engaged in buying, selling or handling cattle in this State shall fail to collect or pay such assessments so deducted to the Commissioner of Agriculture of North Carolina, as herein provided, then and in such event suit may be brought by the duly certified agency concerned in a court of competent jurisdiction to enforce the collection of such assessments. (1959, c. 1176; 1969, c. 184.)

§ 106-564.4. Alternative method for collection of assessments relating to sweet potatoes.

(a) In the event the producers of sweet potatoes approve an assessment pursuant to G.S. 106-564, which assessment shall be paid by the producer based on the number of acres produced, the producer shall report the number of acres planted and shall remit the assessment due to the Commissioner of Agriculture. Sweet potato producers shall report acreage planted at a time and place determined by the duly certified agency representing the producers of sweet potatoes.

(b) Assessments shall be due on September 1 of each year. Any producer who fails to pay assessments by September 30 of each year shall also pay a penalty of ten percent (10%) of the unpaid assessment, plus a penalty of one percent (1%) of the unpaid assessment for each month the assessment remains unpaid. The Commissioner of Agriculture shall remit all assessments received to the duly certified agency representing the producers of sweet potatoes. The duly certified agency representing the producers of sweet potatoes may conduct inspections and audits of sweet potato producers in order to verify the number of acres of sweet potatoes planted and may bring an action to recover unpaid assessments and penalties and the reasonable costs of such action, including attorneys' fees.

(c) There shall be no refund of assessments collected pursuant to this section.

(d) For the purposes of this section, "producer" shall be defined as a grower of one acre or more of sweet potatoes. (1995, c. 521, s. 2.)

§ 106-565. Subsequent referendum.

In the event such referendum so to be conducted as herein provided shall not be supported by two thirds or more of those eligible for participation therein and voting therein, then the duly certified agency conducting the said referendum shall have full power and authority to call another referendum for the purposes herein set forth in the next succeeding year, on the question of an annual assessment for three years. (1947, c. 1018, s. 16.)

§ 106-566. Referendum as to continuance of assessments approved at prior referendum.

In the event the first such referendum or any subsequent referendum is carried by the votes of two thirds or more of the eligible farmers participating therein and assessments in pursuance thereof are levied annually for the period set forth in the call for such referendum, then the agency conducting such referendum shall in its discretion have full power and authority to call and conduct during the third year of such first period or the last year of any subsequent period another referendum in which the farmers and producers of such agricultural commodity shall vote upon the question of whether or not such assessments shall be continued for the next ensuing three years or continued for the next ensuing six years. (1947, c. 1018, s. 17; 1965, c. 1046, s. 2.)

§ 106-567. Rights of farmers dissatisfied with assessments; time for demanding refund.

In the event such referendum is carried in the affirmative and the assessment is levied and collected as provided herein and under the regulations to be promulgated by the duly certified agency conducting the same, any farmer or producer upon and against whom such assessments shall have been levied and collected under the provisions of this Article, if dissatisfied with said assessment and the result thereof, shall have the right to demand of and receive from the treasurer of said agency a refund of such assessment so collected from such farmer or producer, provided such demand for refund is made in writing within 30 days from the date on which said assessment is collected or due to be collected, whichever is earlier from such farmer or producer under the rules and regulations of the duly certified commission, council, board or other agency. Provided, however, that as to growers or producers of potatoes, apples or peaches the right of refund of assessments as provided herein shall be contingent upon such growers or producers having paid said assessment on or before the end of the assessment year in which the assessment was levied. The assessment year shall be determined by the duly certified commission, council, board or agency representing the respective commodity: Provided further, that any farmer or producer of potatoes, apples or peaches who fails to make any protest against the assessment and levy in writing, addressed to the duly certified commission, council, board or agency representing the commodity concerned, within 30 days from the date such assessment shall become due and payable, then, and in such event, suit may be brought by the duly certified commission, council, board or agency concerned in a court of competent jurisdiction to enforce the collection of the assessment. Provided further that on and after July 1, 1972, as to growers or producers of apples there shall be no right of refund of assessments levied pursuant to the referendum provided for by Article 50, Chapter 106 of the General Statutes of North Carolina. (1947, c. 1018, s. 18; 1959, c. 311; 1969, c. 605, ss. 1, 2; 1975, c. 708, ss. 3, 4.)

§ 106-567.1. Refund of milk product assessments.

Notwithstanding any other provision of this Article, on and after January 1, 1982, a milk producer shall be entitled to receive a monthly refund of assessments paid by him by making written demand in the first month of each calendar quarter upon the association receiving such assessment. (1981, c. 216, s. 4.)

§ 106-568. Publication of financial statement by treasurer of agency; bond required.

In the event of the levying and collection of assessments as herein provided, the treasurer of the agency conducting same shall within 30 days after the end of any calendar year in which such assessments are collected, publish through the medium of the press of the State a statement of the amount or amounts so received and collected by him under the provisions of this Article. Before collecting and receiving such assessments, such treasurer shall give a bond in the amount of at least the estimated total of such assessments as will be collected, such bond to have as surety thereon a surety company licensed to do business in the State of North Carolina, and to be in the form and amount approved by the agency conducting such referendum and to be filed with the chairman or executive head of such agency. (1947, c. 1018, s. 19.)

Article 50A.

Promotion of Agricultural Research and Dissemination of Findings.

§ 106-568.1. Policy as to joint action of farmers.

It is declared to be in the public interest that North Carolina farmers producing agricultural products of all kinds, including cotton, tobacco, peanuts, soybeans, potatoes, vegetables, berries, fruits, livestock, livestock products, poultry and turkeys, and any other agricultural products having domestic and/or foreign markets, be permitted to act jointly in cooperation with each other in encouraging an expanding program of agricultural research and the dissemination of agricultural research findings. (1951, c. 827, s. 1.)

§ 106-568.2. Policy as to referendum and assessment.

It is declared to be in the public interest and highly advantageous to the economic development of the State that farmers, producers, and growers of agricultural commodities using commercial feed and/or fertilizers or their ingredients be permitted by referendum held among themselves to levy upon themselves an assessment of fifteen cents (15¢) per ton on mixed fertilizers, commercial feed, and their ingredients (except lime and land plaster) to provide funds through the Agricultural Foundation to supplement the established program of agricultural research and dissemination of research facts.

It is further declared to be in the public interest and highly advantageous to the economic development of the State that tobacco producers be permitted by referendum to levy upon themselves an assessment not to exceed ten cents (10¢) per hundred pounds of tobacco marketed to provide funds through the North Carolina Tobacco Research Commission for research and dissemination of research facts concerning tobacco. (1951, c. 827, s. 2; 1981, c. 181, s. 1; 1991, c. 102, s. 1; 1999-172, s. 1.)

§ 106-568.3. Action of Board of Agriculture on petition for referendum; creation of the Tobacco Research Commission.

(a)   The State Board of Agriculture, upon a petition being filed with it so requesting and signed by the governing boards of the North Carolina Farm Bureau Federation, the North Carolina State Grange, and the North Carolina Agricultural Foundation, Inc., shall examine such petition and upon finding that it complies with the provisions of this Article shall authorize the holding of a referendum as hereinafter set out and the governing boards of the North Carolina Farm Bureau Federation, the North Carolina State Grange, and the North Carolina Agricultural Foundation, Inc., shall thereupon be fully authorized and empowered to hold and conduct on the part of the producers and growers of the commodities herein mentioned a referendum on the question of whether or not such growers and producers shall levy upon themselves an assessment under and subject to and for the purposes stated in this Article. Provided, that the petition for a tobacco referendum shall be signed by and, once approved, shall authorize the holding of a referendum by the governing boards of the North Carolina Farm Bureau Federation, Inc., the North Carolina State Grange, the North Carolina Tobacco Foundation, Inc., and the Tobacco Growers Association of North Carolina, Incorporated.

(b)   There is hereby created a North Carolina Tobacco Research Commission within the Department of Agriculture and Consumer Services. The Commission shall consist of the Commissioner of Agriculture, or his designee; the President of the North Carolina Farm Bureau Federation, Inc., or his designee; the President of the Tobacco Growers Association of North Carolina, Incorporated, or his designee; the Master of the North Carolina State Grange, or his designee; and, the President of the North Carolina Tobacco Foundation, Inc., or his designee. (1951, c. 827, s. 3; 1991, c. 102, s. 2; 1997-261, s. 109.)

§ 106-568.4. By whom referendum to be managed; announcement.

The governing boards of the North Carolina Farm Bureau Federation, the North Carolina State Grange, and the North Carolina Agricultural Foundation, Inc., shall arrange for and manage any referendum conducted under the provisions of this Article but shall, 60 days before the date upon which it is to be held, fix, determine, and publicly announce in each county the date, hours, and polling places in that county for voting in such referendum, the amount and basis proposed to be collected, the means by which such assessment shall be collected as authorized by the growers and producers, and the general purposes for which said funds so collected shall be applied. Provided, that the governing boards of the North Carolina Farm Bureau Federation, Inc., the North Carolina State Grange, the North Carolina Tobacco Foundation, Inc., and the Tobacco Growers Association of North Carolina, Incorporated, shall arrange for and manage any referendum for tobacco poundage assessments under the provisions of this Article. (1951, c. 827, s. 4; 1991, c. 102, s. 3.)

§ 106-568.5. When assessment shall and shall not be levied.

If in such referendum more than one third of the farmers and producers eligible to participate therein and voting therein shall vote in the negative and against the levying or collection of such assessment, then in such event no assessment shall be levied or collected, but if two thirds or more of such farmers and producers voting therein shall vote in the affirmative and in favor of the levying or collection of such assessment, then such assessment shall be collected in the manner hereinafter provided. (1951, c. 827, s. 5.)

§ 106-568.6. Determination and notice of date, area, hours, voting places, etc.

The three organizations herein designated to hold such referendum shall fix the date, area, hours, voting places, rules and regulations with respect to the holding of such referendum and cause the same to be published in the press of the State at least 60 days before holding such referendum and shall certify such information to the State Commissioner of Agriculture and to each of the farm organizations of the State. Such notice, so published and furnished to the several agencies, shall contain, in addition to the other information herein required, a statement of the amount of annual assessment proposed to be levied, and the purposes for which such assessment shall be applied. Provided, that the four organizations designated to hold the referendum for tobacco poundage assessments shall perform the functions set forth in this section. (1951, c. 827, s. 6; 1991, c. 102, s. 4.)

§ 106-568.7. Preparation and distribution of ballots; poll holders; canvass and announcement of results.

The governing boards of the North Carolina Farm Bureau Federation, the North Carolina State Grange, and the North Carolina Agricultural Foundation, Inc., shall prepare and distribute in advance of such referendum all necessary ballots and shall under rules and regulations, adopted and promulgated by the organizations holding such referendum, arrange for the necessary poll holders and shall, within 10 days after the date of such referendum, canvass and publicly declare the results thereof. Provided, that for the tobacco poundage assessment referendum, the North Carolina Farm Bureau Federation, Inc., the North Carolina State Grange, the North Carolina Tobacco Foundation, Inc., and the Tobacco Growers Association of North Carolina, Incorporated, shall perform the functions set forth in this section. (1951, c. 827, s. 7; 1991, c. 102, s. 5.)

§ 106-568.8. Collection and disposition of assessment; report of receipts and disbursements; audit.

(a) Fertilizer and feed assessments. In the event two-thirds or more of the eligible farmers and producers participating in said referendum vote in favor of such assessment, then said assessment shall be collected for a period of six years under rules, regulations, and methods as provided for in this Article. The assessments shall be added to the wholesale purchase price of each ton of fertilizer, commercial feed, and/or their ingredients (except lime and land plaster) by the manufacturer of said fertilizer and feed. The assessment so collected shall be paid by the manufacturer into the hands of the North Carolina Commissioner of Agriculture on the same tonnage and at the same time and in the same manner as prescribed for the reporting of the inspection tax on commercial feeds and fertilizers as prescribed by G.S. 106-284.40 and 106-671. The Commissioner shall then remit the assessment for the total tonnage as reported by all manufacturers of commercial feeds, fertilizers, and their ingredients to the treasurer of the North Carolina Agricultural Foundation, Inc., who shall disburse such funds for the purposes herein enumerated and not inconsistent with provisions contained in the charter and bylaws of the North Carolina Agricultural Foundation, Inc. Signed copies of the receipts for such remittances made by the Commissioner to the treasurer of the North Carolina Agricultural Foundation, Inc., shall be furnished the Commissioner of Agriculture, the North Carolina Farm Bureau Federation, and the North Carolina State Grange. The treasurer of the North Carolina Agricultural Foundation, Inc., shall make an annual report at each annual meeting of the Foundation directors of total receipts and disbursements for the year and shall file a copy of said report with the Commissioner of Agriculture and shall make available a copy of said report for publication.

It shall be the duty of the Commissioner of Agriculture to audit and check the remittances of the assessment by the manufacturer to the Commissioner in the same manner and at the same time as audits and checks are made of remittances of the inspection tax on commercial feeds and fertilizers.

Any commercial feed excluded from the payment of the inspection fee required by G.S. 106-284.40 shall nevertheless be subject to the assessment provided for by this Article and to quarterly tonnage reports to the Department of Agriculture and Consumer Services as provided for in G.S. 106-284.40(c).

(b) Tobacco Poundage Assessments. In the event two-thirds or more of the eligible farmers and producers participating in the tobacco referendum vote in favor of the tobacco poundage assessment authorized under this Article, then said assessment shall be collected for a period of six years under rules, regulations, and methods adopted by the North Carolina Tobacco Research Commission. The North Carolina Tobacco Research Commission is exempt from the provisions of Chapter 150B of the General Statutes.

The assessments collected shall be remitted to the Department of Agriculture and Consumer Services to be expended under the direction of the Tobacco Research Commission for research and dissemination of research facts concerning tobacco. Any person that receives assessment funds from the Tobacco Research Commission shall file quarterly written reports with the Tobacco Research Commission on the receipt and expenditure of assessment funds. The Tobacco Research Commission may transfer assessments to the North Carolina Tobacco Foundation, Inc., to be held and invested by the Tobacco Foundation until such time as the Commission shall direct their expenditure for the purposes set forth in this section. (1951, c. 827, s. 8; 1967, c. 631, s. 1; 1975, c. 646; 1981, c. 181, s. 1; 1989, c. 770, s. 27; 1991, c. 102, s. 6; 1995, c. 239, s. 1; 1997-261, s. 109; 1999-172, s. 2.)

§ 106-568.9. Refunds to farmers.

In the event such a referendum is carried in the affirmative and the assessment is levied and collected as herein provided and under the regulations to be promulgated by the duly certified agencies conducting the same, any farmer upon whom and against whom any such assessment shall have been added and collected under the provisions of this Article, if dissatisfied with the said assessment, shall have the right to demand of and receive from the treasurer of said North Carolina Agricultural Foundation, Inc., a refund of such amount so collected from such farmer or producer provided such demand for refund is made in writing within 30 days from the date of which said assessment is collected from such farmer or producer. Provided, that the Department of Agriculture and Consumer Services shall make tobacco poundage assessment refunds to tobacco farmers when such demand for refund is made in writing by the tobacco farmer within 30 days of the close of the marketing season. (1951, c. 827, s. 9; 1991, c. 102, s. 7; 1997-261, s. 109.)

§ 106-568.10. Subsequent referenda; continuation of assessment.

If the assessment is defeated in the referendum, the governing boards of the North Carolina Farm Bureau Federation, the North Carolina State Grange, and the North Carolina Agricultural Foundation, Inc., shall have full power and authority to call another referendum for the purposes herein set out in the next succeeding year on the question of the annual assessment for six years. In the event the assessment carried in a referendum by two-thirds or more of the eligible farmers participating therein, such assessment shall be levied annually for the six years set forth in the call for such referendum and a new referendum may be called and conducted during the sixth year of such period on the question of whether or not such assessment shall be continued for the next ensuing six years. Provided, that if the tobacco poundage assessment is defeated in the referendum, the governing boards of the North Carolina Farm Bureau Federation, Inc., the North Carolina State Grange, the North Carolina Tobacco Foundation, Inc., and Tobacco Growers Association of North Carolina, Incorporated, may call another referendum in the next succeeding year on the question of the annual assessment for six years. If the tobacco assessment carried in a referendum by two-thirds or more of the eligible farmers participating therein, the assessment shall be levied annually for the six years set forth in the call for the referendum and a new referendum may be called and conducted during the sixth year of the period on the question of whether or not the assessment shall be continued for the next ensuing six years. (1951, c. 827, s. 10; 1967, c. 631, s. 2; 1991, c. 102, s. 8.)

§ 106-568.11. Effect of more than one-third vote against assessment.

If in such referendum called under the provisions of this Article more than one third of the farmers and producers in the State of North Carolina, eligible to participate and voting therein, shall vote in the negative and against the levying or collection of such assessment, then in such an event no assessment shall be levied or collected. (1951, c. 827, s. 11.)

§ 106-568.12. Effect of two-thirds vote in favor of assessment.

If in such referendum called under the provisions of this Article two thirds or more of the farmers or producers in the State of North Carolina, eligible to participate and voting therein, shall vote in the affirmative and in favor of the levying and collection of such assessment proposed in such referendum on the commodities covered thereby, then such assessment shall be collected in the manner prescribed herein (determined and announced by the agencies conducting such referendum). (1951, c. 827, s. 12.)

Article 50B.

North Carolina Agricultural Hall of Fame.

§ 106-568.13. North Carolina Agricultural Hall of Fame created.

There is hereby created and established as an agency of the State of North Carolina the North Carolina Agricultural Hall of Fame. (1953, c. 1129, s. 1.)

§ 106-568.14. Board of directors; membership; compensation.

The North Carolina Agricultural Hall of Fame shall be under the general supervision and control of a board of directors consisting of the following: the Commissioner of Agriculture of the State of North Carolina, who shall act as chairman; the Director of the North Carolina Agricultural Extension Service; the State Supervisor of Vocational Agriculture; the President of the North Carolina Farm Bureau Federation; the Master of the State Grange, the foregoing being ex officio members; and three members who shall be appointed by the Governor of North Carolina. All of said members shall serve without compensation. (1953, c. 1129, s. 2.)

§ 106-568.15. Terms of directors.

One of the appointive members shall be appointed for a term of two years, one for a term of four years and one for a term of six years. The successor to each of the appointive members shall be appointed for a term of six years, and in case of a vacancy, the Governor is authorized to appoint a successor for the remainder of the unexpired term. The ex officio members shall serve so long as they hold their respective offices or positions which entitle them to ex officio membership on said board of directors. (1953, c. 1129, s. 3.)

§ 106-568.16. Admission of candidates to Hall of Fame.

The said board is hereby empowered to formulate rules and regulations governing acceptance and admission of candidates to said North Carolina Agricultural Hall of Fame, provided that no name shall be accepted until an authentic and written record of achievements of said person in agricultural activities shall have been presented to and accepted by a majority vote of said board created by this Article, and provided that both men and women are eligible for recognition. (1953, c. 1129, s. 4.)

§ 106-568.17. Acceptance of gifts, devises, and awards; display thereof.

The said board is hereby empowered to accept and receive gifts, devises, and awards which are to become the sole property of said North Carolina Agricultural Hall of Fame and are to be kept in a proper manner in a suitable room or hall in some state-owned building in Raleigh, provided that duplicates of such gifts, devises, and awards may be displayed in a suitable room or hall in the School of Agriculture of the North Carolina State College of Agriculture and Engineering at Raleigh, North Carolina. (1953, c. 1129, s. 5; 2011-284, s. 73.)

Article 50C.

Promotion of Sale and Use of Tobacco.

§ 106-568.18. Policy as to joint action of farmers.

It is hereby declared to be in the public interest that the farmers of North Carolina who produce flue-cured tobacco be permitted and encouraged to act jointly in promoting and stimulating, by organized methods and through the medium established for such purpose, export trade for flue-cured tobacco and the use of tobacco everywhere. (1959, c. 309, s. 1.)

§ 106-568.19. Policy as to referendum on question of annual assessment.

For the purpose of raising reasonable and necessary funds for producer participation in the operations of the agency set up under farmer sponsorship for the promotion of export trade in flue-cured tobacco and the use of tobacco everywhere, it is proper, desirable, necessary and in the public interest that the farmers in this State engaged in the production of flue-cured tobacco shall have the opportunity and privilege of participating in a referendum to be held as hereinafter provided, in which referendum there shall be determined the question of whether or not the farmers of the State engaged in the production of flue-cured tobacco shall levy upon themselves an annual assessment for the purposes herein stated. (1959, c. 309, s. 2.)

§ 106-568.20. Referendum on assessment for next three years.

During the year 1989 or 1990 upon the exact date in such year as may be determined in the manner hereinafter set forth and under rules and regulations as established under the provisions of this Article, there shall be held in every county in North Carolina in which flue-cured tobacco is produced a referendum to be participated in by all farmers engaged in the production of flue-cured tobacco in which referendum said farmers shall vote upon the question of whether or not there shall be levied an annual assessment for a period of three years 1989, 1990 and 1991, or 1990, 1991, and 1992, such amount as may have been theretofore or as may be thereafter determined by the Board of Directors of Tobacco Associates, Inc., but not more than four dollars ($4.00) per acre per year on all flue-cured tobacco acreage in the State of North Carolina. Those farmers entitled to share in the crop of flue-cured tobacco or in the proceeds of such crop because of sharing in the risk of production shall be deemed to be engaged in the production of such tobacco. (1959, c. 309, s. 3; 1987, c. 294, s. 1; 1989, c. 349, s. 1.)

§ 106-568.21. Effect of more than one-third vote against assessment in referendum.

If in such referendum more than one-third of the tobacco farmers eligible to participate therein and voting therein shall vote in the negative and against the levying or collection of such assessment, then no assessment shall be levied or collected pursuant to that referendum. (1959, c. 309, s. 4; 1987, c. 294, s. 2.)

§ 106-568.22. Effect of two-thirds vote for assessment in referendum.

If in such referendum two-thirds or more of the eligible tobacco farmers voting therein shall vote in the affirmative and in favor of the levying or collection of such assessment to be determined by the board of directors of Tobacco Associates, Incorporated, but in an amount of not more than four dollars ($4.00) per acre per year on all flue-cured tobacco acreage in the State of North Carolina, then such assessment shall be collected in the manner hereinafter provided. (1959, c. 309, s. 5; 1987, c. 294, s. 3; 1989, c. 349, s. 2.)

§ 106-568.23. Regulations as to referendum; notice to farm organizations and county agents.

The exact date, on which such referendum shall be held and the hours, voting places, and rules and regulations under which such referendum shall be conducted, shall be established and determined by the board of directors of the North Carolina corporation known and designated as Tobacco Associates, Incorporated, established under the leadership of farm organizations in the State of North Carolina for the purpose of stimulating, developing and expanding export trade for flue-cured tobacco and the use of tobacco everywhere; the said referendum date, hours, voting places, rules and regulations with respect to the holding of such referendum shall be published through the medium of the public press in the State of North Carolina by said board of directors at least 15 days before the holding of such referendum, and direct written notice thereof shall likewise be given to all farm organizations within the State of North Carolina and to each county agent in any county in which flue-cured tobacco is grown. (1959, c. 309, s. 6; 1987, c. 294, s. 4.)

§ 106-568.24. Distribution of ballots; arrangements for holding referendum; declaration of results.

The said board of directors of Tobacco Associates, Incorporated, shall likewise prepare and distribute in advance of said referendum all necessary ballots for the purpose thereof, and shall under the rules and regulations promulgated by said board arrange for the necessary poll holders for conducting the said referendum; and following such referendum and within 10 days thereafter the said board of directors shall canvass and publicly declare the results of such referendum. (1959, c. 309, s. 7; 1987, c. 294, s. 5.)

§ 106-568.25. Question at referendum.

Said referendum shall be upon the question of whether or not the farmers eligible for participation therein and voting therein shall favor an assessment upon themselves for the period of the next three tobacco marketing years, in an amount in each of said years as determined by or to be determined by the board of directors of Tobacco Associates, Incorporated but not more than four dollars ($4.00) per acre per year on all flue-cured tobacco acreage in the State of North Carolina, for the purpose of providing farmer participation in the fund and through the agency established for the stimulation, expansion and development of export markets for flue-cured tobacco and the encouragement of the use of flue-cured tobacco everywhere. (1959, c. 309, s. 8; 1987, c. 294, s. 6; 1989, c. 349, s. 3.)

§ 106-568.26. Collection of assessments; custody and use of funds.

In the event two-thirds or more of the eligible farmers voting therein shall vote in favor of such assessment, then the said assessment shall be collected annually for the years herein set forth and under such method, rules and regulations as may be determined by the board of directors of the said Tobacco Associates, Incorporated, and the said assessment so collected shall be paid into the treasurer [treasury] of said Tobacco Associates, Incorporated, to be used along with funds from other sources, for the purpose of stimulating, developing and expanding export trade for flue-cured tobacco and encouraging the use of flue-cured tobacco everywhere. (1959, c. 309, s. 9.)

§ 106-568.27. Required affirmative vote of directors of Tobacco Associates, Incorporated.

No assessment shall be made pursuant to this Article unless same shall receive the affirmative vote of not less than two-thirds of the members of the board of directors of Tobacco Associates, Incorporated, including the affirmative vote of not less than two thirds of such board members who were elected by North Carolina farm organizations. (1959, c. 309, s. 10.)

§ 106-568.28. Right of farmers dissatisfied with assessments; time for demanding refund.

In the event any referendum authorized by this Article is carried in the affirmative by such two-thirds vote and the assessment is levied and collected as herein provided and under the regulations to be promulgated by the board of directors of Tobacco Associates, Incorporated, any farmer or tobacco producer upon whom and against whom any such annual assessment shall have been levied and collected under the provisions of this Article, if dissatisfied with the said assessment, shall have the right to demand of and receive from the treasurer of said Tobacco Associates, Incorporated, a refund of such annual assessment so collected from such farmer or producer of tobacco, provided such demand for refund is made in writing within 30 days from the last date on which such assessment is collected from such farmer or producer or deducted from the proceeds of the sale of tobacco of such farmer or producer. (1959, c. 309, s. 11; 1987, c. 294, s. 7.)

§ 106-568.29. Subsequent referendum after defeat of assessment.

In the event any referendum conducted as provided for in this Article shall not be supported by two-thirds or more of those voting therein, then the board of directors of Tobacco Associates, Incorporated shall have full power and authority to call another referendum for the purposes herein set forth in any succeeding year, on the question of an annual assessment for the next three tobacco marketing years or less. If the referendum is carried as provided in this Article, then the assessments may be levied and collected as provided in this Article. (1959, c. 309, s. 12; 1989, c. 349, s. 4.)

§ 106-568.30. Referendum as to continuance of assessments approved at prior referendum.

In the event any referendum, held at any time under the provisions of this Article, is carried by the vote of two-thirds or more of the eligible farmers participating therein and assessments in pursuance thereof are being levied annually, then the board of directors of Tobacco Associates, Incorporated shall, in its discretion, have full power and authority to call and conduct another referendum in which the farmers and producers of flue-cured tobacco shall vote upon the question of whether or not assessments under this Article shall be continued for the next three tobacco marketing years. If the referendum is carried as provided in this Article, then assessments may be levied and collected as provided in this Article. (1959, c. 309, s. 13; 1987, c. 294, s. 8.)

§ 106-568.31. Filing and publication of financial statement by treasurer of Tobacco Associates, Incorporated.

The treasurer of Tobacco Associates, Incorporated shall, within 60 days after the end of any fiscal year, file with the State Auditor a financial statement as of the end of the fiscal year and a detailed statement of operations for the year ended. Further a condensed statement of the financial condition and operating expenses for said fiscal year shall be published in a newspaper of general circulation, if one exists, in each county from which assessments are collected. (1959, c. 309, s. 14; 1987, c. 294, s. 9.)

§ 106-568.32. Repealed by Session Laws 1987, c. 294. s. 11.

§ 106-568.33. Effect of Article on prior acts.

Insofar as the provisions of this Article are different from and in conflict with the provisions of Chapter 511, Session Laws of 1947 and Chapter 63, Session Laws of 1951, to the extent of such conflict the provisions of this Article shall be applicable and shall supersede and prevail over the provisions of said former acts and all provisions of this Article shall be in full effect. So long as assessments are made under this Article, no assessment shall be made and collected under the provisions of Chapter 511, Session Laws of 1947, as amended. (1959, c. 309, s. 16.)

§ 106-568.34. Alternate method for levy of assessment.

At any time when it may be found by the Board of Directors of Tobacco Associates, that it is not reasonably feasible to base the authorization of an assessment or the making of an assessment or the collection of an assessment on a "per-acre" unit, then the Board of Directors of Tobacco Associates, by an affirmative vote of not less than two thirds of its members (which vote shall include the affirmative vote of not less than two thirds of the board members who were elected by North Carolina farm organizations), may use a "tobacco poundage" unit as the basis for the authorization or making or collecting an assessment. No alternative assessment for any year after 1988 shall exceed one-fifth cent (1/5¢) per pound of the flue-cured tobacco marketed by each farmer. The amount of any alternate assessment, based upon a "tobacco poundage" unit as permitted by the provisions of this section shall not be related to or limited by the amount of the assessment which could be authorized, made or collected if it were based upon a "per-acre" unit. (1973, c. 81; 1979, c. 474, s. 1; 1987, c. 294, s. 10; 1989, c. 349, s. 5.)

§ 106-568.35. Alternate provision for referendum voting by mail.

(a) At any time when it may be found that it is not desirable or reasonably possible to conduct a referendum by written ballots to be cast at polling places (as provided in G.S. 106-568.23 and 106-568.24 of this Article), the board of directors of Tobacco Associates, Incorporated, by an affirmative vote of not less than two-thirds of its members (which vote shall include the affirmative vote of not less than two thirds of such board members who were elected by North Carolina farm organizations), may prescribe and provide for a vote by mail by written or printed ballot.

(b)   In the event that the board of directors shall decide to conduct the referendum by mail vote, the board shall prescribe the rules and regulations under which such mail referendum shall be conducted; shall provide the necessary ballots and cause them to be mailed to the farmers of North Carolina who are engaged in the production of flue-cured tobacco; shall provide envelopes for the return of such ballots by individual voters; shall cause to be published through the medium of the public press in the State of North Carolina notice of the holding of such referendum at least 15 days before the mailing out of the ballots; shall give direct written notice of such proposed mail referendum to all statewide farm organizations within the State of North Carolina and to each county agent in each county in which flue-cured tobacco is grown; shall provide a closing date for the return of the ballots; shall provide for the receipt and safeguarding of such ballots; and, within 30 days of the date set as the latest date for the return of such ballots, shall canvass the ballots and publish and declare the results of such referendum. (1975, c. 125; 1987, c. 294, s. 12.)

§ 106-568.36. Maximum levy after 1988.

The maximum amount which may be authorized in any referendum held pursuant to the provisions of this Article during 1989 or thereafter, and the maximum amount which may be assessed, collected or levied for any year after 1988 by the Board of Directors of Tobacco Associates pursuant to the provisions of this Article, is four dollars ($4.00) per acre per year on all flue-cured tobacco acreage in the State, or, under the alternate method for levy of assessment set out in G.S. 106-568.34, one-fifth cent (1/5¢) per pound of the flue-cured tobacco marketed by each farmer. (1979, c. 474, s. 2; 1987, c. 294, s. 13; 1989, c. 349, s. 6.)

§ 106-568.37. Report on use of assessments.

The Board of Directors of the Tobacco Associates, Incorporated shall make an annual written report of the financial transactions and a financial statement concerning the receipts and disbursements of the revenue from the assessment. A copy of the report shall be provided by the Board of Directors of the Tobacco Associates, Incorporated to the Commissioner of Agriculture, the Dean of the College of Agriculture and Life Sciences at North Carolina State University, the North Carolina Farm Bureau Federation, the North Carolina State Grange, and the Bright Belt Warehouse Association. (1989, c. 349, s. 7.)

§ 106-568.38: Reserved for future codification purposes.

§ 106-568.39: Reserved for future codification purposes.

Article 50D.

Tobacco Growers Assessment Act.

§ 106-568.40. Title.

This Article shall be known as the "Tobacco Growers Assessment Act." (2013-311, s. 1.)

§ 106-568.41. Purpose.

It is in the public interest for the State to enable growers of tobacco to assess themselves in order to raise funds to promote the interests of tobacco growers. This assessment shall be in addition to the assessment authorized by Article 50C of Chapter 106 of the General Statutes to promote export sales of tobacco and the assessment authorized by Article 50A of Chapter 106 of the General Statutes for tobacco research. (2013-311, s. 1.)

§ 106-568.42. Definitions.

The following definitions apply in this Article:

(1) Association. - The Tobacco Growers Association of North Carolina, Inc., a North Carolina nonprofit corporation.

(2) Buyer. - Any person engaged in the business of buying tobacco from a producer of tobacco grown in North Carolina, including a broker, dealer, or agent of the buyer.

(3) Department. - The North Carolina Department of Agriculture and Consumer Services.

(4) Person. - An individual, a partnership, a firm, or a corporation.

(5) Tobacco. - Flue-cured tobacco.

(6) Tobacco grower. - A person who (i) is a North Carolina resident, (ii) owns, manages, or has a financial interest in tobacco production, and (iii) is actively involved in tobacco production. (2013-311, s. 1.)

§ 106-568.43. Referendum.

(a) The Association may conduct among tobacco growers a referendum upon the question of whether an assessment shall be levied on tobacco sold in this State.

(b) The Association shall determine the amount of the proposed assessment and the date by which the referendum ballot must be returned by mail as provided in this section.

(c) The amount of the proposed assessment shall be stated on the referendum ballot. The amount may not exceed fifteen cents (15¢) for each hundred pounds of tobacco marketed in this State. If the assessment is approved in the referendum, the Association may set the assessment at an amount equal to or less than the amount stated on the ballot. If the Association sets a lower amount than the amount approved by referendum, it may increase the amount annually without a referendum by no more than one cent (1¢) for each hundred pounds of tobacco marketed. The increased rate may not exceed the amount approved by referendum and may not exceed the maximum allowable rate of fifteen cents (15¢) for each hundred pounds.

(d)   The Association shall mail a referendum ballot to all known tobacco growers in the State for whom the Association has a current and valid mailing address at least three months prior to the date the ballot must be returned. Additionally, the Association must, for the greater of three months or 90 days before the date the ballot must be returned, (i) provide a printable referendum ballot on the Association's official Web site and (ii) make hard copies of the referendum ballot available at all county North Carolina Cooperative Extension Service offices. The ballots shall be returned to the Commissioner of Agriculture by the date set by the Association. The Department shall be responsible for counting the votes and reporting the results of the referendum to the Association.

(e)   All tobacco growers may vote in the referendum. Any dispute over eligibility to vote or any other matter relating to the referendum shall be determined by the Association. The Association shall make reasonable efforts to provide tobacco growers with notice of the referendum and an opportunity to vote. (2013-311, s. 1.)

§ 106-568.44. Payment and collection of assessment.

(a)   The assessment shall not be collected unless more than two-thirds of the votes cast in the referendum are in favor of the assessment. If more than two-thirds of the votes cast in the referendum are in favor of the assessment, then the Association shall notify the Department of the amount of the assessment and the effective date of the assessment. The Department shall notify all tobacco buyers of the assessment.

(b)   Each tobacco producer shall pay the assessment on all tobacco sold to a buyer.

(c)   A buyer shall collect the assessment when buying tobacco by deducting the assessment from the price paid to the producer. The buyer shall remit collected assessments to the Department no later than the 10th day of the following month. The Department shall provide forms to buyers for reporting the assessment. If the total assessments collected by a buyer in a month are less than twenty-five dollars ($25.00), the buyer may keep the assessments until the total amount due is at least twenty-five dollars ($25.00) or the end of the calendar quarter, whichever comes first. All buyers shall file at least one report in each calendar quarter in which they purchase tobacco from a producer, regardless of the amount due.

(d)   A buyer shall keep records of the amount of tobacco purchased and the date purchased. All information or records regarding purchases of tobacco by individual buyers shall be kept confidential by employees or agents of the Department and the Association and shall not be disclosed except by court order.

(e)   The Association may bring an action to recover any unpaid assessments, plus the reasonable costs, including attorneys' fees, incurred in the action. (2013-311, s. 1.)

§ 106-568.45. Use of assessments; refunds; annual audit.

(a)   At least once per month, the Department shall remit all funds collected under this Article to the Association. The Association shall use the funds to promote the interests of tobacco growers. The Association shall prepare an annual report on the assessment funds collected and the use of assessment funds. The Association shall publicly post the annual report on its official Web site at least 30 days before the Association's annual meeting. Copies of the annual report shall be made available to growers at the Association's annual meeting, and a copy shall also be sent to the Commissioner of Agriculture.

(b)   A tobacco grower may request a refund of the assessment collected under this Article by submitting a written request for a refund to the Association postmarked on or before December 31 of the same year. A refund request shall be accompanied by proof of payment of the assessment satisfactory to the Association. The Association shall mail a refund to the grower within 30 days of receipt of a properly documented refund request.

(c)   The Association shall designate a third party to conduct an annual audit of the implementation of this Article. The Association shall also designate the time at which the audit may be conducted each year, provided that the results of the audit be available before or in conjunction with the annual report. (2013-311, s. 1.)

§ 106-568.46. Termination of assessment.

Upon receipt of a petition signed by at least ten percent (10%) of the tobacco growers in North Carolina known to the Association, the Department shall notify the Association, and the Association shall, within six months, conduct a referendum upon the question of continuing the assessment. If a majority of the votes cast in the referendum are against continuing the assessment, or if the Association fails to conduct a referendum within the six-month period, the assessment expires at the end of the six-month period. If a majority of the votes cast in the referendum are in favor of continuing the assessment, then no subsequent referendum shall be held for at least three years. (2013-311, s. 1.)

Article 51.

Inspection and Regulation of Sale of Antifreeze Substances and Preparations.

§§ 106-569 through 106-579: Repealed by Session Laws 1975, c. 179, s. 16.

Article 51A.

North Carolina Antifreeze Law of 1975.

§ 106-579.1. Short title.

This Article shall be known as the "North Carolina Antifreeze Law of 1975." (1975, c. 719, s. 1.)

§ 106-579.2. Purpose.

It is desirable that there should be uniformity between the requirements of the several states. Therefore, the Board and Commission are directed, consistent with the purposes of this Article, to so enforce this Article as to strive for achievement of such uniformity and are also authorized and empowered to cooperate with and enter into agreements with any other agency of this State, or any other state regulating antifreeze, for the purpose of carrying out the provisions of this Article and securing uniformity of regulations in conformity to the primary standards established by this Article. (1975, c. 719, s. 2.)

§ 106-579.3. Definitions.

As used in this Article, the following words and phrases have the following meanings:

(1) "Advertisement" means all representations disseminated in any manner or by any means, other than by labeling, for the purpose of inducing, or which are likely to induce, directly or indirectly, the purchase of antifreeze products.

(2) "Antifreeze" means any substance or preparation sold, distributed or intended for use as the cooling liquid, or to be added to the cooling liquid, in the cooling system of internal combustion engines of motor vehicles to prevent freezing of the cooling liquid or to lower its freezing point.

(3) "Antifreeze-coolant" or "antifreeze and summer coolant" or "summer coolant" means any substance as defined in (2) above which also is sold, distributed or intended for raising the boiling point of water or for the prevention of engine overheating whether or not used as a year-round cooling system fluid. Unless otherwise stated, the term "antifreeze" includes "antifreeze," "antifreeze-coolant," "antifreeze and summer coolant," and "summer coolant."

(4) "Board" means the North Carolina State Board of Agriculture, as defined by G.S. 106-2.

(5) "Commissioner" means the Commissioner of Agriculture of the State of North Carolina.

(6) "Distribute" means to hold with intent to sell, offer for sale, to sell, barter or otherwise supply to the consumer.

(7) "Home consumer-sized package" as used in G.S. 106-579.9(12) shall refer to packages of one fluid U.S. gallon or less.

(8) "Label" means any display of written, printed, or graphic matter on, or attached to, a package, or to the outside individual container or wrapper of the package.

(9) "Labeling" means (i) the labels and (ii) any other written, printed or graphic matter accompanying a package.

(10) "Package" means (i) a sealed tamperproof retail package, drum, or other container designed for the sale of antifreeze directly to the consumer or (ii) a container from which the antifreeze may be installed directly by the seller into the cooling system, but does not include shipping containers containing properly labeled inner containers.

(11) "Person," as used in this Article, shall be construed to mean both the singular and plural as the case demands, and shall include individuals, partnerships, corporations, companies and associations. (1949, c. 1165; 1975, c. 719, s. 3.)

§ 106-579.4. Registrations.

On or before the first day of July of each year, and before any antifreeze may be distributed for the permit year beginning July 1, the manufacturer, packager, or person whose name appears on the label shall make application to the Commissioner on forms provided by the latter for registration for each brand of antifreeze which he desires to distribute. The application shall be accompanied by specimens or facsimiles of labeling for all container sizes to be distributed, when requested by the Commissioner; a license and inspection fee of five hundred dollars ($500.00) for each brand of antifreeze and a properly labeled sample of the antifreeze shall also be submitted at this time. The Commissioner may inspect, test, or analyze the antifreeze and review the labeling. If the antifreeze is not adulterated or misbranded, if it meets the standards established and promulgated by the Board, and if the said antifreeze is not such a type or kind that is in violation of this Article, the Commissioner shall thereafter issue a written license or permit authorizing the sale of such antifreeze in this State for the fiscal year in which the license or inspection fee is paid. If the antifreeze is adulterated or misbranded, if it fails to meet standards promulgated by the Board, or is in violation of this Article or regulations thereunder, the Commissioner shall refuse to register the antifreeze, and he shall return the application to the applicant, stating how the antifreeze or labeling is not in conformity. If the Commissioner shall, at a later date, find that a properly registered antifreeze product has been materially altered or adulterated, or a change has been made in the name, brand or trademark under which the antifreeze is sold, or that it violates the provisions of this Article, or that it violates regulations, definitions or standards duly promulgated by the Board, he shall notify the applicant that the license authorizing sale of the antifreeze is canceled. No antifreeze license shall be canceled unless the registrant shall have been given an opportunity to be heard before the Commissioner or his duly designated agent and to modify his application in order to comply with the requirements of this Article and regulations, definitions, and standards promulgated by the Board. All fees received by the Commissioner shall be placed in the Department of Agriculture and Consumer Services fund for the purpose of supporting the antifreeze enforcement and testing program. (1949, c. 1165; 1975, c. 719, s. 4; 1997-261, s. 109; 2011-145, s. 31.10.)

§ 106-579.5. Adulteration.

Antifreeze shall be deemed to be adulterated:

(1) If, in the form in which it is sold and directed to be used, it would be injurious to the cooling system in which it is installed, or if, when used in such cooling system, it would make the operation of the engine dangerous to the user.

(2) If its strength, quality, or purity falls below the standard of strength, quality, or purity established by the Board for the particular type or composition of antifreeze product. (1949, c. 1165; 1975, c. 719, s. 5.)

§ 106-579.6. Misbranding.

Antifreeze shall be deemed to be misbranded:

(1) If it does not bear a label which (i) specifies the identity of the product, (ii) states the name and place of business of the registrant, (iii) states the correct net quantity of contents (in terms of liquid measure) separately and accurately in a uniform location upon the principal display panel, and (iv) contains a statement warning of any hazard of substantial injury to human beings which

may result from the intended use or reasonably foreseeable misuse of the antifreeze, as provided by applicable federal and State product safety laws.

(2)   If the label on a container of less than five gallons, or the labeling for a container of five gallons or more, does not contain a statement or chart showing the appropriate amount, percentage, proportion or concentration of the antifreeze to be used to provide (i) claimed protection from freezing at a specified degree or degrees of temperature, (ii) claimed protection from corrosion, or (iii) claimed increase of boiling point or protection from overheating.

(3)   If its labeling contains any claim that it has been approved or recommended by the Commissioner or the State of North Carolina.

(4)   If its labeling is false, deceptive, or misleading. (1949, c. 1165; 1975, c. 719, s. 6.)

§ 106-579.7. Rules and regulations.

(a)   The Board is authorized to promulgate such reasonable rules, regulations and standards for antifreezes as are specifically authorized in this Article and such other reasonable rules and regulations as may be necessary for the efficient enforcement of this Article and the protection of the public. The Board is authorized to promulgate regulations banning the distribution in North Carolina of any type of product not suitable for antifreeze usage in modern internal combustion engines or motor vehicles, whether by reason of potential damage to the cooling system, improper heat transfer from the engine, absence of a convenient and suitable test method for measuring freeze protection, or other reason bearing upon the ultimate effect of the product when used in such automotive cooling systems. Before the issuance, amendment, or repeal of any rule, regulation or standard authorized by this Article, the Board shall publish the proposed regulation, amendment, or notice to repeal an existing regulation in a manner reasonably calculated to give interested parties, including all current registrants, adequate notice and shall afford all interested persons an opportunity to present their views thereon, orally or in writing, within a reasonable period of time. After consideration of all views presented by interested persons, the Board shall take appropriate action as dictated by the material weight of objective information presented to the Board.

(b) The Commissioner shall administer this Article by inspections, chemical analyses and other appropriate methods. The Commissioner shall also execute all orders, rules and regulations established by the Board. All authority vested in the Commissioner by virtue of the provisions of this Article may, with like force and effect, be executed by such agents of the Commissioner as he shall designate for such purpose; provided, however, that confidential formula information referred to in G.S. 106-579.11 must be confined to the files of the administrative chemist specifically designated by the Commissioner to handle such information. (1949, c. 1165; 1975, c. 719, s. 7.)

§ 106-579.8. Inspection, sampling and analysis.

The Commissioner, or his authorized agent, shall have free access at reasonable hours to all places and property in this State where antifreeze is manufactured, stored, transported, or distributed, or offered or intended to be offered, for sale, including the right to inspect and examine all antifreeze there found, and to take reasonable samples of such antifreeze for analysis together with specimens of labeling. All samples so taken shall be properly sealed and sent to the Department of Agriculture and Consumer Services laboratories for examination together with all labeling appertaining thereto. It shall be the duty of the Commissioner to examine promptly all samples received in connection with the administration and enforcement of this Article and to report the results of such examination to the owner and registrant of the antifreeze. (1949, c. 1165; 1975, c. 179, s. 8; 1997-261, s. 109.)

§ 106-579.9. Prohibited acts.

It shall be unlawful to:

(1) Distribute any antifreeze which is adulterated or misbranded.

(2) Distribute any antifreeze which has been banned by the Board.

(3) Distribute any antifreeze which has not been registered in accordance with G.S. 106-579.4 or whose labeling is different from that accepted for registration; provided, that any antifreeze declared to be discontinued by the registrant must be registered by the registrant for one full year after distribution

is discontinued; provided further, that any antifreeze in channels of distribution after the aforesaid registration period may be confiscated and disposed of by the Commissioner, unless the antifreeze is acceptable for registration and is continued to be registered by the manufacturer or the person offering the antifreeze for wholesale or retail sale.

(4)   Refuse to permit entry or inspection or to permit the acquisition of a sample of antifreeze as authorized by G.S. 106-579.8.

(5)   Dispose of any antifreeze that is under "stop sale" or "withdrawal from distribution" order in accordance with G.S. 106-579.10.

(6)   Distribute any antifreeze unless it is in the registrant's or manufacturer's unbroken package or is installed by the seller into the cooling system of the purchaser's vehicle directly from the registrant's or manufacturer's package, and the label on such package if less than five gallons, or the labeling of such package if five gallons or more, does not bear the information required by G.S. 106-579.6(1), (2), (3), and (4).

(7)   Use the term "ethylene glycol" in connection with the name of a product which contains other glycols unless it is qualified by the word "base," "type," or similar word, and unless the product meets the following requirements:

a.   It consists essentially of ethylene glycol;

b.   If it contains suitable glycols other than ethylene glycol, that no more than a maximum of fifteen percent (15%) of such other glycols be present;

c.   It contains a minimum total glycol content of ninety-three percent (93%) by weight;

d.   The specific gravity is corrected to give reliable freezing-point readings on a commercial ethylene glycol type hydrometer; and

e.   The freezing point of a fifty percent (50%) by volume aqueous mixture of the antifreeze shall not be above -34° F.

(8)   Refuse, when requested, to permit a purchaser to see the container from which antifreeze is drawn for installation into the purchaser's vehicle.

(9) Refill any container bearing a registered label, unless by the registrant or his duly designated jobber, under regulations established by the Board.

(10) Distribute any antifreeze for which a practical, rapid means for measuring the freeze protection by the user is not readily available, whether by hydrometer or other means.

(11) Distribute antifreeze which is in violation of the Federal Poison Prevention Packaging Act and regulations and related federal and State product safety laws and regulations.

(12) Distribute antifreeze in home consumer-sized packages which are constructed of either transparent or translucent packaging materials.

(13) Disseminate any false or misleading advertisement relating to an antifreeze product. (1975, c. 719, s. 9.)

§ 106-579.10. Enforcement.

(a) When the Commissioner finds any antifreeze being distributed in violation of any of the provisions of this Article or of any of the rules and regulations duly promulgated and adopted under this Article by the Board, he may issue and enforce a written or printed "stop sale" or "withdrawal from distribution" order, warning the distributor not to dispose of any of the lot of antifreeze in any manner until written permission is given by the Commissioner or the court. Copies of such orders shall also be sent by certified mail to the registrant and to the person whose name and address appears on the labeling of the antifreeze. The Commissioner shall release for distribution the lot of antifreeze so withdrawn when said provisions of this Article and applicable rules and regulations have been complied with. If compliance is not obtained within 30 days of the date of notification to the registrant and the person whose name and address appears on the label, the Commissioner may begin proceedings for condemnation.

(b) Notwithstanding the provisions of subsection (a) of this section, any lot of antifreeze not in compliance with said provisions and regulations shall be subject to seizure upon complaint of the Commissioner to the district court in the county in which said antifreeze is located. In the event the court finds said antifreeze to be in violation of this Article and its duly adopted regulations, it may then order the condemnation of said antifreeze and the same shall be disposed of in any manner consistent with the rules and regulations of the Board and the laws of the State at the expense of the claimants thereof, under the supervision of the Commissioner; and all court costs and fees, and storage and other proper expenses, shall be taxed against the claimant of such article or his agent; provided, however, that in no instance shall the disposition of said antifreeze be ordered by the court without first giving 30 days' notice, by certified mail at his last known address, to the owner of same, if he is known to the Commissioner, and to the registrant, if the antifreeze is registered, at the address shown on the label or on the registration certificate, so that such persons may apply to the court for the release of said antifreeze or for permission to process or relabel said antifreeze so as to bring it into compliance with this Article. When the violation can be corrected by proper labeling, processing of the product, or other action, the court, after all costs, fees and expenses incurred by the Commissioner have been paid and a good and sufficient bond, conditioned that such article shall be so corrected, has been executed, may by order direct that such article be delivered to the claimant thereof for such action as necessary to bring it into compliance with this Article and regulations under the supervision of the Commissioner. The expense of such supervision shall be paid by the claimant. Such bond shall be returned to the claimant of the article on representation to the court by the Commissioner that the antifreeze is no longer in violation of this Article, and that the expenses of such supervision have been paid.

(c)   A copy of the analysis made by any chemist of the Department of Agriculture and Consumer Services of any antifreeze certified to by him shall be administered as evidence in any court of the State on trial of any issue involving the merits of antifreeze as defined and covered by this Article.

(d)   When the Commissioner finds any antifreeze being distributed in violation of any of the provisions of this Article or of any of the rules and regulations duly promulgated and adopted by the Board, he may request, and the person whose name and address appears on the labeling or the person who is primarily responsible for the product must promptly supply to him, the distribution data for such product in this State, so as to assure that violative products are not further distributed herein and that an orderly withdrawal from distribution may be attained where necessary to protect the public interest. (1949, c. 1165; 1975, c. 719, s. 10; 1997-261, s. 109.)

§ 106-579.11. Submission of formula.

When application for a license or permit to sell antifreeze in this State is made to the Commissioner, he may require the applicant to furnish a statement of the formula or contents of such antifreeze, which said statement shall conform to rules and regulations established by the Commissioner; provided, however, that the statement of formula or contents may state the content of inhibitor ingredients in generic terms if such inhibitor ingredients total less than five percent (5%) by weight of the antifreeze and if in lieu thereof the manufacturer, packer, seller or distributor furnishes the Commissioner with satisfactory evidence, other than by disclosure of the actual chemical names and percentages of the inhibitor ingredients, that the said antifreeze is in conformity with this Article and any rules and regulations promulgated and adopted by the Board. All statements of content, formulas or trade secrets furnished under this section shall be privileged and confidential and shall not be made public or open to the inspection of any person, firm, association or corporation other than the Commissioner. All such statements of contents shall not be subject to subpoena nor shall the same be exhibited or disclosed before any administrative or judicial tribunal by virtue of any order or subpoena of such tribunal unless with the consent of the applicant furnishing such statements to the Commissioner; provided, however, that in emergency situations information may be revealed to physicians or to other qualified persons for use in preparation of antidotes. The disclosure of any such information, except as provided in this section, shall be a Class 2 misdemeanor. (1949, c. 1165; 1975, c. 719, s. 11; 1993, c. 539, s. 806; 1994, Ex. Sess., c. 24, s. 14(c).)

§ 106-579.12. Violation.

(a) Any person who shall be adjudged to have violated any provision of this Article, or any regulation of the Board adopted pursuant to this Article, shall be guilty of a Class 2 misdemeanor. In addition, if any person continues to violate or further violates any provision of this Article after written notice from the Commissioner, the court may determine that each day during which the violation continued or is repeated constitutes a separate violation subject to the foregoing penalties.

(b) Nothing in this Article shall be construed as requiring the Commissioner to: (i) report for prosecution, or (ii) institute seizure proceedings, or (iii) issue a "stop sale" or "withdrawal from distribution" order, as a result of minor violations of the Article, or when he believes the public interest will best be served by suitable notice of warning in writing to the registrant or the person whose name and address appears on the labeling.

(c) It shall be the duty of each district attorney to whom any violation is reported to cause appropriate proceedings to be instituted and prosecuted in a court of competent jurisdiction without delay.

(d) The Commissioner is hereby authorized to apply for and the court to grant a temporary restraining order and a preliminary or permanent injunction restraining any person from violating or continuing to violate any of the provisions of this Article or any rules or regulations promulgated under the Article notwithstanding the existence of other remedies at law.

(e) Any person adversely affected by an act, order, or ruling made pursuant to the provisions of this Article may within 30 days thereafter bring action in the Superior Court of Wake County for judicial review of such act, order or ruling according to the provisions of Article 33 of Chapter 143 of the General Statutes. (1949, c. 1165; 1973, c. 47, s. 2; 1975, c. 719, s. 12; 1993, c. 539, s. 807; 1994, Ex. Sess., c. 24, s. 14(c).)

§ 106-579.13. Publications.

(a) The Commission [Commissioner] may publish or furnish, upon request, a list of the brands and classes or types of antifreeze inspected by the State Chemist during the fiscal year which have been found to be in accord with this Article and for which a license or permit for sale has been issued.

(b) The Commissioner may cause to be published from time to time reports summarizing all judgments, decrees, and court orders which have been rendered under this Article including the nature of the charge and the disposition thereof.

(c) The Commissioner may also cause to be disseminated such information regarding antifreezes as he deems necessary in the interest of protection of the public. Nothing in this section shall be construed to prohibit the Commissioner from collecting, reporting, and illustrating the results of the investigations of the Department. (1975, c. 719, s. 13.)

§ 106-579.14. Exclusive jurisdiction.

Jurisdiction in all matters pertaining to the distribution, sale and transportation of antifreeze by this Article are vested exclusively in the Board and Commissioner. (1975, c. 719, s. 15.)

Article 52.

Agricultural Development.

§ 106-580. Short title.

This Article may be cited as the "Agricultural Development Act." (1959, c. 1177, s. 1.)

§ 106-581. Intent and purpose.

It is hereby declared to be the intent and purpose of this Article to provide for a plan of assistance to the farmers and other citizens of this State in increasing agricultural income by making available to the various counties of the State the full resources of the Agricultural Extension Service, and other facilities, within the said counties, by means of the Farm and Home Development Program and the Rural Development Program as authorized by Title 7, United States Code, and other existing agricultural agencies. (1959, c. 1177, s. 2.)

§ 106-581.1. Agriculture defined.

For purposes of this Article, the terms "agriculture", "agricultural", and "farming" refer to all of the following:

(1) The cultivation of soil for production and harvesting of crops, including but not limited to fruits, vegetables, sod, flowers and ornamental plants.

(2) The planting and production of trees and timber.

(3) Dairying and the raising, management, care, and training of livestock, including horses, bees, poultry, and other animals for individual and public use, consumption, and marketing.

(4) Aquaculture as defined in G.S. 106-758.

(5) The operation, management, conservation, improvement, and maintenance of a farm and the structures and buildings on the farm, including building and structure repair, replacement, expansion, and construction incident to the farming operation.

(6) When performed on the farm, "agriculture", "agricultural", and "farming" also include the marketing and selling of agricultural products, agritourism, the storage and use of materials for agricultural purposes, packing, treating, processing, sorting, storage, and other activities performed to add value to crops, livestock, and agricultural items produced on the farm, and similar activities incident to the operation of a farm.

(7) A public or private grain warehouse or warehouse operation where grain is held 10 days or longer and includes, but is not limited to, all buildings, elevators, equipment, and warehouses consisting of one or more warehouse sections and considered a single delivery point with the capability to receive, load out, weigh, dry, and store grain. (1991, c. 81, s. 1; 2005-390, s. 18; 2006-255, s. 6; 2013-347, s. 2.)

§ 106-582. Counties authorized to utilize facilities to promote programs.

The several counties of this State are hereby authorized to utilize the facilities of existing extension and other agricultural advisory committees for the purpose of installing and promoting the Farm and Home Development Program and/or the Rural Development Program, or other program within the purview of this Article, in the said counties; or, the several counties may, within their discretion, with the cooperation of the Agricultural Extension Service, create such new additional committees as may be needed for this purpose. (1959, c. 1177, s. 3.)

§ 106-583. Policy of State; cooperation of departments and agencies with Agricultural Extension Service.

It is declared to be the policy of the State of North Carolina to promote the efficient production and utilization of the products of the soil as essential to the health and welfare of our people and to promote a sound and prosperous agriculture and rural life as indispensable to the maintenance of maximum prosperity. For the attainment of these objectives the North Carolina Department of Agriculture and Consumer Services, the School of Agriculture of North Carolina College and each and every other department and agency of the State of North Carolina is hereby empowered to cooperate with the Agricultural Extension Service and the committees authorized by this Article to provide: Development of new and improved methods of production, marketing, distribution, processing and utilization of plant and animal commodities at all stages from the original producer through to the ultimate consumer; development of present, new, and extended uses and markets for agricultural commodities and by-products as food or in commerce, manufacture or trade; introduction and breeding of new and useful agricultural crops, plants and animals, particularly those plants and crops which may be adapted to utilization in chemical and manufacturing industries; research, counsel and advice on new and more profitable uses of our resources of agricultural manpower, soils, plants, animals and equipment than those to which they are now devoted; methods of conservation, development, and use of land, forest, and water resources for agricultural purposes; guidance in the design, development, and more efficient and satisfactory use of farm buildings, farm homes, farm machinery, including the application of electricity, water and other forms of power; techniques relating to the diversification of farm enterprises, both as to the type of commodities produced, and as to the types of operations performed, on the individual farm; and assistance in appraising opportunities for making fuller use of the natural, human and community resources in the various counties of this State to the end that the income and level of living of rural people be increased. (1959, c. 1177, s. 4; 1997-261, s. 109; 1997-443, s. 11A.118(a).)

§ 106-584. Maximum use of existing research facilities.

In effectuating the purposes of this Article, maximum use may be made of existing research facilities owned or controlled by the State of North Carolina or by the federal government and of the facilities of the State and federal extension services. (1959, c. 1177, s. 5.)

§ 106-585. Appropriations by counties; funds made available by Congress.

The several counties of this State are hereby authorized to make such appropriations and expend such funds as shall be necessary to defray any part of the expenses of the programs authorized by this Article, including the salaries of the extension agents, special agents and other necessary personnel, and any funds made available by the Congress of the United States for this purpose may be accepted and used therefor. (1959, c. 1177, s. 6.)

§ 106-586. Authority granted by Article supplementary.

The authority granted by this Article is in addition to that granted to the Extension Service by the Congress of the United States and in no way infringes upon the administrative authority of the director of the Extension Service or the existing policies of the Extension Service. (1959, c. 1177, s. 7.)

§ 106-587. Local appropriations.

Each county and city in this State is authorized to make appropriations for the purposes of this Article and to fund them by levy of property taxes pursuant to G.S. 153A-149 and G.S. 160A-209 and by the allocation of other revenues whose use is not otherwise restricted by law. (1959, c. 1177, s. 8; 1973, c. 803, s. 10.)

§§ 106-588 through 106-600. Reserved for future codification purposes.

Article 53.

Grain Dealers.

§ 106-601. Definitions.

(a) "Cash buyer" means any grain dealer who pays the producer, or his representative at the time of obtaining title, possession or control of grain, the full agreed price of such grain in coin or currency, lawful money of the United States, certified checks, cashier's checks or drafts issued by a bank.

(b) "Commissioner" means the North Carolina Commissioner of Agriculture.

(c) "Department" means the North Carolina Department of Agriculture and Consumer Services.

(d) "Grain" as used herein shall be construed to include, but not by way of limitation, corn, wheat, rye, oats, sorghum, barley, mixed grain and soybeans.

(e) "Grain dealer" means any person owning, controlling or operating an elevator, mill, warehouse or other similar structure or truck or tractor-trailer unit or both who buys, solicits for sale or resale, processes for sale or resale, contracts for storage or exchange, or transfers grain of a North Carolina producer. The term "grain dealer" shall exclude producers or groups of producers buying grain for consumption on their farms.

(f) "Person" means an individual, partnership, corporation, association, syndicate or other legal entity.

(g) "Producer" means the owner, tenant or operator of land in this State who has an interest in and receives all or any part of the proceeds from the sale of the grain produced thereon. (1973, c. 665, s. 1; 1997-261, s. 109.)

§ 106-602. License required.

No person shall act or hold himself out as a grain dealer without first having obtained a license as herein provided. (1973, c. 665, s. 2.)

§ 106-603. Application for license or renewal thereof.

Every grain dealer before transacting business within the State of North Carolina shall on or before July 1, 1974, and annually on or before June 15 of each year thereafter, file a written application for a license or for the renewal of a license with the Commissioner. The application shall be on a form furnished by the Commissioner and shall contain the following information:

(1) The name and address of the applicant and that of its local agent or agents, if any, and the location of its principal place of business within this State.

(2) The kinds of grain the applicant proposes to handle.

(3) The type of grain business proposed to be conducted. (1973, c. 665, s. 3.)

§ 106-604. License fee; bond required; exemption.

All applications shall be accompanied by an initial or renewal license fee of fifty dollars ($50.00) plus thirty dollars ($30.00) per certificate or decal for each separate buying station or truck and a good and sufficient bond in the amount of one hundred thousand dollars ($100,000) to satisfy the initial license application. A fee of five dollars ($5.00) shall be charged for each duplicate license, certificate or decal. "Cash buyers" upon written request to the Commissioner showing proof satisfactory to the Commissioner that the person is a "cash buyer" under this Article shall be exempted from the bonding requirements of this section. The exemption shall be granted within 20 days of the receipt of the exemption request or unless the Commissioner requests the dealer to provide additional necessary information or unless the request is denied. (1973, c. 665, s. 4; 1989, c. 544, s. 1; 2013-102, s. 1.)

§ 106-605. Execution, terms and form of bond; action on bond.

(a) Such bond shall be signed by the grain dealer and by a company authorized to execute surety bonds in North Carolina and shall be made payable to the State of North Carolina. The bond shall be conditioned on the grain dealer's faithful performance of his duties as a grain dealer and his compliance with this Article, and shall be for the use and benefit of any person from whom the grain dealer has purchased grain and who has not been paid by the grain dealer. The bond shall be given for the period for which the grain dealer's license is issued.

(b) Any person claiming to be injured by nonpayment, fraud, deceit, negligence or other misconduct of a grain dealer may institute a suit or suits against said grain dealer and his sureties upon the bond in the name of the State, without any assignment thereof. (1973, c. 665, s. 5; 1979, c. 589, s. 1.)

§ 106-606. Posting of license; decal on truck, etc.

The grain dealer license shall be posted in a conspicuous place in the place of business. In the case of a licensee operating a truck or tractor-trailer unit, the licensee is required to have a decal that the license is in effect and that a bond has been filed, such decal to be carried in each truck or tractor-trailer unit used in connection with the purchase of grain from producers. (1973, c. 665, s. 6.)

§ 106-607. Renewal of license.

Licenses shall be renewed upon application and payment of renewal fees on or before the fifteenth day of June following the date of expiration of any license hereunder issued. Applications received after June 15 of any year shall be subject to a late filing fee of twenty dollars ($20.00) in addition to other applicable fees. (1973, c. 665, s. 7; 1989, c. 544, s. 3.)

§ 106-608. Disposition of fees.

All fees payable under this Article shall be collected by the North Carolina Department of Agriculture and Consumer Services for the administration of this Article. (1973, c. 665, s. 8; 1997-261, s. 109.)

§ 106-609. Records to be kept by dealers; uniform scale ticket.

It shall be the duty of every person doing business as a grain dealer in this State to keep records of grain transactions for reasonable periods of time and in accordance with good business practices.

The Board of Agriculture may, by regulation, require the use of, and prescribe the form of a uniform scale ticket by all grain dealers. (1973, c. 665, s. 9; 1983, c. 482.)

§ 106-610. Grounds for refusal, suspension or revocation of license.

The Commissioner may refuse to grant or renew any license, may suspend or may revoke any license upon a showing by substantial and competent evidence of any of the following:

(1) The dealer has suffered a final money judgment to be entered against him and such judgment remains unsatisfied.

(2) The dealer has failed to promptly and properly account and pay for grain.

(3) The dealer has failed to keep and maintain business records of his grain transactions as required by this Article.

(4) The dealer has engaged in fraudulent or deceptive practices in the transaction of his business as a dealer.

(5) The dealer has failed to collect from a producer and remit to the Commissioner of Agriculture such assessments as have been approved by the producers and are required to be collected under the provisions of Article 50 of Chapter 106 of the General Statutes.

(6) The dealer or applicant has been convicted, pled guilty or nolo contendere within three years in any state or federal court of a crime involving moral turpitude.

(7) The dealer has failed either to file the required bond or to keep such bond in force.

(8) The applicant has acted or held himself or herself out as a grain dealer without first having obtained a license under the provisions of this Article.

(9) The dealer has hired a person who has been convicted of a crime involving fraud, deceit, or misrepresentation in any capacity involving the buying or selling of grain, or the handling of payments for grain.

(10) The dealer or applicant has violated any provision of this Article or rules adopted pursuant to this Article. (1973, c. 665, s. 10; 1979, c. 589, s. 2; 2013-102, s. 2.)

§ 106-611. Procedure for denial, suspension, or revocation of license; effect of revocation.

(a) A denial, suspension, or revocation of a license under this Article shall be made in accordance with Chapter 150B of the General Statutes.

(b) A license may not be suspended for more than one year. A person whose license is revoked may not obtain another license under this Article until at least two years have elapsed from the date of the final decision revoking the license or, if the decision is appealed, from the date of the final judgment sustaining the revocation. (1973, c. 611, s. 11; c. 1331, s. 3; 1987, c. 827, s. 38.)

§ 106-612. Commissioner's authority to investigate.

In furtherance of any such investigation, inspection or hearing, the Commissioner or his duly authorized agent shall have full authority to make any and all necessary investigations relative to the complaint or matter being investigated; and they shall have free and unimpeded access during normal business hours to all buildings, yards, warehouses, storage and transportation facilities in which grain is kept, stored, handled, or transported, or where records of grain transactions are kept. (1973, c. 665, s. 12.)

§ 106-613. Rules and regulations.

The Board of Agriculture may adopt such rules and regulations as may be necessary to carry out the administration and enforcement of this Article. (1973, c. 665, s. 13.)

§ 106-614. Violation a misdemeanor.

Any person who violates any provision of this Article or any rule or regulation of the Board of Agriculture promulgated hereunder shall be guilty of a Class 2 misdemeanor. In case of a continuing violation or violations, each day and each violation occurring constitutes a separate and distinct offense. (1973, c. 665, s. 14; 1993, c. 539, s. 808; 1994, Ex. Sess., c. 24, s. 14(c).)

§ 106-615. Operation without license unlawful; injunction for violation.

It shall be unlawful for any person to be a grain dealer without securing a license as herein provided. In addition to the criminal penalties provided for herein, the Commissioner of Agriculture may apply to any superior court judge and the court may temporarily restrain or preliminarily or permanently enjoin any violation of this Article. (1973, c. 665, s. 15.)

§§ 106-616 through 106-620. Reserved for future codification purposes.

Article 54.

Adulteration of Grains.

§ 106-621. Definitions.

For purposes of this Article, the following words or terms shall mean as follows:

(1) Adulterated grain: Grain which contains any substance, such as, but not limited to, Captan, carbon tetrachloride, Malathion, Parathion, DDT, Dieldrin, Thiram, Endrin, Heptachlor, Maneb, Methoxychlor, 2, 6-dichloro, 4-nitroaniline, pentachloronitrobenzene, hexachlorobenzene, Demeton, Phorate, Carbophenothion, in excess of the tolerance for human or animal consumption established for such substances by the laws of the State or the regulations of the North Carolina Department of Agriculture and Consumer Services, or both the State and the Department.

(2) Commissioner: North Carolina Commissioner of Agriculture.

(3) Grain: Corn, soybeans, milo, barley, oats, rye, and mixtures of them.

(4) Grain dealer: Any person owning, controlling or operating an elevator, mill, warehouse or other similar structure or truck or tractor-trailer unit or both who buys, solicits for sale or resale, processes for sale or resale, contracts for storage or exchange or transfers grain after obtaining title to the grain of a North Carolina producer. The term "grain dealer" shall exclude producers, groups of producers, or contract feeders buying grain for consumption in their operations.

(5) Person: Any individual, partnership, corporation, association, syndicate or other legal entity. (1975, c. 659, s. 1; 1997-261, s. 109.)

§ 106-622. Prohibited acts.

It shall be unlawful for any person to commit a prohibited act under G.S. 106-122 with adulterated grain as defined in this Article and as the particular grain qualifies as adulterated food under G.S. 106-129. (1975, c. 659, s. 2.)

§ 106-623. Penalty.

Any person violating the provisions of this Article shall be subject to the provisions of G.S. 106-123, 106-124 and 106-125. (1975, c. 659, s. 3.)

§ 106-624. Sign furnished by Commissioner.

It shall be the duty of the Commissioner to cause to be prepared and furnished for a fee of ten dollars ($10.00) each to all grain dealers, as defined in this Article, in the State a sign not less than 11 x 15 inches, which shall contain information that it is a violation of law for any person to sell, offer for sale or deliver adulterated grain. Said sign shall also set out the penalties for violation of this Article. Duplicate signs, and replacement for signs lost, stolen, worn or otherwise unusable, shall be purchased from the Department of Agriculture and Consumer Services for a fee of five dollars ($5.00) per sign. (1975, c. 659, s. 4; 1989, c. 544, s. 2; 1997-261, s. 109.)

§ 106-625. Posting of sign.

It shall be the duty of the owner, manager, or person in charge of the elevator, mill, warehouse or other similar structure to post in a conspicuous place, in view of the public, a sign or signs furnished to the grain dealer by the Commissioner pursuant to this Article. (1975, c. 659, s. 5.)

§ 106-626. Nonposting not a defense.

It shall not be a defense to a prosecution under this Article that the sign required to be posted by G.S. 106-625 hereof was not posted on the date of the alleged violation. (1975, c. 659, s. 6.)

§ 106-627. Determination of adulteration.

For purposes of evidence under this Article, the grain dealer or his agent, upon receipt or pending receipt of suspected adulterated grain, may, at his discretion, call any law-enforcement officer to verify the sampling technique, [and] origin of sampled grain and subsequently send or request the law-enforcement officer to send the sample of grain in a sealed package to the Department of Agriculture and Consumer Services for inspection and analysis in order to protect only the chain of evidence.

Upon [a] finding by the Department that said sample is adulterated grain, the Department shall notify the grain dealer of the results and return the sample to the original sender in a sealed package. (1975, c. 659, s. 7; 1997-261, s. 66.)

§ 106-628. Applicability of Article.

The terms of this Article shall not apply to grain sold, offered for sale or delivered for purposes of planting. (1975, c. 659, s. 8.)

§§ 106-629 through 106-633. Reserved for future codification purposes.

Article 55.

North Carolina Bee and Honey Act of 1977.

§ 106-634. Declaration of policy.

The General Assembly hereby declares that it is in the public interest to promote and protect the bee and honey industry in North Carolina and to authorize the Commissioner of Agriculture and the Board of Agriculture to perform services and conduct activities to promote, improve, and enhance the bee and honey industry in North Carolina particularly relative to small beekeepers; to regulate all bees of the superfamily Apoidea in any stage of development; the causal agents of their disease or disorders, and their pests; to protect the bee and honey industry in North Carolina from bee diseases and disorders and to provide regulatory services in the areas of pollination of plants, honeybee poisonings, thefts, bee management and marketing. (1977, c. 238, s. 1.)

§ 106-635. Definitions.

As used in this Article:

(1) The term "apiary" means bees, comb, hives, appliances, or colonies, wherever they are kept, located, or found.

(2) The term "bee(s)" means insects of the superfamily Apoidea; in particular, the honeybees, Apis mellifera (L). It includes all life stages of such insects, their genetic material, and dead remains.

(3) The term "beeyard" means a location or site where bees are located in hives.

(4) The term "Board" means the North Carolina Board of Agriculture.

(5) The term "Brazilian or African bee" means bees of the subspecies Apis mellifera Adansonii and their progeny.

(6) The term "colony" means one hive and its contents, including bees, comb, and appliances.

(7) The term "comb" includes all materials which are normally deposited into hives by bees. It does not include extracted honey or royal jelly, trapped pollen, and processed beeswax.

(8) The term "commercial beekeeper" means a beekeeper who owns or operates 200 or more colonies of bees, or a beekeeper who moves bees across state lines.

(9) The term "Commissioner" means the North Carolina Commissioner of Agriculture or his designated agents.

(10) The term "Department" means the North Carolina Department of Agriculture and Consumer Services.

(11) The term "disease" means any infectious disease, parasite, or pest that detrimentally affects bees.

(12) The term "disorder" means any disease, poisoning, pest, parasite, or predator damage, toxic substance injury, or undesirable trait or genetic strain of the bee that detrimentally affects bees or the bee and honey industry.

(13) The term "exposed" means having been in circumstances where the possibility of infection or damage by a disease or disorder occurred. Bees in an

apiary where disease or disorder is present or where there has been an exchange of equipment with a diseased apiary may be considered exposed.

(14) The term "health certificate" means a statement issued by the State Entomologist certifying that bees or regulated articles are apparently free of disease or disorder based on an inspection or freedom from exposure to disease or disorder.

(15) The term "hive" means any receptacle or container, or part of receptacle or container, which is made or prepared for the use of bees, or which is inhabited by bees.

(16) The term "honey" means for the purpose of defining honey as a regulated article in the control of bee diseases or disorders, the natural food product made by the honeybees from the nectar of flowers, the saccharine exudation of plants, honeydew, sugar, corn syrup, or any other material along with any adulterants.

(17) The term "honeybees" means honey-producing insects of the genus Apis.

(18) The term "honeyflow" means the seasonal yielding of nectar by honey plants.

(19) The term "honey plants" means blooming plants from which bees gather nectar or pollen.

(20) The term "infested or infected" means showing symptoms of or having been exposed to the causal agent of a bee disease or disorder to such a degree that there is a possibility of the infected organisms or material transmitting the disease or disorder to other bees.

(21) The term "moveable frame hive" means any hive where the frames can be removed without damaging the comb.

(22) The term "permit" means an authorization to allow movement or other action involving bees or regulated articles.

(23) The term "regulated article" means any bees, bee equipment, comb, beeswax, honey, pollen, causal agents of disease, toxic substances, products of

the hive, containers, and any other item regulated under this Article or pursuant regulations.

(24) The term "symptomless carrier" means to possess or bear a disease or disorder in a suppressed state having the potential for spreading the disease or disorder. (1977, c. 238, s. 2; 1997-261, s. 67.)

§ 106-636. Powers and duties of Commissioner generally.

The Commissioner shall promote the bee and honey industry in North Carolina. The Commissioner may perform services, cooperate in research activities, conduct investigations, publish information and cooperate with the beekeeping industry to protect and improve beekeeping in North Carolina. He may work toward enhancing honey plants and improving honeybees. He may investigate thefts of honeybees, equipment or products; cooperate in preventative measures; and assist in prosecution of suspects. (1977, c. 238, s. 3.)

§ 106-637. Authority of Board to accept gifts, enter contracts, etc.

The Board is authorized to accept gifts, grants, or donations from any source for the purpose of promoting and protecting the bee and honey industry. The Board is authorized to issue grants or enter contracts or agreements for the furtherance of the purpose of this Article. (1977, c. 238, s. 4.)

§ 106-638. Authority of Board to adopt regulations, standards, etc.

The Board may adopt regulations and set procedures for the purpose of carrying out the provisions of this Article. The Board may adopt minimum standards for colony strength and disease tolerance levels for hives rented for pollination of crops, and the Commissioner shall certify hives meeting those standards. The Board may adopt regulations to regulate or prohibit entrance into North Carolina of bees or regulated articles to protect the bee and honey industry from bee diseases, disorders, overcrowding of honey pasture, or other encroachments deemed by the Board not to be in the best interest of the beekeepers of North Carolina. The Board may adopt regulations relating to, but shall not be limited to, providing for inspection of bees; and surveying and developing regulations to control, eradicate, abate, prevent exposure to, or prevent the introduction of or movement into or within North Carolina of bee diseases, disorders, pests or enemies of bees; or products that are a threat to beekeeping in North Carolina. The diseases, disorders, and products regulated shall include, but not be confined to bee diseases, poisons, bee pests, pollen, causal agents of disease, bee parasites and predators and toxic substances. The Board may regulate undesirable species or strains of bees including but not limited to Brazilian or African strains of bees. Regulations may include articles, exposed to infection or infestation, bees, honey, honeycomb, beeswax, beeswax refuse, royal jelly, containers, and beekeeping equipment to include sale, exposure and shipment of said and like items. The Board may adopt regulations governing beeyards or sites of commercial beekeepers. The Board is authorized to adopt regulations and set fees for extra or special inspections, issuance of certificates, permits, registrations, and regulatory activities. (1977, c. 238, s. 5.)

§ 106-639. Regulations for control and prevention of diseases and disorders.

The Board may adopt regulations and procedures for the disposition of bees infected or infested with diseases or disorders, beekeeping equipment, and other regulated articles kept or moved in violation of this Article and pursuant regulations. Such regulations may authorize the Commissioner to quarantine, destroy, confiscate, or otherwise dispose of, eradicate, establish cleanup areas, and require owners to disinfect, fumigate, treat with drugs, or destroy bees or articles at their own expense or to take measures to eradicate bee diseases or disorders.

The Board shall have authority to either allow, require, or forbid use of drugs in the control of bee diseases or disorders, and may define as infested or infected symptomless carriers of a disease or disorder, declare bees that have been treated with disease-masking drugs to be infested or infected, and consider bees or articles which have been exposed to a disease or disorder to be infected or infested.

The Board may also adopt regulations governing beeswax salvage operations and honey house sanitation for disease prevention. (1977, c. 238, s. 6.)

§ 106-639.1. Permit to sell bees.

Prior to selling bees in North Carolina, a person shall obtain a permit from the Commissioner. Application for the permit shall be made on a form provided by the Commissioner, and shall be accompanied by a nonrefundable fee of twenty-five dollars ($25.00). The Commissioner may deny, suspend, or revoke a permit for any violation of this Article or rules adopted to implement the Article. Permits shall expire annually on December 31 and may be renewed upon payment of a fee of twenty-five dollars ($25.00). All proceedings concerning the denial, suspension, or revocation of a permit shall be conducted in accordance with the Administrative Procedure Act, Chapter 150B of the General Statutes. No permit shall be required for (i) the sale of less than 10 bee hives in a calendar year, (ii) a one-time going-out-of-business sale of less than 50 bee hives, or (iii) the renting of bees for pollination purposes or the movement of bees to gather honey. (1991, c. 349, s. 1.)

§ 106-640. Authority of Commissioner to protect industry from diseases and disorders, etc.

The Commissioner shall protect the bee and honey industry from diseases and disorders of the honeybee (Apis mellifera) and other insects in the superfamily (Apoidea) and shall provide services and enforce provisions of this Article and pursuant regulations. The Commissioner may adopt regulations for prohibiting or regulating the movement of bees and regulated articles into and from quarantine or cleanup areas and enforce procedures for control and cleanup of diseases or disorders in such areas.

The Commissioner is authorized to establish postentry quarantines and issue hold orders for inspection of bees or regulated articles imported into North Carolina. (1977, c. 238, s. 7.)

§ 106-641. Giving false information to Commissioner; hives; certificates, permits, etc.

It is unlawful to knowingly give false information to the Commissioner concerning diseased bees or bees exposed to disease, their treatment, or disposition.

The Commissioner may require that bees be kept in moveable frame hives and be maintained in an inspectable condition or in other hives where an inspection for disease or disorder can be readily made.

The Board may adopt regulations for issuance of health certificates, moving permits, and the registration of honeybees and may require marking or identification of honeybee colonies or apiaries. (1977, c. 238, s. 8.)

§ 106-642. Emergency action by Commissioner.

The Commissioner may take emergency action with respect to Board authority in the provisions of this Article if needed to protect the bee and honey industry in North Carolina. Such action shall remain in force until rescinded by the Commissioner or acted on by the Board. (1977, c. 238, s. 9.)

§ 106-643. Designation of persons to administer Article; inspections, etc.

The Commissioner shall have the authority to designate such employees of the Department or persons collaborating with the Department as may seem expedient to carry out the duties and exercise the powers provided by this Article. The Commissioner is authorized to survey or inspect premises for the presence of bees or other regulated articles, inspect colonies for bee diseases and disorders, and otherwise enforce the provisions of this Article and pursuant regulations. The Commissioner or his designated agent shall have authority to inspect vehicles or other means of transportation and their cargo suspected of carrying bees or regulated articles, and enter upon any premises to inspect any bees or regulated articles to determine the presence or absence of diseases or disorders.

Such inspections and other activities may be conducted with the permission of the owner or person in charge. If permission is denied the Commissioner or his designated agent, such inspections and other activities may be conducted in a reasonable manner, with a warrant, with respect to any premises or vehicles. Such warrant shall be issued pursuant to Article 4A of Chapter 15. A superior court or district court judge may issue confiscation orders on any bees or articles for which confiscation is authorized in this Article or pursuant regulations. (1977, c. 238, s. 10.)

§ 106-644. Penalties.

(a) If anyone shall attempt to prevent inspection as provided in this Article or shall otherwise interfere with the Commissioner of Agriculture, or any of his agents, while engaging in the performance of his duties under this Article, or shall violate any provisions of this Article or any regulation of the Board of Agriculture adopted pursuant to this Article, he shall be guilty of a Class 3 misdemeanor. Each day's violation shall constitute a separate offense.

(b) The Commissioner may assess a civil penalty of not more than ten thousand dollars ($10,000) against a person who violates this Article or a rule adopted to implement this Article. In determining the amount of the penalty, the Commissioner shall consider the degree and extent of harm caused by the violation. No civil penalty may be assessed under this section unless the person has been given the opportunity for a hearing pursuant to the Administrative Procedure Act, Chapter 150B of the General Statutes. If not paid within 30 days after the effective date of a final decision by the Commissioner, the penalty may be collected by any lawful means for the collection of a debt.

The clear proceeds of civil penalties assessed pursuant to this subsection shall be remitted to the Civil Penalty and Forfeiture Fund in accordance with G.S. 115C-457.2. (1977, c. 238, s. 11; 1991, c. 349, s. 2; 1993, c. 539, s. 809; 1994, Ex. Sess., c. 24, s. 14(c); 1998-215, s. 20.)

§§ 106-645 through 106-654. Reserved for future codification purposes.

Article 56.

North Carolina Commercial Fertilizer Law.

§ 106-655. Short title.

This Article shall be known as the "North Carolina Commercial Fertilizer Law." (1977, c. 303, s. 1.)

§ 106-656. Purpose of Article.

The purpose of this Article shall be to assure the manufacturer, distributor, and consumer of the correct quality and quantity of all commercial fertilizer sold in this State, and to assure the safe handling of fluid fertilizers. (1977, c. 303, s. 2.)

§ 106-657. Definitions.

When used in this Article:

(1) The term "brand name" means the name under which any individual mixed fertilizer or fertilizer material is offered for sale, and may include a trademark, but shall not include any numeral other than the grade of the fertilizer.

(2) The term "bulk fertilizer" means a commercial fertilizer distributed in non-package form.

(3) The term "commercial fertilizer" includes both fluid and dry mixed fertilizer and/or fertilizer materials.

(4) The term "contractor" means any person, firm, corporation, wholesaler, retailer, distributor or any other person, who for hire or reward applies commercial fertilizer to the soil or crop of a consumer; provided, that this shall not apply to any consumer applying commercial fertilizer to only the land or crop that he owns or to which he otherwise holds rights, for the production of his own crops.

(5) The term "distributor" means any person who offers for sale, sells, barters, or otherwise supplies mixed fertilizer or fertilizer materials.

(6) The term "fertilizer material" means any substance containing either nitrogen, phosphorus, potassium, or any other recognized plant food element or compound which is used primarily for its plant food content or for compounding mixed fertilizers. Not included in this definition are all types of unmanipulated animal and vegetable manures and mulches for which no plant food content is claimed.

(7) The term "fluid fertilizer" means a nonsolid commercial fertilizer.

(8) The term "fortified mulch" means substances composed primarily of plant remains or mixtures of such substances to which plant food has been added and for which plant food is claimed.

In "fortified mulches" the minimum percentages of total nitrogen, available phosphate and soluble or available potash are to be guaranteed and the guarantee stated in multiples of quarter (.25) percentages; provided, however, that such percentages shall not exceed one percent (1%), respectively, subject to the same limits and tolerances set forth in this Chapter.

(9) The term "grade" means the percentage of total nitrogen, available phosphate and soluble potash only stated in the order given in this subdivision, and, when applied to mixed fertilizers, shall be in whole numbers only for all packages larger than 16 ounces.

(10) The term "manipulated manures" means substances composed primarily of excreta, plant remains or mixtures of such substances which have been processed in any manner, including the addition of plant foods, artificially drying, grinding and other means.

In "manipulated manures" the minimum percentages of total nitrogen, available phosphate and soluble potash are to be guaranteed, and the guarantee stated in multiples of half (.50) percentages. Additions of plant food shall be limited to one-half (.50) percent each of nitrogen, phosphorus and potash.

(11) The term "manufacturer" means a person engaged in the business of preparing, mixing, or manufacturing commercial fertilizers or the person whose name appears on the label as being responsible for the guarantee. The term "manufacture" means preparing, mixing, or combining fertilizer materials chemically or physically, including the simultaneous application of two or more fertilizer materials, by a manufacturer or contract applicator.

(12) The term "mixed fertilizers" means products resulting from the combination, mixture, or simultaneous application of two or more fertilizer materials for use in, or claimed to have value in promoting plant growth.

(13) The term "mulch" means substances composed primarily of plant remains or mixtures of such substances to which no plant food has been added and for which no plant food is claimed.

(14) The term "natural organic fertilizer" means material derived from either plant or animal products containing one or more elements (other than carbon, hydrogen and oxygen) which are essential for plant growth. These materials may be subjected to biological degradation processes under normal conditions of aging, rainfall, sun-curing, air drying, composting, rotting, enzymatic, or anaerobic/aerobic bacterial action, or any combination of these. These materials shall not be mixed with synthetic materials, or changed in any physical or chemical manner from their initial state except by physical manipulations such as drying, cooking, chopping, grinding, shredding or pelleting.

(15) The term "official sample" means any sample of commercial fertilizer taken by the Commissioner or his authorized agent according to the method prescribed in subsection (b) of G.S. 106-662.

(16) The term "organic fertilizer" means a material containing carbon and one or more elements other than hydrogen and oxygen essential for plant growth.

(17) The term "percent" or "percentage" means the percentage by weight.

(18) The term "person" includes individuals, partnerships, associations, firms, agencies, and corporations, or other legal entity.

(19) The term "retailer" means any person who sells or delivers fertilizer to a consumer.

(20) The term "sale" means any transfer of title or possession, or both, exchange or barter of tangible personal property, conditional or otherwise for a consideration paid or to be paid, and this shall include any of said transactions whereby title or ownership is to pass and shall further mean and include any bailment, loan, lease, rental or license to use or consume tangible personal property for a consideration paid in which possession of said property passes to the bailee, borrower, lessee, or licensee.

(21) The term "sell" means the alienation, exchange, transfer or contract for such transfer of property for a fixed price in money or its equivalent.

(22) The term "specialty fertilizer" means any fertilizer distributed primarily for use on noncommercial crops such as gardens, lawns, shrubs, flowers, golf courses, cemeteries and nurseries.

(23) The term "ton" means a net ton of two thousand pounds avoirdupois.

(24) The term "unmanipulated manures" means substances composed primarily of excreta, plant remains or mixtures of such substances which have not been processed in any manner.

(25) The term "wholesaler" shall mean any person who sells to any other person for the purpose of resale, and who also may sell to a consumer.

(26) Words importing the singular number may extend and be applied to several persons or things, and words importing the plural number may include the singular.

(27) The term "fertilizer coated seed" means seed which has been coated with commercial fertilizer. (1947, c. 1086, s. 3; 1951, c. 1026, ss. 1, 2; 1955, c. 354, s. 1; 1959, c. 706, ss. 1, 2; 1961, c. 66, ss. 1, 2; 1977, c. 303, s. 3; 1981, c. 448, ss. 1-4; 1983, c. 146, s. 1; 1993, c. 216, s. 3.)

§ 106-658. Enforcing official.

This Article shall be administered by the Commissioner of Agriculture of the State of North Carolina, or his authorized agent, hereinafter referred to as the "Commissioner." (1947, c. 1086, s. 2; 1977, c. 303, s. 4.)

§ 106-659. Minimum plant food content.

Except as provided in this section, superphosphate containing less than eighteen percent (18%) available phosphate, or any mixed fertilizer in which the guarantees for the nitrogen, available phosphate, or soluble potash are in fractional percentages shall not be offered for sale, sold, or distributed in this State. Packages of 32 fluid ounces or less when in liquid form, or 32 ounces or less avoirdupois when in a dry form, may be sold in fractional percentages, but these packages are not exempt from any other requirements of this Article. (1947, c. 1086, s. 10; 1951, c. 1026, s. 7; 1973, c. 611, s. 6; 1975, c. 126; 1977, c. 303, s. 5; 1983, c. 146, s. 4; 1987, c. 292, s. 1; 1993, c. 216, s. 4; 2003-71, s. 1.)

§ 106-660. Registration of brands; licensing of manufacturers and distributors; fluid fertilizers.

(a) Each brand of commercial fertilizer for tobacco, specialty fertilizer, fertilizer materials, manipulated manure and fortified mulch shall be registered by the person whose name appears upon the label before being offered for sale, sold or distributed in this State, except those brands expressly produced for experimental and demonstration purposes only. Other fertilizers may be manufactured and sold without registration after obtaining a license as required in G.S. 106-661(a). The application for registration shall be submitted in duplicate to the Commissioner for his approval on forms furnished by the Commissioner, and shall include a fee of five dollars ($5.00) per brand and grade for all packages greater than five pounds. The registration fee for packages of five pounds or less shall be fifty-five dollars ($55.00). All approved registrations expire on June 30 of each year. The application shall include such information as deemed necessary by the Board of Agriculture.

(b) The distributor of any brand and grade of commercial fertilizer shall not be required to register the same if it has already been registered under this Article by a person entitled to do so and such registration is then outstanding.

(c) The grade of any brand of mixed fertilizer shall not be changed during the registration period, but the guaranteed analysis may be changed in other respects and the sources of materials may be changed: Provided, prompt notification of such change is given to the Commissioner and the change is noted on the container or tag: Provided, further, that the guaranteed analysis shall not be changed if it, in any way, lowers the quality of the fertilizer: Provided, further, that if at a subsequent registration period, the registrant desires to make any change in the registration of a given brand and grade of fertilizer, said registrant shall notify the Commissioner of such change 30 days in advance of such registration. If the Commissioner, after consultation with the director of the agricultural experiment station decides that such change materially lowers the crop producing value of the fertilizer, he shall notify the registrant of his conclusions, and if the registrant registers the brand and grade with the proposed changes, then the Commissioner shall give due publicity to said changes through the Agricultural Review or by such other means as he may deem advisable.

(d) Any person desiring to manufacture or distribute fertilizers not required to be registered shall first secure a license. Application for said license shall be made on forms provided by the Commissioner and shall be accompanied by a reasonable fee to be determined by the Board of Agriculture. The Board shall charge a maximum of one hundred dollars ($100.00) for said license. Said license shall be renewable annually on the first day of July. Said license may be suspended, revoked or terminated for a violation of this Article or any rule promulgated thereunder.

(e) When fluid fertilizer is offered for sale or sold in this State, the method of transfer of custody shall be by weight expressed in pounds, and shall be invoiced in such a manner as to show the name of the seller, the name of the purchaser, the date of sale, the grade, and the net weight; provided, however, that fluid fertilizer may be measured in gallons of 231 cubic inches and its equivalent expressed in pounds, with a formula for converting from gallons to pounds shown on the invoice.

(f) Repealed by Session Laws 1983, c. 146, s. 2.

(g) Before any anhydrous ammonia installation that handles, stores, distributes, or applies anhydrous ammonia for fertilizer use shall be built in this State, a general layout of the installation shall be submitted in duplicate and approved by the Commissioner. In order that the layout may be approved it must conform to the minimum standards and rules and regulations, relating to safe handling, storage, distribution, or application adopted by the Board of Agriculture. All storage tanks, transfer or transport containers, applicator containers, and attached equipment for fertilizer use shall conform to the minimum standards adopted by the Board of Agriculture. It shall be the duty of a contractor, as defined in G.S. 106-657 to obtain, maintain and operate in accordance with the minimum standards and rules and regulations adopted by the Board of Agriculture, any equipment that the contractor may use in the application of anhydrous ammonia. It shall be the duty of the Commissioner to inspect and ascertain whether or not the provisions of this section are complied with. (1947, c. 1086, s. 4; 1949, c. 637, s. 1; 1951, c. 1026, ss. 3-6; 1959, c. 706, ss. 3-5; 1961, c. 66, ss. 3, 4; 1973, c. 611, ss. 1-4; 1977, c. 303, s. 6; 1981, c. 448, ss. 5, 6; 1983, c. 146, ss. 2, 3; 1987, c. 292, s. 2; 1989, c. 544, s. 5; 2001-440, s. 2; 2013-360, s. 13.9(a).)

§ 106-661. Labeling.

(a) Any commercial fertilizer offered for sale, sold, or distributed in this State in bags, barrels, or other containers shall have placed on or affixed to the container the net weight and the data in written or printed form, required by G.S. 106-660(a), either (i) on tags to be affixed to the end of the package or (ii) directly on the package. In case the brand name appears on the package, the grade shall also appear on the package, immediately preceding the guaranteed analysis or as a part of the brand name. The size of the type of numerals indicating the grade on the containers shall not be less than two inches in height for containers of 100 pounds or more; not less than one inch for containers of 50 to 99 pounds; and not less than 1/2 inch for packages of 25 to 49 pounds. On packages of less than 25 pounds, the grade must appear in numerals at least one half as large as the letters in the brand name. In case of fertilizers sold in containers on which the brand name or other designations of the distributor do not appear, the grade must appear in a manner prescribed by the Commissioner on tags attached to the container.

(b)   If transported in bulk, the net weight and the data, in written or printed form, as required by G.S. 106-660(a), shall accompany delivery and be supplied to the purchaser.

(c)   If mixed fertilizer is sold or intended to be sold in bags weighing more than 100 pounds, each bag must have a tag attached thereto, of a type approved by the Commissioner, showing the grade of the fertilizer contained therein. Such tag must be attached on the end of each bag, approximately at the center of the sewed end of the bag: Provided, that in lieu of such tag the grade of the fertilizer may be printed on the end of the bag in readily legible numerals.

(d)   All labels and registrations shall carry identical guarantees for each fertilizer product requiring registration. (1947, c. 1086, s. 5; 1949, c. 637, s. 2; 1955, c. 354, s. 2; 1975, c. 127; 1977, c. 303, s. 7; 1981, c. 448, s. 7; 1989, c. 770, s. 28.)

§ 106-662. Sampling, inspection and testing.

(a)   It shall be the duty of the Commissioner to sample, inspect, make analysis of, and test commercial fertilizers offered for sale, sold, or distributed within the State at such time and place and to such an extent as he may deem necessary to determine whether such commercial fertilizers are in compliance with the provisions of this Article. The Commissioner is authorized with permission or under court warrant to enter upon any public or private premises during regular business hours or at any time business is being conducted therein in order to have access to commercial fertilizers subject to the provisions of this Article and the rules and regulations thereto.

(b) The methods of sampling shall be as follows:

(1) For the purposes of analysis by the Commissioner and for comparison with the guarantee supplied to the Commissioner in accordance with G.S. 106-660 and 106-661, the Commissioner, shall take an official sample of not less than one pound from containers of commercial fertilizer. No sample shall be taken from less than five containers. Portions shall be taken from containers as shown in the following table:

5 to 10 containers	all containers
11 to 20 containers	10 containers
21 to 40 containers	15 containers
above 40 containers	20 containers

Ten cores from bulk lots or as specified by the Association of Official Analytical Chemists (A.O.A.C.).

(2) A core sampler shall be used that removes a core from a bag or other container in a horizontal position from a corner to the diagonal corner at the other end of the package, and the cores taken shall be mixed, and if necessary, shall be reduced after thoroughly mixing, to the quantity of sample required. The composite sample taken from any lot of commercial fertilizer under the provisions of this subdivision shall be placed in a tight container and shall be forwarded to the Commissioner with proper identification marks.

(3) The Board of Agriculture may modify the provisions of this subsection to bring them into conformity with any changes that may hereafter be made in the official methods of and recommendations for sampling commercial fertilizers which shall have been adopted by the Association of Official Analytical Chemists or by the Association of American Plant Food Control Officials. Thereafter, such methods and recommendations shall be used in all sampling done in connection with the administration of this Article in lieu of those prescribed in subdivisions (1) and (2) of this subsection.

(4) All samples taken under the provisions of this section shall be taken from original unbroken bags or containers, the contents of which have not been damaged by exposure, water or otherwise; provided, that any commercial fertilizer offered for sale, sold or distributed in bulk may be sampled in a manner approved by the Commissioner.

(5) The Commissioner shall refuse to analyze all samples except those taken under the provisions of this section and no sample, unless so taken, shall be admitted as evidence in the trial of any suit or action wherein there is called into question the value or composition of any lot of commercial fertilizer distributed under the provisions of this Article.

(6) In the trial of any suit or action wherein there is called in question the value or composition of any lot of commercial fertilizer, a certificate signed by the fertilizer chemist and attested with the seal of the Department of Agriculture and Consumer Services, setting forth the analysis made by the chemist of the Department of any sample of said commercial fertilizer, drawn under the provisions of this section and analyzed by them under the provisions of the same, shall be prima facie proof that the lot of fertilizer represented by the sample was of the value and constituency shown by said analysis. And the said certificate of the chemist shall be admissible in evidence.

(c) The methods of analysis shall be those adopted as official by the Board of Agriculture and shall conform to sound laboratory practices as evidenced by methods prescribed by the Association of Official Analytical Chemists of the United States. In the absence of methods prescribed by the Board, the Commissioner shall prescribe the methods of analysis.

(d) The result of official analysis of any commercial fertilizer which has been found to be subject to penalty shall be forwarded by the Commissioner to the registrant at least 10 days before the report is submitted to the purchaser. If, during that period, no adequate evidence to the contrary is made available to the Commissioner, the report shall become official. Upon request the Commissioner shall furnish to the registrant a portion of any sample found subject to penalty.

(e) Any purchaser or consumer may take and have a sample of mixed fertilizer or fertilizer material analyzed for available plant food, if taken in accordance with the following rules and regulations:

(1) At least five days before taking a sample, the purchaser or consumer shall notify the manufacturer or seller of the brand in writing, at his permanent address, of his intention to take such a sample and shall request the manufacturer or seller to designate a representative to be present when the sample is taken.

(2) The sample shall be drawn in the presence of the manufacturer, seller, or representative designated by either party together with two disinterested adult persons; or in case the manufacturer, seller, or representative of either refuses or is unable to witness the drawing of such a sample, a sample may be drawn in the presence of three disinterested adult persons; provided, any such sample shall be taken with the same type of sampler as used by the inspector of the Department of Agriculture and Consumer Services in taking samples and shall be drawn, mixed, and divided, as directed in subdivisions (1), (2), (3), and (4) of subsection (b) of this section, except that the sample shall be divided into two parts each to consist of at least one pound. Each of these is to be placed into a separate, tight container, securely sealed, properly labeled, and one sent to the Commissioner for analysis and the other to the manufacturer. A certificate statement in a form which will be prescribed and supplied by the Commissioner must be signed by the parties taking and witnessing the taking of the sample. Such certificate is to be made and signed in duplicate and one copy sent to the Commissioner and the other to the manufacturer or seller of the brand sampled. The witnesses of the taking of any sample, as provided for in this section, shall be required to certify that such sample has been continuously under their observation from the taking of the sample up to and including the delivery of it to an express agency, a post office or to the office of the Commissioner.

(3) Samples drawn in conformity with the requirements of this section shall have the same legal status in the courts of the State, as those drawn by the Commissioner or any official inspector appointed by him as provided for in subsection (b) of this section.

(4) No suit for damages claimed to result from the use of any lot of mixed fertilizer or fertilizer material may be brought unless it shall be shown by an analysis of a sample taken and analyzed in accordance with the provisions of this Article, that the said lot of fertilizer as represented by a sample or samples taken in accordance with the provisions of this section does not conform to the provisions of this Article with respect to the composition of the mixed fertilizer or fertilizer material, unless it shall appear to the Commissioner that the manufacturer of the fertilizer in question has, in the manufacture of other goods offered in this State during such season, employed such ingredients as are

prohibited by the provisions of this Article, or unless it shall appear to the Commissioner that the manufacturer of such fertilizer has offered for sale during that season any kind of dishonest or fraudulent goods or unless it shall appear to the Commissioner that the manufacturer of the fertilizer in question, or a representative, agent or employee of the manufacturer, has violated any provisions of G.S. 106-663. (1947, c. 1086, s. 7; 1955, c. 354, s. 3; 1973, c. 1304, s. 1; 1977, c. 303, s. 8; 1981, c. 448, s. 8; 1997-261, ss. 68, 69.)

§ 106-663. False or misleading statements.

It shall be unlawful to make, in any manner whatsoever, any false or misleading statement or representation with regard to any commercial fertilizer offered for sale, sold, or distributed in this State, or to use any misleading or deceptive trademark or brand name in connection therewith. The Commissioner is authorized to refuse, suspend, revoke or terminate the license of any manufacturer or to refuse, suspend, revoke or terminate the registration of such commercial fertilizer for any violations of this section. (1947, c. 1086, s. 12; 1977, c. 303, s. 9; 1981, c. 448, s. 9.)

§ 106-664. Determination and publication of commercial values.

For the purpose of determining the commercial values to be applied under the provisions of G.S. 106-665, the Commissioner shall determine and publish annually the values per pound of nitrogen, available phosphate, and soluble potash in commercial fertilizers in this State. The values so determined and published shall be used in determining and assessing penalties. (1947, c. 1086, s. 9; 1977, c. 303, s. 10; 1993, c. 216, s. 5.)

§ 106-665. Plant food deficiency.

(a) The Commissioner, in determining for administrative purposes, whether any commercial fertilizer is deficient in plant food, shall be guided solely by the official sample as defined in subdivision (15) of G.S. 106-657, and as provided for in subsections (b), (c), and (d) of G.S. 106-662.

(b) If the analysis shall show that any commercial fertilizer falls short of the guaranteed analysis in any ingredient, a penalty shall be assessed in accordance with the following provisions:

(1) For total nitrogen, available phosphate, or available potash: A penalty of three times the value of the deficiency if the deficiency is in excess of the following investigational allowances.

Guarantee Percentage	Total Nitrogen	Available Phosphate	Soluble Potash Percentage
4 or less	0.49	0.67	0.41
5	0.51	0.67	0.43
6	0.52	0.67	0.47
7	0.54	0.68	0.53
8	0.55	0.68	0.60
9	0.57	0.68	0.65
10	0.58	0.69	0.70
12	0.61	0.69	0.79
14	0.63	0.70	0.87
16	0.67	0.70	0.94
18	0.70	0.71	1.01
20	0.73	0.72	1.08
22	0.75	0.72	1.15
24	0.78	0.73	1.21

26	0.81	0.73	1.27
28	0.83	0.74	1.33
30	0.86	0.75	1.39
32 or more	0.88	0.76	1.44

Provided that when the found relative value of a sample is equal to or exceeds the guaranteed relative value, an overage in primary nutrients may compensate for a deficiency in another primary nutrient up to 10% of the guarantee of the deficient nutrient, not to exceed two units. No compensation shall be allowed toward a deficiency if the overage does not compensate for the entire amount of the deficiency or if the deficiency exceeds 10% of the guarantee or the deficiency exceeds two units. If more than one primary nutrient is in penalty status, no compensation shall be allowed.

(2) Should the basicity or acidity as equivalent of calcium carbonate of any sample of fertilizer be found upon analysis to differ more than five percent (5%) (or 100 pounds of calcium carbonate equivalent per ton) from the guarantee, a penalty of fifty cents (50¢) per ton for each 50 pounds calcium carbonate equivalent, or fraction thereof in excess of the 100 pounds allowed, shall be assessed and paid as is prescribed in subsection (c) of this section.

(3) Chlorine: If the chlorine content of any lot of fertilizer branded for tobacco shall exceed the maximum amount guaranteed by more than 0.5 of one percent, a penalty shall be assessed equal to ten percent (10%) of the value of the fertilizer for each additional 0.5 of one percent of excess or fraction thereof.

(4) Water insoluble nitrogen: A penalty of three times the value of the deficiency shall be assessed, if such deficiency is in excess of 0.15 of one percent on goods guaranteed up to and including five-tenths percent; 0.20 of one percent on goods guaranteed from five-tenths percent to one percent; 0.30 of one percent on goods guaranteed from one percent to two percent; 0.50 of one percent on goods guaranteed above two percent and up to and including five percent; and 1.00 percent on goods guaranteed over five percent.

(5) Nitrate nitrogen: A penalty of three times the value of the deficiency shall be assessed if the deficiency shall exceed 0.20 of one percent for goods guaranteed up to and including five-tenths percent; 0.25 of one percent for

goods guaranteed from five-tenths to one percent; 0.30 of one percent for goods guaranteed from one to two percent; and 0.35 of one percent for goods guaranteed above two percent up to four percent. Tolerances for goods guaranteed above four percent shall be the same as for total nitrogen.

(6)   Total magnesium: If the magnesium content is as much as 0.2 unit plus 5 percent of the guarantee below the minimum amount guaranteed, a penalty of one dollar ($1.00) per ton shall be assessed for each 0.15 of one percent additional deficiency or fraction thereof.

(7)   Total calcium: If the calcium content is as much as 0.2 unit plus 5 percent of the guarantee below the minimum amount guaranteed, a penalty of one dollar ($1.00) per ton shall be assessed for each 0.35 of one percent additional deficiency or fraction thereof.

(8)   Sulfur: If the sulfur content is as much as 0.2 unit plus 5 percent of the guarantee below the minimum amount guaranteed in the case of all mixed fertilizers, including mixed fertilizers branded for tobacco, a penalty of one dollar ($1.00) per ton for each 0.50 of one percent additional excess or fraction thereof, shall be assessed.

(9)   Deficiencies or excesses in any other constituent or constituents covered under subdivisions (6) and (7), subsection (a), G.S. 106-660 which the registrant is required to or may guarantee shall be evaluated by the Commissioner and penalties therefor shall be prescribed by the Commissioner in fertilizer regulations.

(10)   For micro-nutrients as are not specifically covered in this Article, a tolerance of twenty-five percent (25%) of the guarantee will be allowed for each element, not to exceed 1/2 unit (.5%) on guarantees up to 15 units or percent and not to exceed one unit (1%) on guarantees above 15 units or percent.

(c)   All penalties assessed under this section shall be paid to the consumer of the lot of fertilizer represented by the sample analyzed within three months from the date of notice by the Commissioner to the distributor, receipts taken therefor, and promptly forwarded to the Commissioner; provided, that in no case shall the total assessed penalties exceed the commercial value of the goods to which it applies. If said consumer cannot be found, the clear proceeds of the penalty assessed shall be remitted to the Civil Penalty and Forfeiture Fund in accordance with G.S. 115C-457.2. Such sums as shall be found to be payable to consumers on lots of fertilizer against which said penalties were assessed shall not be subject to claim by the consumer after 12 months from the date of assessment. (1947, c. 1086, s. 8; 1955, c. 354, s. 4; 1977, c. 303, s. 11; 1983, c. 146, s. 5; 1993, c. 216, s. 6; 1997-261, s. 109; 1998-215, s. 21.)

§ 106-666. "Stop sale," etc., orders.

(a) When the Commissioner finds that a lot of commercial fertilizer is being offered or exposed for sale in violation of any of the provisions of this Article, the Commissioner shall issue and enforce a written or printed "stop sale, use, or removal" order to the owner or custodian of any lot of commercial fertilizer and shall cause the fertilizer to be held at a designated place until (i) the law has been complied with and the commercial fertilizer is released in writing by the Commissioner or (ii) the violation has been otherwise legally disposed of by written authority. The Commissioner shall release the commercial fertilizer so withdrawn when the requirements of the provisions of this Article have been complied with and upon payment of all costs and expenses incurred in connection with the withdrawal.

(b) If any manufacturer, dealer, or agent fails to pay a penalty owed on commercial fertilizer within 90 days after notice of assessment by the Commissioner, the Commissioner may issue and enforce a written or printed "stop sale, use, or removal" order to that manufacturer, dealer, or agent and shall cause any commercial fertilizer distributed and offered by that manufacturer, dealer, or agent for sale in the State to be held until (i) the penalties are paid in full and the commercial fertilizer is released in writing by the Commissioner or (ii) the penalties have been otherwise legally disposed of by written authority. The Commissioner shall release the commercial fertilizer so withdrawn when the requirements of the provisions of this Article have been complied with and upon payment of all costs and expenses incurred in connection with the withdrawal. (1947, c. 1086, s. 18; 1955, c. 354, s. 5; 1977, c. 303, s. 12; 1993, c. 216, s. 1.)

§ 106-667. Seizure, condemnation and sale.

Any lot of commercial fertilizer not in compliance with the provisions of this Article shall be subject to seizure on complaint of the Commissioner to a court of competent jurisdiction in the area in which said commercial fertilizer is located.

In the event the court finds the said commercial fertilizer to be in violation of this Article and orders the condemnation of said commercial fertilizer, it shall be disposed of in any manner consistent with the quality of the commercial fertilizer and the laws of the State; provided, that in no instance shall the disposition of said commercial fertilizer be ordered by the court without first giving the claimant an opportunity to apply to the court for the release of said commercial fertilizer or for permission to process or relabel said commercial fertilizer to bring it into compliance with this Article. (1947, c. 1086, s. 19; 1977, c. 303, s. 13.)

§ 106-668. Punishment for violations.

Each of the following offenses shall be a Class 1 misdemeanor and any person upon conviction thereof shall be punished as provided by law for the punishment of Class 1 misdemeanors:

(1) To manufacture, offer for sale, or sell in this State any mixed fertilizer or fertilizer materials containing any substance that is injurious to crop growth or deleterious to the soil, or to use in such mixed fertilizer or fertilizer materials as a filler any substance with the effect of defrauding the purchaser.

(2) To offer for sale or to sell in this State for fertilizer purposes any raw or untreated leather, hair, wool waste, hoof, horn, rubber or similar nitrogenous materials, the plant food content of which is largely unavailable, either as such or mixed with other fertilizer materials.

(3) To make any false or misleading representation in regard to any mixed fertilizer or fertilizer material shipped, sold or offered for sale by him in this State, or to use any misleading or deceptive trademark or brand in connection therewith. The sale or offer for sale of any mixture of nitrogenous fertilizer materials under a name or other designation descriptive of only one of the components of the mixture shall be considered deceptive and fraudulent.

The Commissioner is authorized to refuse registration for any commercial fertilizer with respect to which this section is violated.

(4) The filing with the Commissioner of any false statement of fact in connection with the registration under G.S. 106-660 of any commercial fertilizer.

(5) Forcibly obstructing the Commissioner or any official inspector authorized by the Commissioner in the lawful performance by him of his duties in the administration of this Article.

(6) Knowingly taking a false sample of commercial fertilizer for use under provisions of this Article; or knowingly submitting to the Commissioner for analysis a false sample thereof; or making to any person any false representation with regard to any commercial fertilizer sold or offered for sale in this State for the purpose of deceiving or defrauding such other person.

(7) The fraudulent tampering with any lot of commercial fertilizer so that as a result thereof any sample of such commercial fertilizer taken and submitted for analysis under this Article may not correctly represent the lot; or tampering with any sample taken or submitted for analysis under this Article, if done prior to such analysis and disposition of the sample under the direction of the Commissioner.

(8) The delivery to any person by the fertilizer chemist or his assistants or other employees of the Commissioner of a report that is willfully false and misleading on any analysis of commercial fertilizer made by the Department in connection with the administration of this Article.

(9) Selling or offering for sale in this State commercial fertilizer without marking the same as required by G.S. 106-661.

(10) Selling or offering for sale in this State commercial fertilizer containing less than the minimum content required by G.S. 106-659.

(11) Failure of any manufacturer, importer, jobber, agent, or dealer to have applied for and to have been issued a permit as required by G.S. 106-671 before selling, offering, or exposing for sale or distributing commercial fertilizers in this State.

(12) Failure of any manufacturer or contractor to procure a license under the provisions of G.S. 106-660(d) before beginning operations within the State. (1947, c. 1086, s. 20; 1959, c. 706, ss. 10, 11; 1977, c. 303, s. 14; 1993, c. 539, s. 810; 1994, Ex. Sess., c. 24, s. 14(c).)

§ 106-669. Effect of violations on license and registration.

The Commissioner is authorized to suspend, revoke or terminate the license of any manufacturer or to refuse, suspend, revoke or terminate the registration of any commercial fertilizer upon proof that the manufacturer has been guilty of fraudulent or deceptive practices, or in the evasion or attempted evasion of this Article or any rule promulgated thereunder. (1947, c. 1086, s. 17; 1977, c. 303, s. 15; 1981, c. 448, s. 10.)

§ 106-670. Appeals from assessments and orders of Commissioner.

Nothing contained in this Article shall prevent any person from appealing to a court of competent jurisdiction from any assessment of penalty or other final order or ruling of the Commissioner or Board of Agriculture. (1947, c. 1086, s. 22; 1977, c. 303, s. 16.)

§ 106-671. Inspection fees; reporting system.

(a)   For the purpose of defraying expenses on the inspection and of otherwise determining the value of commercial fertilizers in this State, there shall be paid to the Department of Agriculture and Consumer Services a charge of fifty cents (50¢) per ton on all commercial fertilizers other than packages of five pounds or less. Inspection fees shall be paid on all tonnage distributed into North Carolina to any person not having a valid reporting permit. Individual packages of five pounds or less shall be exempt from the tonnage fee; provided that any per annum (fiscal) tonnage of any brand sold in excess of one hundred tons shall be subject to the charge of fifty cents (50¢) per ton on any amount in excess of one hundred tons as provided herein. Whenever any manufacturer of commercial fertilizer shall have paid the charges required by this section his goods shall not be liable to further tax, whether by city, town, or county; provided, this shall not exempt the commercial fertilizers from an ad valorem tax.

(b)   Reporting System. - Each manufacturer, importer, jobber, firm, corporation or person who distributes commercial fertilizers in this State shall make application to the Commissioner for a permit to report the tonnage of commercial fertilizer sold and shall pay to the North Carolina Department of Agriculture and Consumer Services an inspection fee of fifty cents (50¢) per ton. The Commissioner is authorized to require each such distributor to keep such records as may be necessary to indicate accurately the tonnage of commercial fertilizers sold in the State, and as are satisfactory to the Commissioner. Such records shall be available to the Commissioner, or his duly authorized representative, at any and all reasonable hours for the purpose of making such examination as is necessary to verify the tonnage statement and the inspection fees paid. Each registrant shall report monthly the tonnage sold to non-registrants on forms furnished by the Commissioner. Such reports shall be made and inspection fees shall be due and payable monthly on the fifteenth of each month covering the tonnage and kind of commercial fertilizers sold during the past month. If the report is not filed and the inspection fee paid by the last day of the month it is due, the amount due shall bear a penalty of ten percent (10%), which shall be added to the inspection fee due. If the report is not filed and the inspection fee paid within 60 days of the date due, or if the report or tonnage be false, the Commissioner may revoke the permit. (1947, c. 1086, s. 6; 1949, c. 637, s. 3; 1959, c. 706, ss. 6, 7; 1973, c. 611, s. 5; 1977, c. 303, s. 17; 1991, c. 98, s. 2; 1997-261, s. 109; 2009-451, s. 11.1; 2011-145, s. 31.8(a); 2013-360, s. 13.9(b).)

§ 106-672. Declaration of policy.

The General Assembly hereby finds and declares that it is in the public interest that the State regulate the activities of those persons engaged in the business of preparing, mixing, or manufacturing commercial fertilizers, in order to insure the manufacturer, distributor and consumer of the correct quantity and quality of all commercial fertilizer sold or offered for sale in this State. It shall therefore be the policy of this State to regulate the activities of those persons engaged in the business of preparing, mixing or manufacturing commercial fertilizer. (1977, c. 303, s. 18.)

§ 106-673. Authority of Board of Agriculture to make rules and regulations.

Because legislation with regard to commercial fertilizer sold or offered for sale in this State must be adapted to complex conditions and standards involving numerous details with which the General Assembly cannot deal directly and in order to effectuate the purposes and policies of this Article, and in order to insure the manufacturer, distributor, and consumer of the correct quality and quantity of all commercial fertilizer sold or offered for sale in this State, the

Board of Agriculture shall have the authority to make rules and regulations with respect to:

(1)   The maximum chlorine guarantee permitted for tobacco fertilizer;

(2)   The maximum chlorine guarantee permitted in tobacco top dressers;

(3)   Which grades of fertilizer may be branded top dressers;

(4)   The labeling of the grade of fertilizer when such fertilizer is sold in plain or unbranded bags;

(5)   The labeling requirements for all containers of liquid commercial fertilizer for direct application to the soil;

(6)   The bag sizes which may be used in the sale of commercial fertilizer;

(7)   The labeling requirements for packages containing a combination of any nonfertilizer material and mixed tobacco fertilizer;

(8)   Registration and labeling requirements for grades and brands of fertilizer carrying any guarantee of boron; the tolerance allowances for the percentage of boron in fertilizer mixtures;

(9)   The required composition for boron-landplaster mixtures before they may be registered and sold for use on peanuts in this State; the labeling requirements for each container of such mixture;

(10)   The monetary penalties assessed for excesses or deficiencies of boron and all other minor elements above or below the tolerances allowed;

(11)   The registration and labeling of general crop grades and tobacco grades;

(12)   The method, and the time limitations for the reporting to the Commissioner of Agriculture of the tonnage of each grade of fertilizer shipped to each destination in the State by each manufacturer or firm having fertilizer registered in this State;

(13)   The required composition, before such mixtures may be registered and sold in this State, of fertilizer-pesticide, landplaster-pesticide, and fertilizer-landplaster-pesticide, when to be used for peanuts alone;

(14)   The labeling and bag requirements of fertilizer-landplaster-pesticide mixtures;

(15)   The standards and requirements which must be met before fertilizer-pesticide mixtures may be registered in this State. These requirements may include, but are not limited to, approval in North Carolina of both the pesticide and the fertilizer grades, approval of the mixture by the Board of Agriculture, and any labeling requirements;

(16)   The standards and requirements which must be complied with before fertilizers-pesticides may, without registering the mixture, be mixed for direct application at the farmer's request;

(17)   Requests for mixing any pesticide with fertilizer, for products not previously approved by the Board of Agriculture;

(18)   Packaging requirements for fertilizer-pesticide mixtures sold either in bulk or in bags, such that dusting, spillage, sifting, or a loss of any fertilizer-pesticide mixture will not occur;

(19)   The percentages of nitrogen required to be in nitrogen solutions, before such solutions may be registered and sold in this State;

(20)   The labeling of fertilizer products to ascertain their compliance to the Fertilizer or Lime and Landplaster Law;

(21)   Requesting substantiating data to back up claims made about a fertilizer product; registration may be denied if such data is not furnished;

(22)   The denial of approval of the registration of fertilizer products when such products will not, when used as directed, supply deficient needs of a plant;

(23)   Safety requirements for the movement, handling and storage of fluid fertilizers;

(24)   Standards and requirements for equipment and tanks for handling liquid fertilizer;

(25) Refusing registration as a result of information or recommendations from the director of research stations;

(26) Establishing minimum guarantees permissible for registering secondary elements and micronutrients;

(27) Establishing minimum standards for containment of fertilizer materials in storage to prevent contamination of groundwater and surface water; and

(28) Standards and labeling requirements for specialty fertilizers. (1947, c. 1086, s. 15; 1949, c. 637, s. 4; 1977, c. 303, s. 19; 1991, c. 100; 1993, c. 216, s. 2.)

§ 106-674. Short weight.

If any commercial fertilizer in the possession of the consumer is found by the Commissioner to be short in weight, the registrant of said commercial fertilizer shall within 30 days after official notice from the Commissioner pay to the consumer a penalty equal to four times the value of the actual shortage. The Commissioner may in his discretion allow reasonable tolerance for short weight due to loss through handling and transporting. (1947, c. 1086, s. 16; 1977, c. 303, s. 20.)

§ 106-675. Publication of information concerning fertilizers.

The Commissioner shall publish at least annually, in such forms as he may deem proper, complete information concerning the sales of commercial fertilizers, together with a report of the results of the analyses based on official samples of commercial fertilizers sold or offered for sale within the State; such data on their production and use as he may consider advisable; provided, however, that the information concerning production and use of commercial fertilizers shall be shown separately for periods July first to December thirty-first and January first to June thirtieth of each year, and that no disclosure shall be made of the operations of any person. (1947, c. 1086, s. 14; 1959, c. 706, s. 9; 1977, c. 303, s. 21.)

§ 106-676. Sales or exchanges between manufacturers, etc.

Nothing in this Article shall be construed to restrict or avoid sales or exchanges of commercial fertilizers to each other by importers or manufacturers who mix fertilizer materials for sale or as preventing the free and unrestricted shipments of commercial fertilizers to manufacturers who have registered their brands as required by the provisions of this Article. (1947, c. 1086, s. 21; 1977, c. 303, s. 22.)

§ 106-677. Grade-tonnage reports.

Each person registering commercial fertilizers under this Article shall furnish the Commissioner with a written statement of the tonnage of each grade of fertilizer sold by him in this State. This information shall be held in confidence by the Commissioner. Said statement shall include all sales for the periods of July first to and including December thirty-first and of January first to and including June thirtieth of each year. The Commissioner may suspend, revoke or terminate the registration of said commercial fertilizer and suspend, revoke or terminate the license of any person failing to comply with this section within 30 days of the close of each period. All information published by the Department of Agriculture and Consumer Services pursuant to this section shall be classified so as to prevent the identification of information received from individual registrants. All information received pursuant to this section shall be held confidential by the Department and its employees. (1947, c. 1086, s. 13; 1977, c. 303, s. 23; 1981, c. 448, s. 11; 1997-261, s. 109.)

§§ 106-678 through 106-699. Reserved for future codification purposes.

Article 57.

Nuisance Liability of Agricultural and Forestry Operations.

§ 106-700. Legislative determination and declaration of policy.

It is the declared policy of the State to conserve and protect and encourage the development and improvement of its agricultural land and forestland for the production of food, fiber, and other products. When other land uses extend into agricultural and forest areas, agricultural and forestry operations often become the subject of nuisance suits. As a result, agricultural and forestry operations are sometimes forced to cease. Many others are discouraged from making investments in farm and forest improvements. It is the purpose of this Article to reduce the loss to the State of its agricultural and forestry resources by limiting the circumstances under which an agricultural or forestry operation may be deemed to be a nuisance. (1979, c. 202, s. 1; 1991 (Reg. Sess., 1992), c. 892, s. 1.)

§ 106-701. When agricultural and forestry operation, etc., not constituted nuisance by changed conditions in or about the locality outside of the operation.

(a)   No agricultural or forestry operation or any of its appurtenances shall be or become a nuisance, private or public, by any changed conditions in or about the locality outside of the operation after the operation has been in operation for more than one year, when such operation was not a nuisance at the time the operation began.

(a1)   The provisions of subsection (a) of this section shall not apply when the plaintiff demonstrates that the agricultural or forestry operation has undergone a fundamental change. A fundamental change to the operation does not include any of the following:

(1)   A change in ownership or size.

(2)   An interruption of farming for a period of no more than three years.

(3)   Participation in a government-sponsored agricultural program.

(4)   Employment of new technology.

(5)   A change in the type of agricultural or forestry product produced.

(a2)   The provisions of subsection (a) of this section shall not apply whenever a nuisance results from the negligent or improper operation of any agricultural or forestry operation or its appurtenances.

(b) For the purposes of this Article, "agricultural operation" includes, without limitation, any facility for the production for commercial purposes of crops, livestock, poultry, livestock products, or poultry products.

(b1) For the purposes of this Article, "forestry operation" shall mean those activities involved in the growing, managing, and harvesting of trees.

(c) The provisions of subsection (a) shall not affect or defeat the right of any person, firm, or corporation to recover damages for any injuries or damages sustained by him on account of any pollution of, or change in condition of, the waters of any stream or on the account of any overflow of lands of any such person, firm, or corporation.

(d) Any and all ordinances of any unit of local government now in effect or hereafter adopted that would make the operation of any such agricultural or forestry operation or its appurtenances a nuisance or providing for abatement thereof as a nuisance in the circumstance set forth in this section are and shall be null and void; provided, however, that the provisions of this subsection shall not apply whenever a nuisance results from the negligent or improper operation of any such agricultural or forestry operation or any of its appurtenances. Provided further, that the provisions shall not apply whenever a nuisance results from an agricultural or forestry operation located within the corporate limits of any city at the time of enactment hereof.

(e) This section shall not be construed to invalidate any contracts heretofore made but insofar as contracts are concerned, it is only applicable to contracts and agreements to be made in the future.

(f) In a nuisance action against an agricultural or forestry operation, the court shall award costs and expenses, including reasonable attorneys' fees, to:

(1) The agricultural or forestry operation when the court finds the operation was not a nuisance and the nuisance action was frivolous or malicious; or

(2) The plaintiff when the court finds the agricultural or forestry operation was a nuisance and the operation asserted an affirmative defense in the nuisance action that was frivolous and malicious. (1979, c. 202, s. 1; 1991 (Reg. Sess., 1992), c. 892, s. 1; 2013-314, s. 1.)

§§ 106-702 through 106-705. Reserved for future codification purposes.

Article 57A.

Civil Liability of Farmers.

§ 106-706. Exemption from civil liability for farmers permitting gleaning.

Any farmer, as an owner, lessee, occupant, or otherwise in control of land, who allows without compensation another person to enter upon the land for the purpose of removing any crops remaining in the farmer's fields following the harvesting of the crops, owes that person the same duty of care the farmer owes a trespasser. (1991 (Reg. Sess., 1992), c. 868, s. 1.)

Article 58.

North Carolina Biologics Law of 1981.

§ 106-707. Short title and purpose.

This Article shall be known as "The North Carolina Biologics Law of 1981." The purpose of the law is to provide for the production and sale of biologics for the prevention or treatment of disease in animals other than man and to establish controls for the sale and use of biologics in North Carolina. (1981, c. 552, s. 1.)

§ 106-708. Definitions.

For purposes of this Article, the following words, terms and phrases are defined as follows:

(1)   "Animal" means all birds and mammals, other than man, to which biologics may be administered.

(2) "Biologics" means preparations made from living organisms and their products, including serums, vaccines, antigens and antitoxins which are used for the treatment or prevention of diseases in animals other than humans, or in the diagnosis of diseases.

(3) "Board" means the North Carolina Board of Agriculture.

(4) "Commissioner" means the Commissioner of Agriculture.

(5) "Department" means the Department of Agriculture and Consumer Services. (1981, c. 552, s. 1; 1997-261, s. 70.)

§ 106-709. Rules and regulations.

The Board of Agriculture shall adopt rules and regulations necessary for the implementation and administration of this Article. (1981, c. 552, s. 1.)

§ 106-710. Biologics production license.

(a) No person shall engage in the production of biologics except in:

(1) An establishment licensed by the Department;

(2) An establishment licensed by the United States Department of Agriculture; or

(3) An establishment producing biologics only for use by the owner or operator of the establishment for animals owned by him, if the biologics are registered with the Commissioner.

(b) Any establishment applying for a license to produce biologics shall be inspected by the Commissioner. Approval shall be based on compliance with the rules and regulations adopted by the board.

(c) Application for a license to produce biologics shall be made on forms provided by the Commissioner and shall be accompanied by a reasonable fee as established by the board.

(d) Upon approval, a license shall be granted upon payment of the annual license fee of one hundred dollars ($100.00) for each establishment licensed, and an additional fee of fifty dollars ($50.00) for each product produced at any time during the year. This license shall be renewed annually. The annual renewal fee shall be paid on or before the first day of July of each year. (1981, c. 552, s. 1.)

§ 106-711. License revocation or suspension.

The Commissioner, upon a finding that a licensed establishment producing biologics is not in compliance with this Article or any rules or regulations promulgated thereunder, may revoke or suspend the license in accordance with Chapter 150B of the General Statutes. (1981, c. 552, s. 1; 1987, c. 827, s. 1.)

§ 106-712. Registration of biologics.

(a) No person shall offer for sale or use any biologic in North Carolina unless it is registered with the Commissioner. The registration shall be made on forms provided by the Commissioner. The forms shall require the applicant to provide information showing that the biologic:

(1) Is produced under procedures approved by the Commissioner;

(2) Is safe and noninjurious to animals when used as directed;

(3) Is labeled for proper handling, use and contents;

(4) Is produced in an establishment licensed under this Article; and

(5) Is not in violation of this Article or any rule or regulation promulgated thereunder.

(b) The application for registration shall also include a protocol of methods of production in detail which is followed in the production of the biologic, a sample of the label to be placed on the biologic, and any other information prescribed by the board as necessary for the implementation of this Article. (1981, c. 552, s. 1.)

§ 106-713. Revocation or suspension of registration.

The Commissioner, upon a finding that a registered biologic is being produced, sold or distributed in violation of this Article or any rules or regulations promulgated thereunder, may revoke or suspend the regulation in accordance with Chapter 150B of the General Statutes. (1981, c. 552, s. 1; 1987, c. 827, s. 1.)

§ 106-714. Penalties for violation.

(a) Any person adjudged to have violated any provision of this Article or the rules and regulations promulgated thereunder is guilty of a Class 2 misdemeanor. The Attorney General or his representative has concurrent jurisdiction with the district attorneys of this State to prosecute violations under this section.

(b) The Commissioner may apply to the Superior Court for an injunction to restrain and prevent violations of this Article or the rules and regulations promulgated thereunder irrespective of whether there exists an adequate remedy elsewhere at law. (1981, c. 552, s. 1; 1993, c. 539, s. 811; 1994, Ex. Sess., c. 24, s. 14(c).)

§ 106-715. Civil penalties.

The Commissioner may assess a civil penalty of not more than five thousand dollars ($5,000) against any person who violates a provision of this Article or any rule promulgated thereunder. In determining the amount of the penalty, the Commissioner shall consider the degree and extent of harm caused by the violation.

The clear proceeds of civil penalties assessed pursuant to this section shall be remitted to the Civil Penalty and Forfeiture Fund in accordance with G.S. 115C-457.2. (1995, c. 516, s. 15; 1998-215, s. 22.)

§§ 106-716 through 106-718. Reserved for future codification purposes.

Article 59.

Northeastern North Carolina Farmers Market Commission.

§§ 106-719 through 106-725. Repealed by Session Laws 1999-44, s. 6, effective May 13, 1999.

Article 60.

Southeastern North Carolina Farmers Market Commission.

§§ 106-726 through 106-734. Repealed by Session Laws 1999-44, s. 7, effective May 13, 1999.

Article 61.

Agricultural Development and Preservation of Farmland.

Part 1. General Provisions.

§ 106-735. Short title, purpose, and administration.

(a) This Article shall be known as "The Agricultural Development and Farmland Preservation Enabling Act."

(b) The purpose of this Article is to authorize counties and cities to undertake a series of programs to encourage the preservation of qualifying farmland, as defined herein, and to foster the growth, development, and sustainability of family farms.

(c) This Article shall be administered and supervised by the Department of Agriculture and Consumer Services. (1985 (Reg. Sess., 1986), c. 1025, s. 1; 2005-390, ss. 2, 9; 2011-251, s. 1.)

§ 106-736. Agricultural Development/Farmland preservation programs authorized.

(a) A county or a city may by ordinance establish a farmland preservation program under this Article. The ordinance may authorize qualifying farms, as defined in G.S. 106-737, to take advantage of one or more of the benefits authorized by the remaining sections of this Article.

(b) A county or a city may develop programs to promote the growth, development, and sustainability of farming and assist farmers in developing and implementing plans that achieve these goals. For purposes of this Article, the terms "agriculture", "agricultural", and "farming" have the same meaning as set forth in G.S. 106-581.1. (1985 (Reg. Sess., 1986), c. 1025, s. 1; 2005-390, ss. 2, 10.)

Part 2. Voluntary Agricultural Districts.

§ 106-737. Qualifying farmland.

In order for farmland to qualify for inclusion in a voluntary agricultural district or an enhanced voluntary agricultural district under Part 1 or Part 2 of this Article, it must be real property that:

(1) Is engaged in agriculture as that word is defined in G.S. 106-581.1.

(2) Repealed by Session Laws 2005-390, s. 11 effective September 13, 2005.

(3) Is managed in accordance with the Soil Conservation Service defined erosion control practices that are addressed to highly erodable land; and

(4) Is the subject of a conservation agreement, as defined in G.S. 121-35, between the county and the owner of such land that prohibits nonfarm use or development of such land for a period of at least 10 years, except for the creation of not more than three lots that meet applicable county and municipal zoning and subdivision regulations. (1985 (Reg. Sess., 1986), c. 1025, s. 1; 2005-390, ss. 3, 11; 2011-219, s. 1.)

§ 106-737.1. Revocation of conservation agreement.

By written notice to the county, the landowner may revoke this conservation agreement. Such revocation shall result in loss of qualifying farm status. (1985 (Reg. Sess., 1986), c. 1025, s. 1; 2005-390, s. 3.)

§ 106-738. Voluntary agricultural districts.

(a)   An ordinance adopted under this Part shall provide:

(1)   For the establishment of voluntary agricultural districts consisting initially of at least the number of contiguous acres of agricultural land, and forestland or horticultural land that is part of a qualifying farm or the number of qualifying farms deemed appropriate by the governing board of the county or city adopting the ordinance;

(2)   For the formation of such districts upon the execution by the owners of the requisite acreage of an agreement to sustain agriculture in the district;

(3)   That the form of this agreement must be reviewed and approved by an agricultural advisory board established under G.S. 106-739 or some other county board or official;

(4)   That each such district have a representative on the agricultural advisory board established under G.S. 106-739.

(b)   The purpose of such agricultural districts shall be to increase identity and pride in the agricultural community and its way of life and to increase protection from nuisance suits and other negative impacts on properly managed farms. The county or city that adopted an ordinance under this Part may take such action as it deems appropriate to encourage the formation of such districts and to further their purposes and objectives.

(c)   A county ordinance adopted pursuant to this Part is effective within the unincorporated areas of the county. A city ordinance adopted pursuant to this Part is effective within the corporate limits of the city. A city may amend its ordinances in accordance with G.S. 160A-383.2 with regard to agricultural districts within its planning jurisdiction. (1985 (Reg. Sess., 1986), c. 1025, s. 1; 2005-390, ss. 3, 12.)

§ 106-739. Agricultural advisory board.

An ordinance adopted under this Part or Part 3 of this Article shall provide for the establishment of an agricultural advisory board, organized and appointed as the county or city that adopted the ordinance shall deem appropriate. The county or city that adopted the ordinance may confer upon this advisory board authority to:

(1)   Review and make recommendations concerning the establishment and modification of agricultural districts;

(2)   Review and make recommendations concerning any ordinance or amendment adopted or proposed for adoption under this Part or Part 3 of this Article;

(3)   Hold public hearings on public projects likely to have an impact on agricultural operations, particularly if such projects involve condemnation of all or part of any qualifying farm;

(4)   Advise the governing board of the county or city that adopted the ordinance on projects, programs, or issues affecting the agricultural economy or way of life within the county;

(5)   Perform other related tasks or duties assigned by the governing board of the county or city that adopted the ordinance. (1985 (Reg. Sess., 1986), c. 1025, s. 1; 2005-390, ss. 3, 13.)

§ 106-740. Public hearings on condemnation of farmland.

An ordinance adopted under this Part or Part 3 of this Article may provide that no State or local public agency or governmental unit may formally initiate any action to condemn any interest in qualifying farmland within a voluntary agricultural district under this Part or an enhanced voluntary agricultural district under Part 3 of this Article until such agency has requested the local agricultural advisory board established under G.S. 106-739 to hold a public hearing on the proposed condemnation.

(1)   Following a public hearing held pursuant to this section, the board shall prepare and submit written findings and a recommendation to the decision-making body of the agency proposing acquisition.

(2)   The board designated to hold the hearing shall have 30 days after receiving a request under this section to hold the public hearing and submit its findings and recommendations to the agency.

(3)   The agency may not formally initiate a condemnation action while the proposed condemnation is properly before the advisory board within these time limitations. (1985 (Reg. Sess., 1986), c. 1025, s. 1; 2005-390, ss. 3, 14.)

§ 106-741. Record notice of proximity to farmlands.

(a)   Any county that has a computerized land records system may require that such records include some form of notice reasonably calculated to alert a person researching the title of a particular tract that such tract is located within one-half mile of a poultry, swine, or dairy qualifying farm or within 600 feet of any other qualifying farm or within one-half mile of a voluntary agricultural district.

(b)   In no event shall the county or any of its officers, employees, or agents be held liable in damages for any misfeasance, malfeasance, or nonfeasance occurring in good faith in connection with the duties or obligations imposed by any ordinance adopted under subsection (a).

(c)   In no event shall any cause of action arise out of the failure of a person researching the title of a particular tract to report to any person the proximity of the tract to a qualifying farm or voluntary agricultural district as defined in this Article. (1985 (Reg. Sess., 1986), c. 1025, s. 1; 2005-390, s. 3.)

§ 106-742. Waiver of water and sewer assessments.

(a)   A county or a city that has adopted an ordinance under this Part may provide by ordinance that its water and sewer assessments be held in abeyance, with or without interest, for farms, whether inside or outside of a voluntary agricultural district, until improvements on such property are connected to the water or sewer system for which the assessment was made.

(b)   The ordinance may provide that, when the period of abeyance ends, the assessment is payable in accordance with the terms set out in the assessment resolution.

(c)   Statutes of limitations are suspended during the time that any assessment is held in abeyance without interest.

(d)   If an ordinance is adopted under this section, then the assessment procedures followed under Article 9 of Chapter 153A of the General Statutes or Article 10 of Chapter 160A of the General Statutes, whichever applies, shall conform to the terms of this ordinance with respect to qualifying farms that entered into conservation agreements while such ordinance was in effect.

(e)   Nothing in this section is intended to diminish the authority of counties or cities to hold assessments in abeyance under G.S. 153A-201 or G.S. 160A-237. (1985 (Reg. Sess., 1986), c. 1025, s. 1; 2005-390, ss. 3, 15.)

§ 106-743. Local ordinances.

A county or a city adopting an ordinance under this Part or Part 3 of this Article may consult with the North Carolina Commissioner of Agriculture or his staff before adoption, and shall record the ordinance with the Commissioner's office after adoption. Thereafter, the county or city shall submit to the Commissioner at least once a year, a written report including the status, progress and activities of its farmland preservation program under this Part or Part 3 of this Article. (1985 (Reg. Sess., 1986), c. 1025, s. 1; 2005-390, ss. 3, 16.)

Part 3. Enhanced Voluntary Agricultural Districts.

§ 106-743.1. Enhanced voluntary agricultural districts.

(a)   A county or a municipality may adopt an ordinance establishing an enhanced voluntary agricultural district. An ordinance adopted pursuant to this Part shall provide:

(1) For the establishment of an enhanced voluntary agricultural district that initially consists of at least the number of contiguous acres of agricultural land, and forestland and horticultural land that is part of a qualifying farm under G.S. 106-737 or the number of qualifying farms deemed appropriate by the governing board of the county or city adopting the ordinance.

(2) For the formation of the enhanced voluntary agricultural district upon the execution of a conservation agreement, as defined in G.S. 121-35, that meets the condition set forth in G.S. 106-743.2 by the landowners of the requisite acreage to sustain agriculture in the enhanced voluntary agricultural district.

(3) That the form of the agreement under subdivision (2) of this subsection be reviewed and approved by an agricultural advisory board established under G.S. 106-739, or other governing board of the county or city that adopted the ordinance.

(4) That each enhanced voluntary agricultural district have a representative on the agricultural advisory board established under G.S. 106-739.

(b) The purpose of establishing an enhanced voluntary agricultural district is to allow a county or a city to provide additional benefits to farmland beyond that available in a voluntary agricultural district established under Part 2 of this Article, when the owner of the farmland agrees to the condition imposed under G.S. 106-743.2. The county or city that adopted the ordinance may take any action it deems appropriate to encourage the formation of these districts and to further their purposes and objectives.

(c) A county ordinance adopted pursuant to this Part is effective within the unincorporated areas of the county. A city ordinance adopted pursuant to this Part is effective within the corporate limits of the city. A city may amend its ordinances in accordance with G.S. 160A-383.2 with regard to agricultural districts within its planning jurisdiction.

(d) A county or city ordinance adopted pursuant to this Part may be adopted simultaneously with the creation of a voluntary agricultural district pursuant to G.S. 106-738. (2005-390, s. 5.)

§ 106-743.2. Conservation agreements for farmland in enhanced voluntary agricultural districts; limitation.

A conservation agreement entered into between a county or city and a landowner pursuant to G.S. 106-743.1(a)(2) shall be irrevocable for a period of at least 10 years from the date the agreement is executed. At the end of its term, a conservation agreement shall automatically renew for a term of three years, unless notice of termination is given in a timely manner by either party as prescribed in the ordinance establishing the enhanced voluntary agricultural district. The benefits set forth in this Part shall be available to the farmland that is the subject of the conservation agreement for the duration of the conservation agreement. (2005-390, s. 5.)

§ 106-743.3. Enhanced voluntary agricultural districts entitled to all benefits of voluntary agricultural districts.

The provisions of G.S. 106-739 through G.S. 106-741 and G.S. 106-743 apply to an enhanced voluntary agricultural district under this Part, to an ordinance adopted under this Part, and to any person, entity, or farmland subject to this Part in the same manner as they apply under Part 2 of this Article. (2005-390, s. 5.)

§ 106-743.4. Enhanced voluntary agricultural districts; additional benefits.

(a)   Property that is subject to a conservation agreement under G.S. 106-743.2 that remains in effect may receive up to twenty-five percent (25%) of its gross sales from the sale of nonfarm products and still qualify as a bona fide farm that is exempt from zoning regulations under G.S. 153A-340(b). For purposes of G.S. 153A-340(b), the production of any nonfarm product that the Department of Agriculture and Consumer Services recognizes as a "Goodness Grows in North Carolina" product that is produced on a farm that is subject to a conservation agreement under G.S. 106-743.2 is a bona fide farm purpose. A farmer seeking to benefit from this subsection shall have the burden of establishing that the property's sale of nonfarm products did not exceed twenty-five percent (25%) of its gross sales. A county may adopt an ordinance pursuant to this section that sets forth the standards necessary for proof of compliance.

Nothing in this section shall affect the county's authority to zone swine farms pursuant to G.S. 153A-340(b)(3).

(b) A person who farms land that is subject to a conservation agreement under G.S. 106-743.2 that remains in effect is eligible under G.S. 106-850(b) to receive the higher percentage of cost-share funds for the benefit of that farmland under the Agriculture Cost Share Program established pursuant to Article 72 of this Chapter for funds to benefit that farmland.

(c) State departments, institutions, or agencies that award grants to farmers are encouraged to give priority consideration to any person who farms land that is subject to a conservation agreement under G.S. 106-743.2 that remains in effect. (2005-390, s. 5; 2011-145, s. 13.22A(cc).)

§ 106-743.5. Waiver of utility assessments.

(a) In the ordinance establishing an enhanced voluntary agricultural district under this Part, a county or a city may provide that all assessments for utilities provided by that county or city are held in abeyance, with or without interest, for farmland subject to a conservation agreement under G.S. 106-743.2 that remains in effect until improvements on the farmland property are connected to the utility for which the assessment was made.

(b) The ordinance may provide that, when the period of abeyance ends, the assessment is payable in accordance with the terms set out in the assessment resolution.

(c) Statutes of limitations are suspended during the time that any assessment is held in abeyance under this section without interest.

(d) If an ordinance is adopted by a county or a city under this section, then the assessment procedures followed under Article 9 of Chapter 153A or Article 10 of Chapter 160A of the General Statutes, respectively, shall conform to the terms of this ordinance with respect to qualifying farms that entered into conservation agreements while such ordinance was in effect.

(e) Nothing in this section is intended to diminish the authority of counties or cities to hold assessments in abeyance under G.S 153A-201 and G.S. 160A-237. (2005-390, s. 5.)

Part 4. Agricultural Conservation Easements.

§ 106-744. Purchase of agricultural conservation easements; establishment of North Carolina Agricultural Development and Farmland Preservation Trust Fund and Advisory Committee.

(a) A county may, with the voluntary consent of landowners, acquire by purchase agricultural conservation easements over qualifying farmland as defined by G.S. 106-737.

(b) For purposes of this section, "agricultural conservation easement" means a negative easement in gross restricting residential, commercial, and industrial development of land for the purpose of maintaining its agricultural production capability. Such easement:

(1) May permit the creation of not more than three lots that meet applicable county zoning and subdivision regulations;

(1a) May permit agricultural uses as necessary to promote agricultural development associated with the family farm; and

(2) Shall be perpetual in duration, provided that, at least 20 years after the purchase of an easement, a county may agree to reconvey the easement to the owner of the land for consideration, if the landowner can demonstrate to the satisfaction of the county that commercial agriculture is no longer practicable on the land in question.

(c) There is established a "North Carolina Agricultural Development and Farmland Preservation Trust Fund" to be administered by the Commissioner of Agriculture. The Trust Fund shall consist of all monies received for the purpose of purchasing agricultural conservation easements or funding programs that promote the development and sustainability of farming and assist in the transition of existing farms to new farm families, or monies transferred from counties or private sources. The Trust Fund shall be invested as provided in G.S. 147-69.2 and G.S. 147-69.3. The Commissioner shall use Trust Fund monies for any of the following purposes:

(1) For the purchase of agricultural conservation easements, including transaction costs.

(2)   For the costs of public and private enterprise programs that will promote profitable and sustainable family farms through assistance to farmers in developing and implementing plans for the production of food, fiber, and value-added products, agritourism activities, marketing and sales of agricultural products produced on the farm, and other agriculturally related business activities.

(3)   To fund conservation agreements to bring into or maintain farmland in active production of food, fiber, and other agricultural products.

(4)   For the costs of administering the program under this Article, including the cost of staff and staff support.

(c1)   The Commissioner shall distribute Trust Fund monies for only the purposes under subsection (c) of this section, including transaction costs, as follows:

(1)   To a private nonprofit conservation organization that matches thirty percent (30%) of the Trust Fund monies it receives with funds from sources other than the Trust Fund.

(2)   To counties according to the match requirements under subsection (c2) of this section.

(c2)   A county that is a development tier two or three county, as these tiers are defined in G.S. 143B-437.08, and that has prepared a countywide farmland protection plan shall match fifteen percent (15%) of the Trust Fund monies it receives with county funds. A county that has not prepared a countywide farmland protection plan shall match thirty percent (30%) of the Trust Fund monies it receives with county funds. A county that is a development tier one county, as defined in G.S. 143B-437.08, and that has prepared a countywide farmland protection plan shall not be required to match any of the Trust Fund monies it receives with county funds.

(c3)   The Commissioner of Agriculture shall adopt rules governing the use, distribution, investment, and management of Trust Fund monies.

(d)   This section shall apply to agricultural conservation easements falling within its terms. This section shall not be construed to make unenforceable any restriction, easement, covenant, or condition that does not comply with the requirements of this section.

This section shall not be construed to invalidate any farmland preservation program.

This section shall not be construed to diminish the powers of any public entity, agency, or instrumentality to acquire by purchase, gift, devise, inheritance, eminent domain, or otherwise and to use property of any kind for public purposes.

This section shall not be construed to authorize any public entity, agency, or instrumentality to acquire by eminent domain an agricultural conservation easement.

(e)   As used in subsection (c2) of this section, a countywide farmland protection plan means a plan that satisfies all of the following requirements:

(1)   The countywide farmland protection plan shall contain a list and description of existing agricultural activity in the county.

(2)   The countywide farmland protection plan shall contain a list of existing challenges to continued family farming in the county.

(3)   The countywide farmland protection plan shall contain a list of opportunities for maintaining or enhancing small, family-owned farms and the local agricultural economy.

(4)   The countywide farmland protection plan shall describe how the county plans to maintain a viable agricultural community and shall address farmland preservation tools, such as agricultural economic development, including farm diversification and marketing assistance; other kinds of agricultural technical assistance, such as farm infrastructure financing, farmland purchasing, linking with younger farmers, and estate planning; the desirability and feasibility of donating agricultural conservation easements, and entering into voluntary agricultural districts.

(5)   The countywide farmland protection plan shall contain a schedule for implementing the plan and an identification of possible funding sources for the long-term support of the plan.

(f)   A countywide farmland protection plan that meets the requirements of subsection (e) of this section may be formulated with the assistance of an agricultural advisory board designated pursuant to G.S. 106-739.

(g) There is established the Agricultural Development and Farmland Preservation Trust Fund Advisory Committee. The Advisory Committee shall be administratively located within the Department of Agriculture and Consumer Services and shall advise the Commissioner on the prioritization and allocation of funds, the development of criteria for awarding funds, program planning, and other areas where monies from the Trust Fund can be used to promote the growth and development of family farms in North Carolina. The Advisory Committee shall be composed of 19 members as follows:

(1) The Commissioner of Agriculture or the Commissioner's designee, who shall serve as the Chair of the Advisory Committee.

(2) The Secretary of Commerce or the Secretary's designee.

(3) The Secretary of Environment and Natural Resources or the Secretary's designee.

(4) Three practicing farmers, one appointed by the Governor, one appointed by the President Pro Tempore of the Senate, and one appointed by the Speaker of the House of Representatives.

(5) The Dean of the College of Agriculture and Life Sciences at North Carolina State University or the Dean's designee.

(6) The Dean of the School of Agriculture and Environmental Sciences at North Carolina Agricultural and Technical State University or the Dean's designee.

(7) The chair of the Rural Infrastructure Authority within the Department of Commerce or the chair's designee.

(8) The Executive Director of the Conservation Trust for North Carolina or the Executive Director's designee.

(9) The Executive Director of the North Carolina Farm Transition Network or the Executive Director's designee.

(10) The President of the North Carolina Association of Soil and Water Conservation Districts or the President's designee.

(11) The Executive Director of the Rural Advancement Foundation International - USA or the Executive Director's designee.

(12) The Executive Director of the North Carolina Agribusiness Council or the Executive Director's designee.

(13) The President of the North Carolina State Grange or the President's designee.

(14) The President of the North Carolina Farm Bureau Federation, Inc., or the President's designee.

(15) The President of the North Carolina Black Farmers and Agriculturalists Association or the President's designee.

(16) The President of the North Carolina Forestry Association or the President's designee.

(17) The Executive Director of the North Carolina Association of County Commissioners or the Executive Director's designee.

(h) The Advisory Committee shall meet at least quarterly. The Department of Agriculture and Consumer Services shall provide the Advisory Committee with administrative and secretarial staff. Members of the Advisory Committee shall be entitled to per diem pursuant to G.S. 138-5 or G.S. 138-6, as appropriate. The Advisory Committee shall make recommendations to the Commissioner on the distribution of monies from the Trust Fund at least annually. The Commissioner shall take the recommendations of the Advisory Committee into consideration in making decisions on the distribution of monies from the Trust Fund.

(i) The Advisory Committee shall report no later than October 1 of each year to the Joint Legislative Commission on Governmental Operations, the Environmental Review Commission, and the House of Representatives and Senate Appropriations Subcommittees on Natural and Economic Resources regarding the activities of the Advisory Committee, the agriculture easements purchased, and agricultural projects funded during the previous year. (1991, c. 734, s. 1; 2000-171, ss. 1, 2; 2005-390, ss. 4, 17; 2006-252, s. 2.12; 2007-495, s. 23; 2009-303, ss. 1, 2, 3; 2009-484, s. 12; 2013-360, s. 15.26(a).)

§§ 106-745 through 106-749. Reserved for future codification purposes.

Article 62.

[Redesignated.]

§§ 106-750 through 106-755: Redesignated as Part 2J of Article 10 of Chapter 143B by Session Laws 2005-380, s. 4(a), effective September 8, 2005.

Article 62.

[Redesignated.]

§§ 106-750 through 106-755: Redesignated as part 2J of Article 10 of Chapter 143B by Session Laws 2005-380, s. 4(a), effective September 8, 2005.

Article 62A.

Wine and Grape Growers Council.

§ 106-755.1. North Carolina Wine and Grape Growers Council - Creation; powers and duties.

There is created the North Carolina Wine and Grape Growers Council of the Department of Agriculture and Consumer Services. The North Carolina Wine and Grape Growers Council shall have the following powers and duties:

(1) To identify and implement methods for improving North Carolina's rank as a wine-producing State;

(2) To assure orderly growth and development of North Carolina's grape and wine industry;

(3) To achieve public awareness of the quality of North Carolina grapes and wine;

(4) To coordinate the interaction of North Carolina's grape and wine industry with other segments of the State's economy such as tourism, retail trade, and horticulture;

(5) To conduct methods of quality assurance of North Carolina's grape and wine industry to create a sound foundation for further growth;

(6) To assist in the coordination of the activities of the various State agencies and other organizations contributing to the development of the grape and wine industry;

(7) To receive and disburse funds;

(8) To enter into contracts for the purpose of developing new or improved markets or marketing methods for wine and grape products;

(9) To contract for research services to improve viticultural and enological practices in North Carolina;

(10) To enter into agreements with any local, state, or national organizations or agency engaged in education for the purpose of disseminating information on wine or other viticultural projects;

(11) To enter into contracts with commercial entities for the purpose of developing marketing, advertising, and other promotional programs designed to promote the orderly growth of the North Carolina grape and wine industry;

(12) To acquire any licenses or permits necessary for performance of the duties of the Council; and

(13) To develop a State Viticulture Plan that identifies problems and constraints of the viticultural industry, proposes solutions to those problems and delineates planning mechanisms for the orderly growth of the industry.

(14) By September 1 of each year, to report to the House of Representatives Appropriations Subcommittee on Natural and Economic Resources, the Senate Appropriations Committee on Natural and Economic Resources, the Joint Legislative Commission on Governmental Operations, and the Fiscal Research Division on the activities of the Council, the status of the wine and grape industry in North Carolina and the United States, progress on the development and implementation of the State Viticulture Plan, and any contracts or

agreements entered into by the Council for research, education, or marketing. (1985 (Reg. Sess., 1986), c. 974, s. 1; 1997-261, s. 109; 2005-380, s. 4(a); 2006-264, s. 98.3; 2010-31, s. 14.10; 2011-145, s. 14.3B; 2011-391, s. 38.1(b); 2012-142, s. 13.9A(b).)

§ 106-755.2. North Carolina Wine and Grape Growers Council - Composition; terms; reimbursement.

(a) The North Carolina Wine and Grape Growers Council shall consist of 10 members who shall be appointed by the Commissioner of Agriculture as provided in this section. The members of the Council shall be divided into an advisory committee for the Vinifera Group and an advisory committee for the Muscadines Group for the purpose of performing the powers and duties prescribed in G.S. 143B-437.90 and for the purpose of promoting North Carolina wineries and tourism related to the wineries.

(b) Each advisory committee shall consist of five members, who shall be appointed by the Commissioner of Agriculture to serve two-year terms, which shall be staggered. The members appointed shall be chosen from among individuals who have education or experience in the wine industry or in the field of tourism. No member of an advisory committee may serve for more than two consecutive terms. Initial terms shall commence September 1, 2011.

(c) Each advisory committee shall meet at least twice each calendar year during which time each committee shall discuss issues related to the Council's powers and duties, including ways in which to promote and advertise North Carolina wineries and ways in which to improve, use, and distribute State maps showing winery locations. The Vinifera Group shall meet at the NC Shelton Badgett Viticulture Center at Surry Community College, and the Muscadines Group shall meet at Duplin Community College. After each meeting, each advisory committee shall report to the Commissioner of Agriculture with its recommendations. Notwithstanding any other provision of law, committee members shall receive no salary, per diem, subsistence, travel reimbursement, or other stipend or reimbursement as a result of serving on their respective committees.

(d) Each advisory committee shall elect from the membership of each committee a chair and vice-chair. Vacancies resulting from the resignation of a member or otherwise shall be filled in the same manner in which the original appointment was made, and the term shall be for the balance of the unexpired term. A majority of the members of each committee shall constitute a quorum for the transaction of business. The affirmative vote of a majority of the members present at meetings of each committee shall be necessary for action to be taken by the committee. (1985 (Reg. Sess., 1986), c. 974, s. 1; 1997-261, s. 109; 2005-380, s. 4(a); 2006-264, s. 98.3; 2011-145, s. 14.3B; 2011-391, s. 38.1(b), (c); 2012-142, s. 13.9A(b).)

Article 63.

Aquaculture Development Act.

§ 106-756. Legislative findings and purpose.

The General Assembly finds and declares that it is in the best interest of the citizens of North Carolina to promote and encourage the development of the State's aquacultural resources in order to augment food supplies, expand employment, promote economic activity, increase stocks of native aquatic species, enhance commercial and recreational fishing and protect and better use the land and water resources of the State. (1989, c. 752, s. 147.)

§ 106-757. Short title.

This Article shall be known as the Aquaculture Development Act. (1989, c. 752, s. 147.)

§ 106-758. Definitions.

In addition to the definitions in G.S. 113-129, the following definitions shall apply as used in this Article,

(1) "Aquaculture" means the propagation and rearing of aquatic species in controlled or selected environments, including, but not limited to, ocean ranching;

(2) "Aquaculture facility" means any land, structure or other appurtenance that is used for aquaculture, including, but not limited to, any laboratory, hatchery, rearing pond, raceway, pen, incubator, or other equipment used in aquaculture;

(3) "Aquatic species" means any species of finfish, mollusk, crustacean, or other aquatic invertebrate, amphibian, reptile, or aquatic plant, and including, but not limited to, "fish" and "fishes" as defined in G.S. 113-129(7);

(4) "Commissioner" means the Commissioner of Agriculture;

(5) "Department" means the North Carolina Department of Agriculture and Consumer Services. (1989, c. 752, s. 147; 1993, c. 18, s. 1; 1997-261, s. 71.)

§ 106-759. Lead agency; powers and duties.

(a) For the purposes of this Article, aquaculture is considered to be a form of agriculture and thus the Department of Agriculture and Consumer Services is designated as the lead State agency in matters pertaining to aquaculture.

(b) The Department shall have the following powers and duties:

(1) To provide aquaculturalists with information and assistance in obtaining permits related to aquacultural activities;

(2) To promote investment in aquaculture facilities in order to expand production and processing capacity; and

(3) To work with appropriate State and federal agencies to review, develop and implement policies and procedures to facilitate aquacultural development. (1989, c. 752, s. 147; 1997-261, s. 109.)

§ 106-760: Repealed by Session Laws 2011-266, s. 1.4, effective July 1, 2011.

§ 106-761. Aquaculture facility registration and licensing.

(a) Authority. The North Carolina Department of Agriculture and Consumer Services shall regulate the production and sale of commercially raised freshwater fish and freshwater crustacean species. The Board of Agriculture shall promulgate rules for the registration of facilities for the production and sale of freshwater aquaculturally raised species. The Board may prescribe standards under which commercially reared fish may be transported, possessed, bought, and sold. The Department and Board of Agriculture authority shall be limited to commercially reared fish and shall not include authority over the wild fishery resource which is managed under the authority of the North Carolina Wildlife Resources Commission. The authority granted herein to regulate facilities licensed pursuant to this section does not authorize the Department of Agriculture and Consumer Services or the Board of Agriculture to promulgate rules that (i) are inconsistent with rules adopted by any other State agency; or (ii) exempt such facilities from the rules adopted by any other State agency.

(b) Species subject to this section. The following species are exempt from special restrictions on introduction of exotic species promulgated by the Wildlife Resources Commission except to prevent disease. All other species are prohibited from propagation and production unless the applicant for the permit first obtains written permission from the Wildlife Resources Commission.

(1) Bluegill   Lepomis macrochirus

(2) Redear Sunfish   Lepomis microlophus

(3) Redbreast Sunfish   Lepomis auritus

(4) Green Sunfish   Lepomis cyanellus

(5) Any hybrids using above species of the genus   Lepomis

(6) Black Crappie   Pomoxis nigromaculatus

(7) White Crappie   Pomoxis annularis

(8) Largemouth Bass   Micropterus salmoides
(northern strain)

(9) Smallmouth Bass — Micropterus dolomieui

(10) White Catfish — Ictalurus catus

(11) Channel Catfish — Ictalurus punctatus

(12) Golden Shiner — Notemigonus crysoleucas

(13) Fathead Minnow — Pimephales promelas

(14) Goldfish — Carassius auratus

(15) Rainbow Trout — Oncorhynchus mykiss

(16) Brown Trout — Salmo trutta

(17) Brook Trout — Salvelinus fontinalis

(18) Common Carp — Cyprinus carpio

(19) Crayfish — Procambarus species

(c) Exceptions for Species Not Listed. - The following fish species that are not listed in subsection (b) of this section may be produced and sold as if they were listed in that subsection with the following restrictions:

(1) Hybrid striped bass. - Production, propagation, and holding facilities in the Neuse, Roanoke, or Tar/Pamlico River basins for the hybrid striped bass shall comply with additional escapement prevention measures prescribed by the Wildlife Resources Commission.

(2) Yellow perch. - A letter of approval from the Wildlife Resources Commission is required before the yellow perch, perca flavenscens, may be raised at a facility located west of Interstate Highway 77.

(d) Aquaculture Propagation and Production Facility License. The Board of Agriculture may, by rule, authorize and license the operation of fish hatcheries and production facilities for species of fish listed in subsection (b) of this section. The Board may prescribe standards of operation, qualifications of operators, and the conditions under which fish may be commercially reared, transported, possessed, bought, and sold. Aquaculture Propagation and Production Licenses issued by the Department shall be valid for a period of five years.

(e)   Commercial Catchout Facility License.

(1)   Commercial catchout facilities must be stocked exclusively with hatchery reared fish obtained from hatcheries approved by the Department to prevent the introduction of diseases. The Board of Agriculture may, by rule, prescribe standards of operation and conditions under which fish from such ponds may be taken, transported, possessed, bought, and sold.

(2)   The Commercial Catchout Facility License shall be valid for a period of five years. A pond owner or operator licensed under this subsection shall be authorized to sell fish taken by fishermen from the pond to such fishermen. Fish sold at such facilities shall be limited to those fish covered under this section.

(3)   The holder of the Catchout Facility License shall provide receipts to the purchasers of fish. The receipt shall describe the species, number, total weight, and the location of the catchout facility.

(4)   No fish taken from a commercial catchout facility may be resold by the purchasing angler for any purpose.

(5)   No fishing, special trout, or other license shall be required of anglers fishing in licensed commercial catchout facilities.

(f)   Holding Pond/Tank Permit. All facilities holding live food or bait species for sale must obtain a Holding Pond/Tank Permit. Permits shall be valid for a period of two years and shall only authorize possession of fish specified in this section. All fish held live for sale shall be kept in accordance with rules promulgated by the Board of Agriculture. Possession of an Aquaculture Propagation and Production Facility or Commercial Catchout Facility License shall serve in lieu of a Holding Pond/Tank Permit for possession both on and off their facilities premises. No permit shall be required for holding lobsters for sale.

(g)   Possession of species other than those listed in subsection (b) of this section or as authorized in writing by the Wildlife Resources Commission shall be a violation which shall result in the revocation of the Aquaculture Propagation and Production Facility or Commercial Catchout Facility License until such time that proper authorization is received from the Wildlife Resources Commission or the unauthorized species is removed from the facility. In the event of possession of unauthorized fish species, the Wildlife Resources Commission may take further regulatory action. The Department and the Wildlife Resources Commission shall have authority to enter the premises of such facilities to inspect for the possession of a species other than those authorized in subsection (b) of this section or authorized by written permission of the Wildlife Resources Commission.

(h)   Nothing in this act shall apply to the aquarium or ornamental trade in fish. The Wildlife Resources Commission may by rule identify species for which possession in the State is prohibited. (1993, c. 18, s. 2; 1997-198, s. 1; 1997-261, ss. 73-76.)

§ 106-762. Fish disease management.

(a)   The North Carolina Department of Agriculture and Consumer Services shall, with the assistance of the Wildlife Resources Commission, develop and implement a fish disease management plan to prevent the introduction of fish diseases through aquaculture facilities subject to the provisions and duly adopted rules of this section into the State.

(b)   Release of fish. It shall be unlawful to willfully release domestically raised fish into the waters of the State, other than in private ponds as defined by G.S. 113-129, without written permission of the Wildlife Resources Commission, or the Division of Marine Fisheries of the Department of Environment and Natural Resources. (1993, c. 18, s. 2; 1997-261, s. 77; 1997-443, s. 11A.119(a).)

§ 106-763. Fish passage and residual stream flow.

(a)   Natural watercourses as designated by law or regulation shall not be blocked with a stand, dam, weir, hedge, or other water diversion structure to supply an aquaculture facility that in any way prevents or fails to maintain the free passage of anadromous or indigenous fish.

(b)   Residual flow in a natural watercourse below the point of water withdrawal supplying an aquaculture operation shall be sufficient to prevent destruction or serious diminution of downstream fishery habitat and shall be consistent with rules adopted by the Environmental Management Commission. (1993, c. 18, s. 2.)

§ 106-763.1. Propagation and production of American alligators.

(a) License Required. - A person who intends to raise American alligators commercially must first obtain an Aquaculture Propagation and Production Facility License from the Department. The Board of Agriculture may regulate a facility that raises American alligators to the same extent that it can regulate any other facility licensed under this Article.

(b) Requirements. - A facility that raises American alligators commercially must comply with all of the following requirements:

(1) Before a facility begins operation, it must prepare and implement a confinement plan. After a facility begins operation, it must adhere to the confinement plan. A confinement plan must comply with guidelines developed and adopted by the Wildlife Resources Commission. The Department may inspect a facility to determine if the facility is complying with the confinement plan. As used in this subdivision, "confinement" includes production within a building or similar structure and a perimeter fence.

(2) A facility can possess only hatchlings that have been permanently tagged and have an export permit from their state of origin. The facility must keep records of all hatchlings it receives and must make these records available for inspection by the Wildlife Resources Commission and the Department upon request.

(3) If the facility uses swine, poultry, or other livestock for feed, it must have a disease management plan that has been approved by the State Veterinarian, and it must comply with the plan.

(4) The activities of the facility must comply with the Endangered Species Act and the Convention on International Trade in Endangered Species. The Department is the State agency responsible for the administration of this program for farm-raised alligators.

(c) Sanctions. - The operator of a facility that possesses an untagged or undocumented alligator commits a Class H felony if the operator knows the alligator is untagged or undocumented. Conviction of an operator of a facility under this section revokes the license of the facility for five years beginning on the date of the conviction. An operator convicted under this section may not be the operator of any other facility required to be licensed under this Article for five years beginning on the date of the conviction. (1997-198, s. 2.)

§ 106-764. Violation.

A person who violates this act or a rule of the Board of Agriculture adopted hereunder is guilty of a Class 3 misdemeanor. (1993, c. 18, s. 2; 1994, Ex. Sess., c. 14, s. 56.)

Article 64.

Genetically Engineered Organisms Act.

§§ 106-765 through 106-777: Expired.

§§ 106-778 through 106-780. Reserved for future codification purposes.

Article 65.

Strawberry Assessment Act.

§ 106-781. Title.

This Article shall be known as the "Strawberry Assessment Act." (1989 (Reg. Sess., 1990), c. 1027, s. 1.)

§ 106-782. Findings and purpose.

The General Assembly hereby finds that strawberry production makes an important contribution to the State's economy; and that it is appropriate for the State to provide a means whereby strawberry producers may voluntarily assess themselves in order to provide funds for strawberry research and marketing. (1989 (Reg. Sess., 1990), c. 1027, s. 1.)

§ 106-783. Definitions.

As used in this Article:

(1)   "Association" means the North Carolina Strawberry Association, Inc.

(2)   "Commercial production" means the production of strawberries for sale.

(3)   "Department" means the North Carolina Department of Agriculture and Consumer Services.

(4)   "Strawberry plant seller" means a person who sells strawberry plants to growers for commercial production of strawberries. (1989 (Reg. Sess., 1990), c. 1027, s. 1; 1997-261, s. 78; 1997-371, s. 2.)

§ 106-784. Referendum.

(a)   At any time after the effective date of this Article, the Association may conduct a referendum among strawberry producers upon the question of whether an assessment shall be levied as provided for herein.

(b)   The Association shall determine:

(1)   The amount of the proposed assessment;

(2)   The period for which the assessment shall be levied, not to exceed three years;

(3)   The time and place of the referendum;

(4)   Procedures for conducting the referendum and counting of votes; and

(5) Any other matters pertaining to the referendum.

(c) The amount of the proposed assessment and the method of collection shall be set forth on the ballot; provided that no annual assessment shall exceed five percent (5%) of the value of the previous year's strawberry plant sales.

(d) All persons engaged in the commercial production of strawberries, including owners of farms, tenants and sharecroppers shall be eligible to vote in the referendum. Any questions concerning eligibility to vote shall be resolved by the Board of Directors of the Association. (1989 (Reg. Sess., 1990), c. 1027, s. 1.)

§ 106-785. Two-thirds vote required; collection of assessment; penalties; audits.

(a) The assessment shall not be collected unless at least two-thirds of the votes cast in the referendum are in favor of the assessment. If at least two-thirds of the votes cast in the referendum are in favor of the assessment, then the Department shall notify all strawberry plant sellers of the assessment. The assessment shall be added by the strawberry plant sellers to the price of all strawberry plants sold for commercial planting in North Carolina. The Department shall provide forms to the strawberry plant sellers for reporting the assessment. All strawberry plant sellers shall provide each purchaser of strawberry plants for commercial production with an invoice that sets forth the amount of the assessment on the purchase covered by the invoice. Persons who purchase strawberry plants for commercial production on which the assessment has not been collected by the seller shall report such purchases and pay the assessment to the Department.

(b) Each strawberry plant seller shall remit to the Department no later than the tenth day following the end of each calendar quarter the assessment on strawberry plants sold during that quarter. Any strawberry plant seller who fails to remit the assessment for the previous year's sales by January 10 shall pay a penalty of five percent (5%) of the unpaid assessment plus a penalty of one percent (1%) of the unpaid assessment for each month after January 10 that the assessment remains unpaid.

(c) The Association may conduct inspections or audits of the books of any strawberry plant seller. If the inspection or audit reveals that a strawberry plant seller has willfully failed to remit assessments when due, the seller shall pay the Association the reasonable costs of the inspection or audit.

(d) The Association may bring an action to collect unpaid assessments, penalties, and reasonable costs of any inspection or audit as provided in subsection (c) of this section, against any strawberry plant seller who fails to pay the assessment, penalties, or costs. If successful, the Association shall also recover the cost of such action, including attorneys' fees. (1989 (Reg. Sess., 1990), c. 1027, s. 1; 1997-371, s. 3.)

§ 106-786. Use of funds; refunds.

The Department shall remit all funds collected under this Article to the Association at least monthly.

The Association shall use such funds for research and marketing related to strawberries including such administrative expenses as may be reasonably necessary to carry out this function. A funding committee composed of seven members of the Association appointed by the Commissioner of Agriculture, shall approve all expenditures of such funds. Funding committee members may be reimbursed for necessary expenses as determined by the Association's Board of Directors.

Any person who has purchased strawberry plants upon which the assessment has been paid shall have the right to receive a refund of the assessment by making demand in writing to the Association within 30 days of purchase of the plants. Such demand must be accompanied by proof of purchase satisfactory to the funding committee. (1989 (Reg. Sess., 1990), c. 1027, s. 1.)

§§ 106-787 through 106-789. Reserved for future codification purposes.

Article 66.

Pork Promotion Assessment Act.

§ 106-790. Title.

This Article shall be known as the "Pork Promotion Assessment Act." (1991, c. 605, s. 1.)

§ 106-791. Purpose.

It is in the public interest for the State to enable producers of porcine animals to assess themselves in order to raise funds to promote the interests of the pork industry. (1991, c. 605, s. 1.)

§ 106-792. Definitions.

The following definitions apply in this Article:

(1)   Association. - The North Carolina Pork Producers Association, Inc., a North Carolina nonprofit corporation.

(2)   Buyer. - Any person engaged as (i) a commission merchant, (ii) an auction market, or (iii) a livestock market in the business of receiving porcine animals for sale on commission for or on behalf of a pork producer.

(3)   Department. - The North Carolina Department of Agriculture and Consumer Services.

(4)   Market. - To sell, slaughter for sale, or otherwise dispose of a porcine animal in commerce.

(5)   Person. - An individual, a partnership, a firm, or a corporation.

(6)   Porcine animal. - Swine raised for seed stock, market hogs, or slaughter.

(7)   Pork producer. - A person who (i) is a North Carolina resident, (ii) owns, manages, or has a financial interest in pork production, and (iii) is actively involved in the production of porcine animals. (1991, c. 605, s. 1; 1997-261, s. 79.)

§ 106-793. Referendum.

(a) The Association may conduct among pork producers a referendum upon the question of whether an assessment shall be levied on porcine animals sold in this State.

(b) The Association shall determine:

(1) The amount of the proposed assessment.

(2) The time and place of the referendum.

(3) Procedures for conducting the referendum and counting of votes.

(4) Any other matters pertaining to the referendum.

(c) The amount of the proposed assessment shall be stated on the referendum ballot. The amount may not exceed five cents (5¢) for each porcine animal sold in this State. If the assessment is approved in the referendum, the Association may set the assessment at an amount equal to or less than the amount stated on the ballot. If the Association sets a lower amount than the amount approved by referendum, it may increase the amount annually without a referendum by no more than one cent (1¢) for each porcine animal. The increased rate may not exceed the amount approved by referendum and may not exceed the maximum allowable rate of five cents (5¢) for each porcine animal.

(d) All pork producers may vote in the referendum. Any dispute over eligibility to vote or any other matter relating to the referendum shall be determined by the Association. The Association shall make reasonable efforts to provide pork producers with notice of the referendum and an opportunity to vote. (1991, c. 605, s. 1.)

§ 106-794. Payment and collection of assessment.

(a) The assessment shall not be collected unless more than half of the votes cast in the referendum are in favor of the assessment. If more than half of the votes cast in the referendum are in favor of the assessment, then the Association shall notify the Department of the amount of the assessment and the effective date of the assessment. The Department shall notify all buyers and pork producers of the assessment.

(b)   Each pork producer must pay an assessment on each porcine animal sold to a buyer.

(c)   A buyer of a porcine animal shall collect the assessment when buying a porcine animal by deducting the assessment from the price paid for the animal. The buyer shall remit collected assessments to the Department no later than the 10th day of the following month. The Department shall provide forms to buyers for reporting the assessment. If the total assessments collected by a buyer in a month are less than twenty-five dollars ($25.00), the buyer may keep the assessments until the total amount due is at least twenty-five dollars ($25.00) or the end of the quarter, whichever comes first. All buyers shall file at least one report in each calendar quarter, regardless of the amount due.

(d)   A buyer of porcine animals shall keep records of the number of porcine animals purchased and the date purchased. All information or records regarding purchases of porcine animals by individual buyers shall be kept confidential by employees or agents of the Department and the Association, and shall not be disclosed except by court order.

(e)   The Association may bring an action to recover any unpaid assessments, plus the reasonable costs, including attorney fees, incurred in the action. (1991, c. 605, s. 1.)

§ 106-795. Use of assessments; refunds.

(a)   The Department shall remit all funds collected under this Article to the Association at least monthly. The Association shall use the funds to promote the interests of the pork industry. In order to prevent duplication of effort, these funds shall not be used for activities funded under 7 U.S.C. Chapter 79, Pork Promotion, Research, and Consumer Information.

(b)   A pork producer may request a refund of an assessment deducted from the sales price of a porcine animal sold by the producer by submitting a written request for a refund to the Association within 30 days after the buyer of the animal collected the assessment. A refund request must be accompanied by proof of payment of the assessment satisfactory to the Association. The

Association shall mail a refund to the producer within 30 days of receipt of a properly documented refund request. (1991, c. 605, s. 1.)

§ 106-796. Termination of assessment.

Upon receipt of a petition signed by at least ten percent (10%) of the pork producers in North Carolina known to the Association, the Department shall notify the Association, and the Association shall, within six months, conduct a referendum upon the question of continuing the assessment. If a majority of the votes cast in the referendum are against continuing the assessment, or if the Association fails to conduct a referendum within the six-month period, the assessment expires at the end of the six-month period. If a majority of the votes cast in the referendum are in favor of continuing the assessment, then no subsequent referendum shall be held for at least three years. (1991, c. 605, s. 1.)

§ 106-797. Reserved for future codification purposes.

Article 66A.

Transportation of Swine.

§ 106-798. Identification required to transport swine.

(a) No live swine shall be transported on a public road within the State unless the swine has an official form of identification approved by the State Veterinarian for this purpose.

(b) Any live swine that is transported on a public road within this State without identification as required by this section is presumed to be a feral swine and is also subject to regulation by the Wildlife Resources Commission under Chapter 113 of the General Statutes. Any person transporting a swine without identification is subject to a civil penalty under this Article.

(c) Swine that do not leave the premises of the swine owner are not subject to the identification requirement under this section.

(d) The Board of Agriculture shall adopt rules to charge any swine owner a fee for the identification required under this section. The fee may not exceed the actual cost to the Department of Agriculture and Consumer Services for the identification approved by the State Veterinarian and any direct administrative costs associated with providing the identification to swine owners. The Board of Agriculture shall adopt any other rules necessary to implement this Article. (2011-326, s. 19.7; 2011-369, s. 1.)

§ 106-798.1. Penalty for unlawful transport of swine without identification.

Any person who fails to obtain identification as required under this Article shall be subject to a civil penalty of up to five thousand dollars ($5,000) for each violation. Each swine that has no identification is a separate violation. (2011-326, s. 19.7; 2011-369, s. 1.)

§ 106-798.2. Penalty for misuse of identification.

Any person who misuses the identification required under this Article shall be subject to a civil penalty of one thousand dollars ($1,000) for each occurrence. A person misuses identification required under this Article by knowingly providing it to other than the owner of the swine or by engaging in other activity that is in violation of this Article. (2011-326, s. 19.7; 2011-369, s. 1.)

Article 67.

Swine Farms.

§ 106-800. Title.

This Article shall be known as the "Swine Farm Siting Act". (1995, c. 420, s. 1; 1995 (Reg. Sess., 1996), c. 626, s. 7(a); 1997-458, s. 4.1.)

§ 106-801. Purpose.

The General Assembly finds that certain limitations on the siting of swine houses and lagoons for swine farms can assist in the development of pork production, which contributes to the economic development of the State, by lessening the interference with the use and enjoyment of adjoining property. (1995, c. 420, s. 1; 1995 (Reg. Sess., 1996), c. 626, s. 7(a); 1997-458, s. 4.1.)

§ 106-802. Definitions.

As used in this Article, unless the context clearly requires otherwise:

(1) "Lagoon" means a confined body of water to hold animal byproducts including bodily waste from animals or a mixture of waste with feed, bedding, litter or other agricultural materials.

(2) Repealed by Session Laws 1995 (Regular Session, 1996), c. 626, s. 7.

(3) "Occupied residence" means a dwelling actually inhabited by a person on a continuous basis as exemplified by a person living in his or her home.

(3a) "Outdoor recreational facility" means any plot or tract of land on which there is located an outdoor swimming pool, tennis court, or golf course that is open to either the general public or to the members and guests of any organization having 50 or more members.

(4) "Site evaluation" means an investigation to determine if a site meets all federal and State standards as evidenced by the Waste Management Facility Site Evaluation Report on file with the Soil and Water Conservation District office or a comparable report certified by a professional engineer or a comparable report certified by a technical specialist approved by the North Carolina Soil and Water Conservation Commission.

(5) "Swine farm" means a tract of land devoted to raising 250 or more animals of the porcine species.

(6) "Swine house" means a building that shelters porcine animals on a continuous basis. (1995, c. 420, s. 1; 1995 (Reg. Sess., 1996), c. 626, s. 7(a); c. 743, s. 3; 1997-443, s. 11A.119(a); 1997-456, s. 15; 1997-458, s. 4.1; 1997-496, s. 12.)

§ 106-803. Siting requirements for swine houses, lagoons, and land areas onto which waste is applied at swine farms.

(a) A swine house or a lagoon that is a component of a swine farm shall be located:

(1) At least 1,500 feet from any occupied residence.

(2) At least 2,500 feet from any school; hospital; church; outdoor recreational facility; national park; State Park, as defined in G.S. 113-44.9; historic property acquired by the State pursuant to G.S. 121-9 or listed in the North Carolina Register of Historic Places pursuant to G.S. 121-4.1; or child care center, as defined in G.S. 110-86, that is licensed under Article 7 of Chapter 110 of the General Statutes.

(3) At least 500 feet from any property boundary.

(4) At least 500 feet from any well supplying water to a public water system, as defined in G.S. 130A-313.

(5) At least 500 feet from any other well that supplies water for human consumption. This subdivision does not apply to a well located on the same parcel or tract of land on which the swine house or lagoon is located and that supplies water only for use on that parcel or tract of land or for use on adjacent parcels or tracts of land all of which are under common ownership or control.

(a1) The outer perimeter of the land area onto which waste is applied from a lagoon that is a component of a swine farm shall be at least 75 feet from any boundary of property on which an occupied residence is located and from any perennial stream or river, other than an irrigation ditch or canal.

(a2) No component of a liquid animal waste management system for which a permit is required under Part 1 or 1A of Article 21 of Chapter 143 of the General Statutes, other than a land application site, shall be constructed on land that is located within the 100-year floodplain.

(b) A swine house or a lagoon that is a component of a swine farm may be located closer to a residence, school, hospital, church, or a property boundary than is allowed under subsection (a) of this section if written permission is given by the owner of the property and recorded with the Register of Deeds. (1995, c. 420, s. 1; 1995 (Reg. Sess., 1996), c. 626, s. 7(a); 1997-458, s. 4.1.)

§ 106-804. Enforcement.

(a) Any person who owns property directly affected by the siting requirements of G.S. 106-803 pursuant to subsection (b) of this section may bring a civil action against the owner or operator of a swine farm who has violated G.S. 106-803 and may seek any one or more of the following:

(1) Injunctive relief.

(2) An order enforcing the siting requirements under G.S. 106-803.

(3) Damages caused by the violation.

(b) A person is directly affected by the siting requirements of G.S. 106-803 only if the person owns a facility or property located within the siting requirements specified under G.S. 106-803.

(c) If the court determines it is appropriate, the court may award court costs, including reasonable attorneys' fees and expert witnesses' fees, to any party. If a temporary restraining order or preliminary injunction is sought, the court may require the filing of a bond or equivalent security. The court shall determine the amount of the bond or security.

(d) Nothing in this section shall restrict any other right that any person may have under any statute or common law to seek injunctive or other relief. (1995 (Reg. Sess., 1996), c. 626, s. 7(a); 1997-458, s. 4.1.)

§ 106-805. Written notice of swine farms.

Any person who intends to construct a swine farm whose animal waste management system is subject to a permit under Part 1 or 1A of Article 21 of Chapter 143 of the General Statutes shall, after completing a site evaluation and before the farm site is modified, notify all adjoining property owners; all property owners who own property located across a public road, street, or highway from the swine farm; the county or counties in which the farm site is located; and the local health department or departments having jurisdiction over the farm site of that person's intent to construct the swine farm. This notice shall be by certified mail sent to the address on record at the property tax office in the county in which the land is located. Notice to a county shall be sent to the county manager or, if there is no county manager, to the chair of the board of county commissioners. Notice to a local health department shall be sent to the local health director. The written notice shall include all of the following:

(1)   The name and address of the person intending to construct a swine farm.

(2)   The type of swine farm and the design capacity of the animal waste management system.

(3)   The name and address of the technical specialist preparing the waste management plan.

(4)   The address of the local Soil and Water Conservation District office.

(5)   Information informing the adjoining property owners and the property owners who own property located across a public road, street, or highway from the swine farm that they may submit written comments to the Division of Water Resources, Department of Environment and Natural Resources. (1995 (Reg. Sess., 1996), c. 626, s. 7(a); 1996, 2nd Ex. Sess., c. 18, s. 27.34(d); 1997-443, s. 11A.119(a); 1997-458, s. 4.1; 2013-413, s. 57(d).)

§ 106-806. Construction or renovation of swine houses at preexisting swine farms.

(a)   As used in this section, the following definitions apply:

(1)   "New swine farm" means any swine farm the operations of which were sited on or after October 1, 1995. "New swine farm" does not include any

preexisting swine farm, even if a subsequent site evaluation is performed on or after October 1, 1995, at the preexisting swine farm.

(2)   "Preexisting swine farm" means any swine farm either the operations of which were begun prior to October 1, 1995, or the site evaluation of which was approved prior to October 1, 1995, by the Department of Environment and Natural Resources under Part 1A of Article 21 of Chapter 143 of the General Statutes.

(3)   "Renovation or construction," "renovated or constructed," and any similar phrase mean any activity to renovate, construct, reconstruct, rebuild, modify, alter, change, restructure, upgrade, improve, enlarge, reduce, move, or otherwise perform construction work on a swine house that is a component of a swine farm.

(b)   Notwithstanding any other provisions of this Article, a swine house that is a component of a preexisting swine farm can be constructed or renovated if the construction or renovation of that swine house satisfies all of the following requirements:

(1)   The construction or renovation of the swine house does not result in an increase in the permitted capacity of the swine farm, as measured in the annual steady state live weight capacity of the swine farm.

(2)   The construction or renovation of the swine house does not result in requiring an increase in the total permitted capacity of the animal waste management systems located at the swine farm.

(3)   Except as provided in subsection (c) of this section, for any swine house that fails to meet any siting requirement for a swine house under G.S. 106-803, the construction or renovation of the swine house does not result in any portion of the constructed or renovated swine house being located any closer to the building or the property that is the object of the siting requirement that the swine house fails to meet.

(4)   Regardless of the footprint of the existing swine house, renovation or construction of a swine house shall not be allowed in the 100-year floodplain.

(c)   A swine house that is a component of a preexisting swine farm can be constructed or renovated such that it results in a portion of the constructed or renovated swine house being located closer to a residence, school, hospital, church, or a property boundary than is allowed under subdivision (3) of subsection (b) of this section if written permission is given by the owner or owners of the property directly affected by the siting requirements specified under G.S. 106-803 and recorded with the register of deeds.

(d)   This section does not apply to the construction or renovation of a swine house that is a component of a new swine farm. (2011-118, s. 1.)

§ 106-807. Reserved for future codification purposes.

§ 106-808. Reserved for future codification purposes.

§ 106-809. Reserved for future codification purposes.

Article 68.

Southern Dairy Compact.

§ 106-810. Southern Dairy Compact entered into; form of Compact.

The Southern Dairy Compact is enacted into law and entered into with all other jurisdictions legally joining therein in the form substantially as follows:

ARTICLE I. Statement of Purpose, Findings, and Declaration of Policy

§ 1. Statement of purpose, findings, and declaration of policy.

The purpose of this compact is to recognize the interstate character of the southern dairy industry and the prerogative of the states under the United States Constitution to form an interstate commission for the southern region. The mission of the Commission is to take such steps as are necessary to assure the continued viability of dairy farming in the South, and to assure consumers of an adequate, local supply of pure and wholesome milk.

The participating states find and declare that the dairy industry is an essential agricultural activity of the South. Dairy farms, and associated suppliers, marketers, processors, and retailers, are an integral component of the region's economy. Their ability to provide a stable, local supply of pure, wholesome milk is a matter of great importance to the health and welfare of the region.

The participating states further find that dairy farms are essential, and they are an integral part of the region's rural communities. The farms preserve land for agricultural purposes and provide needed economic stimuli for rural communities.

By entering into this compact, the participating states affirm that their ability to regulate the price that southern dairy farmers receive for their product is essential to the public interest. Assurance of a fair and equitable price for dairy farmers ensures their ability to provide milk to the market and the vitality of the southern dairy industry, with all the associated benefits.

Recent dramatic price fluctuations, with a pronounced downward trend, threaten the viability and stability of the southern dairy region. Historically, individual state regulatory action had been an effective emergency remedy available to farmers confronting a distressed market. The system of federal orders, implemented by the Agricultural Marketing Agreement Act of 1937, establishes only minimum prices paid to producers for raw milk, without preempting the power of states to regulate milk prices above the minimum levels so established.

In today's regional dairy marketplace, cooperative, rather than individual state action is needed to more effectively address the market disarray. Under our constitutional system, properly authorized states acting cooperatively may exercise more power to regulate interstate commerce than they may assert individually without such authority. For this reason, the participating states invoke their authority to act in common agreement, with the consent of Congress, under the compact clause of the Constitution.

In establishing their constitutional regulatory authority over the region's fluid milk market by this compact, the participating states declare their purpose that this compact neither displace the system of federal orders nor encourage the merging of federal orders. Specific provisions of the compact itself set forth this basic principle.

Designed as a flexible mechanism able to adjust to changes in a regulated marketplace, the compact also contains a contingency provision should the system of federal orders be discontinued. In that event, the interstate commission may regulate the marketplace in lieu of the system of federal orders. This contingent authority does not anticipate such a change, however, and should not be so construed. It is only provided should developments in the market other than establishment of this compact result in discontinuance of the system of federal orders.

ARTICLE II. Definitions and Rules of Construction

§ 2. Definitions.

For the purposes of this compact, and of any supplemental or concurring legislation enacted pursuant thereto, except as may be otherwise required by the context:

(1) "Class I milk" means milk disposed of in fluid form or as a fluid milk product, subject to further definition in accordance with the principles expressed in subsection (b) of Section 3.

(2) "Commission" means the Southern Dairy Compact Commission established by this compact.

(3) "Commission marketing order" means regulations adopted by the Commission pursuant to Sections 9 and 10 of this compact in place of a terminated federal marketing order or state dairy regulation. Such order may apply throughout the region or in any part or parts thereof as defined in the regulations of the Commission. Such order may establish minimum prices for any or all classes of milk.

(4) "Compact" means this interstate compact.

(5) "Compact over-order price" means a minimum price required to be paid to producers for Class I milk established by the Commission in regulations adopted pursuant to Sections 9 and 10 of this compact, which is above the price established in federal marketing orders or by state farm price regulation in the regulated area. Such price may apply throughout the region or in any part or parts thereof as defined in the regulations of the Commission.

(6) "Milk" means the lacteal secretion of cows and includes all skim, butterfat, or other constituents obtained from separation or any other process. The term is used in its broadest sense and may be further defined by the Commission for regulatory purposes.

(7) "Partially regulated plant" means a milk plant not located in a regulated area but having Class I distribution within such area. Commission regulations may exempt plants having such distribution or receipts in amounts less than the limits defined therein.

(8) "Participating state" means a state which has become a party to this compact by the enactment of concurring legislation.

(9) "Pool plant" means any milk plant located in a regulated area.

(10) "Region" means the territorial limits of the states which are parties to this compact.

(11) "Regulated area" means any area within the region governed by and defined in regulations establishing a compact over-order price or commission marketing order.

(12) "State dairy regulation" means any state regulation of dairy prices and associated assessments, whether by statute, marketing order, or otherwise.

§ 3. Rules of construction.

(a) This compact shall not be construed to displace existing federal milk marketing orders or state dairy regulation in the region but to supplement them. In the event some or all federal orders in the region are discontinued, the compact shall be construed to provide the Commission the option to replace them with one or more commission marketing orders pursuant to this compact.

(b) This compact shall be construed liberally in order to achieve the purposes and intent enunciated in Section 1. It is the intent of this compact to establish a basic structure by which the Commission may achieve those purposes through the application, adaptation, and development of the regulatory techniques historically associated with milk marketing and to afford the Commission broad flexibility to devise regulatory mechanisms to achieve the purposes of this compact. In accordance with this intent, the technical terms which are associated with market order regulation and which have acquired commonly understood general meanings are not defined herein but the Commission may further define the terms used in this compact and develop additional concepts and define additional terms as it may find appropriate to achieve its purposes.

ARTICLE III. Commission Established

§ 4. Commission established.

There is hereby created a commission to administer the compact, composed of delegations from each state in the region. The Commission shall be known as the Southern Dairy Compact Commission. A delegation shall include not less than three nor more than five persons. Each delegation shall include at least one dairy farmer who is engaged in the production of milk at the time of appointment or reappointment, and one consumer representative. Delegation members shall be residents and voters of, and subject to such confirmation process as is provided for in, the appointing state. Delegation members shall serve no more than three consecutive terms with no single term of more than four years, and be subject to removal for cause. In all other respects, delegation members shall serve in accordance with the laws of the state represented. The compensation, if any, of the members of a state delegation shall be determined and paid by each state, but their expenses shall be paid by the Commission.

§ 5. Voting requirements.

All actions taken by the Commission, except for the establishment or termination of an over-order price or commission marketing order, and the adoption, amendment, or rescission of the Commission's bylaws, shall be by majority vote of the delegations present. Each state delegation shall be entitled to one vote in the conduct of the Commission's affairs. Establishment or termination of an over-order price or commission marketing order shall require at least a two-thirds vote of the delegations present. The establishment of a regulated area that covers all or part of a participating state shall require also the affirmative vote of that state's delegation. A majority of the delegations from the participating states shall constitute a quorum for the conduct of the Commission's business.

§ 6. Administration and management.

(a) The Commission shall elect annually from among the members of the participating state delegations a chairperson, a vice-chairperson, and a treasurer. The Commission shall appoint an executive director and fix his or her duties and compensation. The executive director shall serve at the pleasure of the Commission, and, together with the treasurer, shall be bonded in an amount determined by the Commission. The Commission may establish through its bylaws an executive committee composed of one member elected by each delegation.

(b) The Commission shall adopt bylaws for the conduct of its business by a two-thirds vote and shall have the power by the same vote to amend and rescind these bylaws. The Commission shall publish its bylaws in convenient form with the appropriate agency or officer in each of the participating states. The bylaws shall provide for appropriate notice to the delegations of all Commission meetings and hearings and of the business to be transacted at such meetings or hearings. Notice also shall be given to other agencies or officers of participating states as provided by the laws of those states.

(c) The Commission shall file an annual report with the Secretary of Agriculture of the United States, and with each of the participating states by submitting copies to the Governor, both houses of the legislature, and the head of the state department having responsibilities for agriculture.

(d) In addition to the powers and duties elsewhere prescribed in this compact, the Commission may engage in all of the following:

(1) Sue and be sued in any state or federal court.

(2) Have a seal and alter the same at pleasure.

(3) Acquire, hold, and dispose of real and personal property by gift, purchase, lease, license, or other similar manner, for its corporate purposes.

(4) Borrow money and to issue notes, to provide for the rights of the holders thereof, and to pledge the revenue of the Commission as security therefor, subject to the provisions of Section 18 of this compact.

(5) Appoint such officers, agents, and employees as it may deem necessary, prescribe their powers, duties, and qualifications.

(6) Create and abolish such offices, employments, and positions as it deems necessary for the purposes of the compact and provide for the removal, term, tenure, compensation, fringe benefits, pension, and retirement rights of its officers and employees.

(7) Retain personal services on a contract basis.

§ 7. Rule-making power.

In addition to the power to promulgate a compact over-order price or commission marketing orders as provided by this compact, the Commission is further empowered to make and enforce such additional rules and regulations as it deems necessary to implement any provisions of this compact, or to effectuate in any other respect the purposes of this compact.

ARTICLE IV. Powers of the Commission

§ 8. Powers to promote regulatory uniformity, simplicity, and interstate cooperation.

The Commission may:

(1)   Investigate or provide for investigations or research projects designed to review the existing laws and regulations of the participating states, to consider their administration and costs, to measure their impact on the production and marketing of milk and their effects on the shipment of milk and milk products within the region.

(2)   Study and recommend to the participating states joint or cooperative programs for the administration of the dairy marketing laws and regulations and to prepare estimates of cost savings and benefits of such programs.

(3)   Encourage the harmonious relationships between the various elements in the industry for the solution of their material problems. Conduct symposia or conferences designed to improve industry relations, or a better understanding of problems.

(4)   Prepare and release periodic reports on activities and results of the Commission's efforts to the participating states.

(5)   Review the existing marketing system for milk and milk products and recommend changes in the existing structure for assembly and distribution of milk which may assist, improve, or promote more efficient assembly and distribution of milk.

(6)   Investigate costs and charges for producing, hauling, handling, processing, distributing, selling, and for all other services, performed with respect to milk.

(7)   Examine current economic forces affecting producers, probable trends in production and consumption, the level of dairy farm prices in relation to costs, the financial conditions of dairy farmers, and the need for an emergency order to relieve critical conditions on dairy farms.

§ 9. Equitable farm prices.

(a)   The powers granted in this section and Section 10 shall apply only to the establishment of a compact over-order price, so long as federal milk marketing orders remain in effect in the region. In the event that any or all such orders are terminated, this Article authorizes the Commission to establish one or more commission marketing orders, as herein provided, in the region or parts thereof as defined in the order.

(b)   A compact over-order price established pursuant to this section shall apply only to Class I milk. Such compact over-order price shall not exceed one dollar and fifty cents ($1.50) per gallon at Atlanta, Georgia, however, this compact over-order price shall be adjusted upward or downward at other locations in the region to reflect differences in minimum federal order prices. Beginning in 1990, and using that year as a base, the foregoing one dollar and fifty cents ($1.50) per gallon maximum shall be adjusted annually by the rate of change in the Consumer Price Index as reported by the Bureau of Labor Statistics of the United States Department of Labor. For purposes of the pooling and equalization of an over-order price, the value of milk used in other use classifications shall be calculated at the appropriate class price established pursuant to the applicable federal order or state dairy regulation and the value of unregulated milk shall be calculated in relation to the nearest prevailing class price in accordance with and subject to such adjustments as the Commission may prescribe in regulations.

(c)   A commission marketing order shall apply to all classes and uses of milk.

(d)   The Commission may establish a compact over-order price for milk to be paid by pool plants and partially regulated plants. The Commission also may establish a compact over-order price to be paid by all other handlers receiving milk from producers located in a regulated area. This price shall be established either as a compact over-order price or by one or more commission marketing orders. Whenever such a price has been established by either type of regulation, the legal obligation to pay such price shall be determined solely by the terms and purpose of the regulation without regard to the situs of the transfer of title, possession, or any other factors not related to the purposes of the regulation and this compact. Producer-handlers as defined in an applicable federal market order shall not be subject to a compact over-order price. The Commission shall provide for similar treatment of producer-handlers under commission marketing orders.

(e) In determining the price, the Commission shall consider the balance between production and consumption of milk and milk products in the regulated area, the costs of production including, but not limited to, the price of feed, the cost of labor including the reasonable value of the producer's own labor and management, machinery expense and interest expense, the prevailing price for milk outside the regulated area, the purchasing power of the public, and the price necessary to yield a reasonable return to the producer and distributor.

(f) When establishing a compact over-order price, the Commission shall take such other action as is necessary and feasible to help ensure that the over-order price does not cause or compensate producers so as to generate local production of milk in excess of those quantities necessary to assure consumers of an adequate supply for fluid purposes.

(g) The Commission shall whenever possible enter into agreements with state or federal agencies for exchange of information or services for the purpose of reducing regulatory burden and cost of administering the compact. The Commission may reimburse other agencies for the reasonable cost of providing these services.

§ 10. Optional provisions for pricing order.

Regulations establishing a compact over-order price or a commission marketing order may contain, but shall not be limited to, any of the following:

(1) Provisions classifying milk in accordance with the form in which or purpose for which it is used, or creating a flat pricing program.

(2) With respect to a commission marketing order only, provisions establishing or providing a method for establishing separate minimum prices for each use classification prescribed by the Commission, or a single minimum price for milk purchased from producers or associations of producers.

(3) With respect to an over-order minimum price, provisions establishing or providing a method for establishing such minimum price for Class I milk.

(4) Provisions for establishing either an over-order price or a commission marketing order may make use of any reasonable method for establishing such price or prices including flat pricing and formula pricing. Provision may also be made for location adjustments, zone differentials, and competitive credits with respect to regulated handlers who market outside the regulated area.

(5) Provisions for the payment to all producers and associations of producers delivering milk to all handlers of uniform prices for all milk so delivered, irrespective of the uses made of such milk by the individual handler to whom it is delivered, or for the payment of producers delivering milk to the same handler of uniform prices for all milk delivered by them.

a. With respect to regulations establishing a compact over-order price, the Commission may establish one equalization pool within the regulated area for the sole purpose of equalizing returns to producers throughout the regulated area.

b. With respect to any commission marketing order, as defined in Section 2, subdivision (9), which replaces one or more terminated federal orders or state dairy regulation, the marketing area of now separate state or federal orders shall not be merged without the affirmative consent of each state, voting through its delegation, which is partly or wholly included within any such new marketing area.

(6) Provisions requiring persons who bring Class I milk into the regulated area to make compensatory payments with respect to all such milk to the extent necessary to equalize the cost of milk purchased by handlers subject to a compact over-order price or commission marketing order. No such provisions shall discriminate against milk producers outside the regulated area. The provisions for compensatory payments may require payment of the difference between the Class I price required to be paid for such milk in the state of production by a federal milk marketing order or state dairy regulation and the Class I price established by the compact over-order price or commission marketing order.

(7) Provisions specially governing the pricing and pooling of milk handled by partially regulated plants.

(8) Provisions requiring that the account of any person regulated under the compact over-order price shall be adjusted for any payments made to or received by such persons with respect to a producer settlement fund of any federal or state milk marketing order or other state dairy regulation within the regulated area.

(9) Provision requiring the payment by handlers of an assessment to cover the costs of the administration and enforcement of such order pursuant to subsection (a) of Section 18 of Article VII.

(10) Provisions for reimbursement to participants of the Women, Infants and Children Special Supplemental Food Program of the United States Child Nutrition Act of 1966.

(11) Other provisions and requirements as the Commission may find are necessary or appropriate to effectuate the purposes of this compact and to provide for the payment of fair and equitable minimum prices to producers.

ARTICLE V. Rule-Making Procedure

§ 11. Rule-making procedure.

Before promulgation of any regulations establishing a compact over-order price or commission marketing order, including any provision with respect to milk supply under subsection (f) of Section 9, or amendment thereof, as provided in Article IV, the Commission shall conduct an informal rule-making proceeding to provide interested persons with an opportunity to present data and views. Such rule-making proceeding shall be governed by Section 4 of the Federal Administrative Procedure Act, as amended (5 U.S.C. § 553). In addition, the Commission shall, to the extent practicable, publish notice of rule-making proceedings in the official register of each participating state. Before the initial adoption of regulations establishing a compact over-order price or a commission marketing order and thereafter before any amendment with regard to prices or assessments, the Commission shall hold a public hearing. The Commission may commence a rule-making proceeding on its own initiative or may in its sole discretion act upon the petition of any person including individual milk producers, any organization of milk producers or handlers, general farm organizations, consumer or public interest groups, and local, state or federal officials.

§ 12. Findings and referendum.

(a) In addition to the concise general statement of basis and purpose required by section 4(b) of the Federal Administrative Procedure Act, as amended (5 U.S.C. § 53 (c)), the Commission shall make findings of fact with respect to:

(1) Whether the public interest will be served by the establishment of minimum milk prices to dairy farmers under Article IV.

(2) What level of prices will assure that producers receive a price sufficient to cover their costs of production and will elicit an adequate supply of milk for the inhabitants of the regulated area and for manufacturing purposes.

(3) Whether the major provisions of the order, other than those fixing minimum milk prices, are in the public interest and are reasonably designed to achieve the purposes of the order.

(4) Whether the terms of the proposed regional order or amendment are approved by producers as provided in Section 13.

§ 13. Producer referendum.

(a) For the purpose of ascertaining whether the issuance or amendment of regulations establishing a compact over-order price or a commission marketing order, including any provision with respect to milk supply under subsection (f) of Section 9, is approved by producers, the Commission shall conduct a referendum among producers. The referendum shall be held in a timely manner, as determined by regulation of the Commission. The terms and conditions of the proposed order or amendment shall be described by the Commission in the ballot used in the conduct of the referendum, but the nature, content, or extent of such description shall not be a basis for attacking the legality of the order or any action relating thereto.

(b) An order or amendment shall be deemed approved by producers if the Commission determines that it is approved by at least two-thirds of the voting producers who, during a representative period determined by the Commission, have been engaged in the production of milk the price of which would be regulated under the proposed order or amendment.

(c) For purposes of any referendum, the Commission shall consider the approval or disapproval by any cooperative association of producers, qualified under the provisions of the Act of Congress of February 18, 1922, as amended, known as the Capper-Volstead Act, bona fide engaged in marketing milk, or in rendering services for or advancing the interests of producers of such commodity, as the approval or disapproval of the producers who are members or stockholders in, or under contract with, such cooperative association of producers, except as provided in subdivision (1) of this subsection and subject to the provisions of subdivisions (2) through (5) of this subsection.

(1) No cooperative that has been formed to act as a common marketing agency for both cooperatives and individual producers shall be qualified to block vote for either.

(2) Any cooperative that is qualified to block vote shall, before submitting its approval or disapproval in any referendum, give prior written notice to each of its members as to whether and how it intends to cast its vote. The notice shall be given in a timely manner as established, and in the form prescribed, by the Commission.

(3) Any producer may obtain a ballot from the Commission in order to register approval or disapproval of the proposed order.

(4) A producer who is a member of a cooperative which has provided notice of its intent to approve or not to approve a proposed order, and who obtains a ballot and with such ballot expresses his or her approval or disapproval of the proposed order, shall notify the Commission as to the name of the cooperative of which he or she is a member, and the Commission shall remove such producer's name from the list certified by such cooperative with its corporate vote.

(5) In order to ensure that all milk producers are informed regarding a proposed order, the Commission shall notify all milk producers that an order is being considered and that each producer may register his or her approval or disapproval with the Commission either directly or through his or her cooperative.

§ 14. Termination of over-order price or marketing order.

(a) The Commission shall terminate any regulations establishing an over-order price or commission marketing order issued under this Article whenever it finds that such order or price obstructs or does not tend to effectuate the declared policy of this compact.

(b) The Commission shall terminate any regulations establishing an over-order price or a commission marketing order issued under this Article whenever it finds that such termination is favored by a majority of the producers who, during a representative period determined by the Commission, have been engaged in the production of milk, the price of which is regulated by such order; but such termination shall be effective only if announced on or before such date as may be specified in such marketing agreement or order.

(c) The termination or suspension of any order or provision thereof, shall not be considered an order within the meaning of this Article and shall require no hearing, but shall comply with the requirements for informal rule making prescribed by Section 4 of the Federal Administrative Procedure Act, as amended (5 U.S.C. § 553).

ARTICLE VI. Enforcement

§ 15. Records, reports, access to premises.

(a) The Commission may by rule and regulation prescribe record keeping and reporting requirements for all regulated persons. For purposes of the administration and enforcement of this compact, the Commission may examine the books and records of any regulated person relating to his or her milk business and for that purpose, the Commission's properly designated officers, employees, or agents shall have full access during normal business hours to the premises and records of all regulated persons.

(b) Information furnished to or acquired by the Commission officers, employees, or its agents pursuant to this section shall be confidential and not subject to disclosure except to the extent that the Commission deems disclosure to be necessary in any administrative or judicial proceeding involving the administration or enforcement of this compact, an over-order price, a compact marketing order, or other regulations of the Commission. The Commission may adopt rules further defining the confidentiality of information pursuant to this section. Nothing in this section shall be deemed to prohibit (i) the issuance of general statements based upon the reports of a number of handlers, which do not identify the information furnished by any person, or (ii) the publication by direction of the Commission of the name of any person violating any regulation of the Commission, together with a statement of the particular provisions violated by such person.

(c) No officer, employee, or agent of the Commission shall intentionally disclose information, by inference or otherwise, that is made confidential pursuant to this section. Any person violating the provisions of this section shall, upon conviction, be subject to a fine of not more than one thousand dollars ($1,000) or to imprisonment for not more than one year, or both, and shall be removed from office. The Commission shall refer any allegation of a violation of this section to the appropriate state enforcement authority or United States Attorney.

§ 16. Subpoena, hearings, and judicial review.

(a)   The Commission is hereby authorized and empowered by its members and its properly designated officers to administer oaths and issue subpoenas throughout all signatory states to compel the attendance of witnesses and the giving of testimony and the production of other evidence.

(b)   Any handler subject to an order may file a written petition with the Commission stating that any order or any provision of any such order or any obligation imposed in connection therewith is not in accordance with law and praying for a modification thereof or to be exempted therefrom. The handler shall thereupon be given an opportunity for a hearing upon such petition, in accordance with regulations made by the Commission. After such hearing, the Commission shall make a ruling upon the prayer of such petition which shall be final, if in accordance with law.

(c)   The district courts of the United States in any district in which the handler is an inhabitant, or has his or her principal place of business, are hereby vested with jurisdiction to review such ruling, provided a complaint for that purpose is filed within 30 days from the date of the entry of the ruling. Service of process in these proceedings may be had upon the Commission by delivering to it a copy of the complaint. If the court determines that the ruling is not in accordance with law, it shall remand such proceedings to the Commission with directions either (i) to make such ruling as the court shall determine to be in accordance with law, or (ii) to take such further proceedings as, in its opinion, the law requires. The pendency of proceedings instituted pursuant to this subdivision shall not impede, hinder, or delay the Commission form obtaining relief pursuant to Section 17. Any proceedings brought pursuant to Section 17, except where brought by way of counterclaim in proceedings instituted pursuant to this section, shall abate whenever a final decree has been rendered in proceedings between the same parties, and covering the same subject matter, instituted pursuant to this section.

§ 17. Enforcement with respect to handlers.

(a)   Any violation by a handler of the provisions of regulation establishing an over-order price or a commission marketing order, or other regulations adopted pursuant to this compact shall:

(1)   Constitute a violation of the laws of each of the signatory states. Such violation shall render the violator subject to a civil penalty in an amount as may

be prescribed by the laws of each of the participating states, recoverable in any state or federal court of competent jurisdiction. Each day such violation continues shall constitute a separate violation.

(2) Constitute grounds for the revocation of license or permit to engage in the milk business under the applicable laws of the participating states.

(b) With respect to handlers, the Commission shall enforce the provisions of this compact, regulations establishing an over-order price, a commission marketing order or other regulations adopted hereunder by:

(1) Commencing an action for legal or equitable relief brought in the name of the Commission in any state or federal court of competent jurisdiction; or

(2) Referral to the state agency for enforcement by judicial or administrative remedy with the agreement of the appropriate state agency of a participating state.

(c) With respect to handlers, the Commission may bring an action for injunction to enforce the provisions of this compact or the order or regulations adopted thereunder without being compelled to allege or prove that an adequate remedy of law does not exist.

ARTICLE VII. Finance

§ 18. Finance of start-up and regular costs.

(a) To provide for its start-up costs, the Commission may borrow money pursuant to its general power under Section 6, subdivision (d), paragraph 4. In order to finance the cost of administration and enforcement of this compact, including payback of start-up costs, the Commission may collect an assessment from each handler who purchases milk from producers within the region. If imposed, this assessment shall be collected on a monthly basis for up to one year from the date the Commission convenes, in an amount not to exceed $.015 per hundred weight of milk purchased from producers during the period of the assessment. The initial assessment may apply to the projected purchases of handlers for the two-month period following the date the Commission convenes. In addition, if regulations establishing an over-order price or a compact marketing order are adopted, they may include an assessment for the specific purpose of their administration. These regulations shall provide for establishment of a reserve for the Commission's ongoing operating expenses.

(b) The Commission shall not pledge the credit of any participating state or of the United States. Notes issued by the Commission and all other financial obligations incurred by it, shall be its sole responsibility and no participating state or the United States shall be liable therefor.

§ 19. Audit and accounts.

(a) The Commission shall keep accurate accounts of all receipts and disbursements, which shall be subject to the audit and accounting procedures established under its rules. In addition, all receipts and disbursements of funds handled by the Commission shall be audited yearly by a qualified public accountant and the report of the audit shall be included in and become part of the annual report of the Commission.

(b) The accounts of the Commission shall be open at any reasonable time for inspection by duly constituted officers of the participating states and by any persons authorized by the Commission.

(c) Nothing contained in this Article shall be construed to prevent commission compliance with laws relating to audit or inspection of accounts by or on behalf of any participating state or of the United States.

ARTICLE VIII. Entry into Force; Additional Members and Withdrawal

§ 20. Entry into force; additional members.

The compact shall enter into force effective when enacted into law by any three states of the group of states composed of Alabama, Arkansas, Florida, Georgia, Kentucky, Louisiana, Maryland, Mississippi, North Carolina, Oklahoma, South Carolina, Tennessee, Texas, Virginia, and West Virginia and when the consent of Congress has been obtained.

§ 21. Withdrawal from compact.

Any participating state may withdraw from this compact by enacting a statute repealing the same, but no such withdrawal shall take effect until one year after notice in writing of the withdrawal is given to the Commission and the governors of all the participating states. No withdrawal shall affect any liability already already incurred by or chargeable to a participating state prior to the time of such withdrawal.

§ 22. Severability.

If any part or provision of this compact is adjudged invalid by any court, such judgment shall be confined in its operation to the part or provision directly involved in the controversy in which such judgment shall have been rendered and shall not affect or impair the validity of the remainder of this compact. In the event Congress consents to this compact subject to conditions, said conditions shall not impair the validity of this compact when said conditions are accepted by three or more compacting states. A compact state may accept the conditions of Congress by implementation of this compact. (1997-494, s. 1.)

§ 106-811. Appointment of members to the Southern Dairy Compact Commission.

(a) The delegation from the State of North Carolina to the Southern Dairy Compact Commission, as established in Article IV of the Compact, shall be composed of five members appointed as follows:

(1) One member representing consumers of milk, appointed by the Governor.

(2) One member appointed by the General Assembly upon the recommendation of the Speaker of the House of Representatives.

(3) One member appointed by the General Assembly upon the recommendation of the President Pro Tempore of the Senate.

(4) Two members appointed by the Commissioner of Agriculture, one of whom shall be a dairy farmer engaged in the production of milk at the time of appointment or reappointment.

(b) Members must be registered to vote in the State.

(c) Members shall serve a term of four years and may be reappointed, but no member shall serve more than three consecutive terms. Members shall serve until their successors are duly appointed. Any appointment to fill an unexpired term shall be for the balance of the unexpired term and shall be made by the appropriate appointing authority. A member may be removed by the appointing authority, in accordance with G.S. 143B-13. The Commissioner of

Agriculture shall designate one member of the delegation to serve as chair, at the pleasure of the Commissioner.

(d)   Members of the delegation shall receive per diem and necessary travel and subsistence expenses in accordance with G.S. 138-5.

(e)   A majority of the delegation shall constitute a quorum for the transaction of business.

(f)   All clerical and other services required by the delegation shall be provided by the Commissioner of Agriculture. (1997-494, s. 1.)

Vision Books Order Form

Fax Orders:	1-980-299-5965
Phone Orders:	1-704-898-0770
E-mail Orders:	www.visionbooks.org
Mail Orders:	Vision Books, LLC P.O. Box 42406 Charlotte, NC 28215

Shipp To:
Name_____
Address_____
City_____ State_____ Zip_____
Phone_____ Fax_____
Email_____ @_____

Bill To: We can bill a third party on your behalf.
Name_____
Address_____
City_____ State_____ Zip_____
Phone____( )_____ Fax_____
Email_____ @_____

Pamphlet Number ($15.00 Each)	Qty	Total Cost
_____	_____	_____
_____	_____	_____
_____	_____	_____
_____	_____	_____
_____	_____	_____
_____	_____	_____
_____	_____	_____
_____	_____	_____
Full Volume Set 1-92	**92 Pamphlets**	**1,380.00**

Free Shipping Shipping & Handling on Full Volume Orders
Add $1.00 Shipping & Handling per pamphlet $_____

Total Cost $_____

Thank you for your support. Management!

DID YOU ENJOY THIS BOOK?

Vision Books, LLC would like to hear from you! If you or someone you know has been fasely imprisoned, we would like to hear your story. If the 'North Carolina Criminal Law and Procedure' has had an effect in your life or if you have suggestions, we would like to hear from you. Send your letters to:

Vision Books, LLC
Attn: Staff Writers
P.O. Box 42406
Charlotte, NC 28215
Email: staff@visionbooks.org

Order Additional Copies:

Fax Orders:	1-980-299-5965
Phone Orders:	1-704-898-0770
E-mail Orders:	www.visionbooks.org
Mail Orders:	Vision Books, LLC P.O. Box 42406 Charlotte, NC 28215